Internet in Plain English

Bryan Pfaffenberger

MIS:
PRESS

A Subsidiary of
Henry Holt and Co., Inc.

Editor: Debra Williams Cauley
Techical Editor: Sean Wingerter
Editorial Team: Elissa Keeler and Annette Stroka Devlin
Design and Production: Alan Hill

For Suzanne, always

Acknowledgments

Creating a book like this one isn't a solitary job, and I'd like to convey my thanks to all the folks who helped me, in big ways and small. There isn't room to list the dozens of Internet users who have commented—via electronic mail and Usenet, naturally—on many of the definitions you'll find in the pages to follow, so I'll just say thanks to all. It's ample testimony to the Internet's value, incidentally, that this book could not have been written without Internet email, Usenet discussions, and a heck of a lot of Internet resource discovery; I was on-line to the tune of 16 hours per day. (Sorry my phone was always busy, Mom.)

When the manuscript reached New York (via, incidentally, a high-speed, trans-Atlantic **T1** connection), MIS's seasoned publishing professionals went to work—while I took a much-needed break! Hats off to this book's technical editor, Sean Wingerter, who combed through all that follows to make sure it meets the highest technical standards. Editorial details were tackled by a world-class team, including Elissa Keeler and Annette Sroka Devlin. This book's cool design stems from the work of Alan Hill.

Writing gobbles up huge amounts of time, so I'd like to thank my family—wife Suzanne, daughter Julia, and son Michael—for my having spent many more hours with Archie, Veronica, and Jughead than with them. I appreciate your understanding, and now that I'm done it's time for some fun! How 'bout that backpacking trip we were talking about?

Most of all, I'd like to thank Debra Williams Cauley, this book's editor, whose unflagging enthusiasm and good humor helped me through many a hurdle. Thanks to Debra, writing this book was a wonderful experience—a supportive publisher, a talented staff, and the right mix of editorial guidance and creative freedom.

But let me thank you, the reader, in advance. It's your feedback that will help make the next edition of this book even better. Any terms missing that you think ought to be included? Please send your comments, criticisms, and suggestions to bp@virginia.edu—or, if you prefer **snail mail**, to Bryan Pfaffenberger, TCC, Engineering, University of Virginia, Charlottesville, VA 22903. "See" you on the net!

Table of Contents

Introduction

Internet in Plain English is for anyone who uses the Internet, the network of networks that is fast becoming the world's first global data communications system.

Why a dictionary of Internet terms? As anyone who uses the Internet quickly discovers, the Internet comes with a welter of new, confusing words: For instance, you're not using a computer, you're using a **host**. That's not a program, it's a **client**. Acronyms abound—TCP/IP, SMTP, JPEG. And as if they jumped right out of an Archie comic book, you'll meet **Veronica**, **Jughead**, and—naturally—**Archie** himself. (Betty, for some reason, is conspicuously absent.) And woe unto the poor citizen who's trying to figure out where the Internet is going. Europeans will tell you, condescendingly, that **OSI** is going to run over the Internet like a steamroller (Not!), while the telephone people, starry-eyed, talk incomprehensibly of **ADSL**, **ATM**, and **SONET**.

As maddening as the Internet's terminology can be, it's the key to grasping a new space—**cyberspace**—that's emerging from the linkage of millions of computers. What's more, knowing Internet terms—or being able to look them up—can help you use the Internet more successfully. After all, what are you doing paging through that **newsgroup** at the **article selector** level, when you can view the same **postings** organized by topic at the **thread selector** level? And since those **cascaders** are wasting your time, why don't you just **kill** them?

If you need a quick definition of an Internet-related term, you'll find it here. This dictionary focuses squarely on the Internet—its technology and physical media, its programs and tools, its standards and protocols, its history and context. Where this dictionary defines terms that find use in other computing contexts, such as **operating system** or **database**, they're defined the way Internet people use these terms.

A Dictionary in Depth

Internet in Plain English also gives you something that other dictionaries don't: a thorough explanation of the *concepts* underlying these terms—concepts that can help you use the Internet more effectively, assist you in judging where the Internet is going, and give you an understanding of the issues facing the emerging **National Information Infrastructure (NII)**.

Take a look at one of this dictionary's entries, and you'll see what I'm getting at. First, you see the definition. Then you see an explanation, which tells you *how* the term is used and *why* it's important:

| data transfer rate |

The speed at which a point-to-point transmission line can convey data, measured in **bits per second (bps)**.

Data transfer rates are commonly expressed with the abbreviations Kbps (one thousand bits per second), Mbps (one million bits per second), and Gbps (one billion bits per second). Commonly-used Modems, for example, can transfer data via telephone lines at a speed of 14.4 Kbps. To put these terms in perspective, a **modem** running at 14.4 Kbps would require about 5 minutes to transfer a 50-page essay, but a **gigabit network** running at 2 Gbps could transfer the entire text of the *Encyclopedia Britannica* in less than a second.

Practical Knowledge at Your Fingertips

What's the point in learning new terms and understanding concepts? You want to *apply* your Internet knowledge, so that you can use the Internet more effectively. That's why *Internet in Plain English* is loaded with dozens of practical tips, like this one that appears in the **alias** entry:

Tip: If your electronic mail address has lots of subdomains that are difficult to type, ask your system administrator to create an alias that will allow your correspondents to ignore subdomain names. For example, after creating such an alias a message addressed to *skywalker-@marine.com* will reach *skywalker@babybyte.eng.-marine.com*).

Learning Netiquette

The Internet isn't just a network of computer networks. It's also a moral community, bound by its own sense of right and wrong. In the absence of a controlling central authority, that's what holds the Internet together. Everyone benefits when users follow the community's rules, known as **netiquette**. That's why this book includes plenty of straightforward advice on what to do—and what *not* to do—when you're on-line. Here's an example from the article titled **crosspost**:

Do crosspost when doing so makes sense. For example, a message posted to alt.aquaria might also prove of interest to readers of sci.aquaria.

Here's another example from the article on **anonymous FTP**:

Don't overuse an FTP site, try to explore the system outside the pub directory, or disobey the rules you see when you log on to the FTP site. Repeated abuse may result in the site's termination—and if that happens, everyone loses.

Finding Acronyms

Whatever else one can say about the people who created the Internet, it's clear that they fell victim to a dangerous modern disease, called Acronym Overuse Syndrome (AOS). To be sure, acronyms help us talk about complex new computer entities that just don't exist in the everyday world—it's easy to say, "I just FTPed a neat file." The alternative? "I just got a neat file by means of the File Transfer Protocol." That's a mouthful, and it explains why Internet people use acronyms so much.

Acronyms may make life easier for experienced Internet users, but they aren't welcomed by users trying to learn the Internet or cope with its peculiarities. Sooner or later, you'll run across a new, incomprehensible acronym. Do you understand the following sentence? "Should you prepare your file with **HTML,** or will **SGML** do the trick?" If not, head for the Acronym Finder in the first section of this book.

The Acronym and Abbreviation finders, a unique feature of this book, put dozens of Internet acronyms and abbreviations into handy lists that you can quickly scan. Just looking up the acronym's meaning may be enough to give you the information you need ("Oh, they mean the *hypertext* protocol"). If you're still in the dark, you'll find a cross-reference that guides you to an in-depth definition. HTML, incidentally, stands for **HyperText Markup Language**, and that's how its listed in this book.

Finding Related Information

This book is loaded with boldfaced cross-references, which point you toward additional information. Here's an example:

Archie

A **resource discovery tool** that is designed to help you locate publicly-accessible file directories, as well as the files that are available in them, by means of **anonymous FTP** at more than 1,000 **archive sites** throughout the Internet.

Check out **resource discovery tool**:

resource discovery tool

One of several programs that were developed to help Internet users discover and retrieve **resources** (such as files, documents, programs, sounds, and graphics). The most widely-used resource discovery tools are the following: **Archie** (for finding files in directories that are publicly accessible by means of **anonymous FTP**); **WAIS** (for finding documents in more than 1,000 Internet-accessible databases), **Gopher** (a menu-based **browser** that provides user-friendly access to FTP- and WAIS-accessible resources), and **World Wide Web** (a **hypertext** browser).

In short, this book is organized by **hypertext** principles—the boldfaced words show you where to find additional information on a topic. There are literally thousands of ways that you can browse through this book's contents, tracking down cross-references as your knowledge and understanding grow.

Learning About the Internet

If you're new to the Internet, you can use this book as a learning guide. In what follows, I've identified entries you can read to give yourself an excellent grounding in Internet knowledge.

Getting Started

broadcast model, catenet, community model, computer network, connectionless network, graphical user interface (GUI), internet, Internet, Internet Society (ISOC), internetworking, interoperability, local area network, Open Systems Interconnection (OSI) reference model, TCP/IP

Learning About the Internet

Understanding the Computer

Networks bandwidth, baseband, broadband, client-server model, congestion, connection, Ethernet, gigabit network, host, local area network (LAN), login name, metropolitan area network (MAN), net lag, password, wide area network (WAN)

Getting Connected to the Internet

access, account, dedicated access, dialup access, dialup IP, domain name, domain name system, freenet, gateway, IP address, service provider

Learning Netiquette

abbrev, Acceptable Use Policy (AUP), advertising, anonymous posting, carpet bomb, cascade, Frequently-Asked Questions (FAQ), flame, netiquette

Internet Tools

Archie, archive site, client-server model, electronic mail, File Transfer Protocol (FTP), finger, Gopher, Jughead, LIST-SERVE, mailing list, resource discovery tool, Telnet, Usenet, Veronica, Wide Area Information Server (WAIS), World Wide Web (WWW)

Internet Fun

ASCII art, Internet Relay Chat (IRC), Internet Talk Radio, Multi-User Dungeons (MUD)

Internet Issues

anonymity, commercialization, Clipper chip, cracker, email terrorism, Imminent Death of the Net, Internet Worm, last mile problem, malicious use, National Information Infrastructure (NII), National Research and Education Network (NREN), privacy, privatization, problem user, scale-up problem, security, spamming, trolling, unauthorized access

Acronym Finder

If you're trying to find the meaning of an acronym (such as TCP or PPP) look here first. You'll find cross-references to the entry that defines them. The most commonly-used acronyms (such as ASCII, FTP, and TCP/IP) are also cross-referenced amidst the entries.

ACK   *See* **acknowledgment (ACK)**

ACL   *See* **Access Control List (ACL)**

ADSL   *See* **Asynchronous Digital Subscriber Loop (ADSL)**

AFS   *See* **Andrew File System (AFS)**

ANSI   *See* **American National Standards Institute (ANSI)**

API   *See* **application program interface (API)**

ARP   *See* **Address Resolution Protocol (ARP)**

ARPA   *See* **Advanced Research Projects Agency (ARPA)**

AS   *See* **Autonomous System (AS)**

ASCII   *See* **American Standard Code for Information Interchange (ASCII)**

ATM   *See* **Asynchronous Transfer Mode (ATM)**

AUP   *See* **Acceptable Use Policy (AUP)**

BBN   *See* **Bolt, Beranak, and Newman (BBN)**

BBS   *See* **bulletin board system (BBS)**

BCC   *See* **blind courtesy copy (BCC)**

BER	*See* **Basic Encoding Rules (BER)**
BGP	*See* **Border Gateway Protocol (BGP)**
BISDN	*See* **Broadband ISDN**
BPS	*See* **bits per second (bps)**
BSD	*See* **Berkeley Software Distribution (BSD)**
CATV	*See* **cable television (CATV)**
CC	*See* **courtesy copy (CC)**
CCITT	*See* **Comité Consultif International de Télégraphique et Téléphonique (CCITT)**
CERN	**European Laboratory for Particle Physics (CERN)**
CERT	*See* **Computer Emergency Response Team (CERT)**
CFV	*See* **Call For Votes (CFV)**
CIX	*See* **Commercial Internet Exchange (CIX)**
CNI	*See* **Coalition for Network Information (CNI)**
CPSR	*See* **Computer Professionals for Social Responsibility (CPSR)**
CRC	*See* **Cyclic Redundancy Code (CRC)**
CREN	*See* **Corporation for Research and Educational Networking (CREN)**
CSMA/CD	*See* **Carrier Sense Multiple Access with Collision Detection (CSMA/CD)**
CWIS	*See* **Campus-Wide Information System (CWIS)**

DARPA   *See* **Defense Advanced Research Projects Agency (DARPA)**

DCE   *See* **Data Circuit-Terminating Equipment (DCE)**

DDN   *See* **Defense Data Network (DDN)**

DDN NIC   *See* **Defense Data Network Information Center (DDN NIC)**

DES   *See* **Data Encryption Standard (DES)**

DNS   *See* **Domain Name Service (DNS)**

DTE   *See* **Data Terminal Equipment (DTE)**

EBCDIC   *See* **Extended Binary Coded Decimal Interchange Code (EBCDIC)**

ECPA   *See* **Electronic Communications Privacy Act (ECPA)**

EFF   *See* **Electronic Frontier Foundation (EFF)**

EGP   *See* **Exterior Gateway Protocol (EGP)**

email   *See* **electronic mail**

etext   *See* **electronic text**

FAQ   *See* **Frequently-Asked Questions (FAQ)**

FDDI   *See* **Fiber Distributed Data Interface (FDDI)**

FDM   *See* **Frequency Division Multiplexing (FDM)**

FOIA   *See* **Freedom of Information Act (FOIA)**

FQDN	*See* **Fully Qualified Domain Name (FQDN)**
FTP	*See* **File Transfer Protocol (FTP)**
FYI	*See* **For Your Information (FYI)**
GIF	*See* **Graphics Interchange Format (GIF)**
GUI	*See* **graphical user interface (GUI)**
HDC	*See* **Heterogeneous Distributed Computing (HDC)**
HDSL	*See* **High-speed Digital Subscriber Loop (HDSL)**
HPCC	*See* **High Performance Computing and Communications Program (HPCC)**
HTML	*See* **HyperText Markup Language (HTML)**
HTTP	*See* **HyperText Transport Protocol (HTTP)**
IAB	*See* **Internet Architecture Board (IAB)**
IANA	*See* **Internet Assigned Numbers Authority (IANA)**
ICMP	*See* **Internet Control Message Protocol (ICMP)**
IEN	*See* **Internet Experiment Notes (IEN)**
IESG	*See* **Internet Enginering Steering Group (IESG)**
IETF	*See* **Internet Engineering Task Force (IETF)**
IGP	*See* **Interior Gateway Protocol (IGP)**

IMP   *See* **Interface Message Processor (IMP)**

IMR   *See* **Internet Monthly Report (IMR)**

IP   *See* **Internet Protocol (IP)**

IRC   *See* **Internet Relay Chat (IRC)**

IRSG   *See* **Internet Research Steering Group (IRSG)**

IRTF   *See* **Internet Research Task Force (IRTF)**

ISDN   *See* **Integrated Services Digital Network (ISDN)**

ISO   *See* **International Standards Organization (ISO)**

ISOC   *See* **Internet Society (ISOC)**

ITU-TSS   *See* **Comité Consultif International de Télégraphique et Téléphonique (CCITT)**

ITV   *See* **Interactive TV**

JPEG   *See* **Joint Photographic Experts Group (JPEG) graphics format**

LAN   *See* **local area network (LAN)**

LED   *See* **light emitting diode (LED)**

LPF   *See* **League for Programming Freedom (LPF)**

MAC   *See* **Medium Access Control (MAC)**

MAN   *See* **metropolitan area network (MAN)**

MIL STD   *See* **Military Standards (MIL STD)**

MIME   *See* **Multi-Purpose Internet Mail Extensions (MIME)**

MNP   *See* **Microcom Networking Protocol (MNP)**

MOTIS   *See* **Message-Oriented Text Interchange System (MOTIS)**

MPEG   *See* **Motion Picture Experts Group (MPEG)**

MTA   *See* **Message Transfer Agent (MTA)**

MTU   *See* **Maximum Transmission Unit (MTU)**

MUD   *See* **Multi-User Dungeons (MUD)**

NFS   *See* **Network File System (NFS)**

NIC   *See* **Network Information Center (NIC)**

NII   *See* **National Information Infrastructure (NII)**

NIS   *See* **Network Information Service (NIS)**

NJE   *See* **Network Job Entry (NJE)**

NNTP   *See* **Network News Transfer Protocol (NNTP)**

NOC   *See* **Network Operations Center (NOC)**

NREN   *See* **National Research and Education Network (NREN)**

NSF   *See* **National Science Foundation**

NVT   *See* **Network Virtual Terminal**

OSF   *See* **Open Software Foundation (OSF)**

OSI   *See* **Open Systems Interconnection (OSI) Reference Model**

OSPF   *See* **Open Shortest Path First (OSPF)**

PAR   *See* **Positive Acknowledgment with Re-Transmission (PAR)**

PBX   *See* **Private Branch Exchange (PBX)**

PC   *See* **personal computer (PC)**

PDL   *See* **page description language (PDL)**

PDN   *See* **Public Data Network (PDN)**

PEM   *See* **Privacy Enhanced Mail (PEM)**

PING   *See* **Packet Internet Groper (PING)**

POP   *See* **Post Office Protocol (POP)** or **Point of Presence (POP)**

POTS   *See* **Plain Old Telephone Service (POTS)**

PPP   *See* **Point-to-Point Protocol (PPP)**

RARP   *See* **Reverse Address Resolution Protocol (RARP)**

RBOC   *See* **Regional Bell Operating Company (RBOC)**

RFC   *See* **Request for Comments (RFC)**

RFD   *See* **Request for Discussion (RFD)**

RIP   *See* **Routing Information Protocol (RIP)**

RL   *See* **real life (RL)**

RPC   *See* **Remote Procedure Call (RPC)**

SDH   *See* **Synchronous Digital Hierarchy (SDH)**

SGML   *See* **Standard Generalized Markup Language (SGML)**

SLIP	*See* **Serial Line Interface Protocol (SLIP)**
SLIP/PPP	*See* **Serial Line Interface Protocol (SLIP)** and **Point-to-Point Protocol (PPP)**
SMDS	*See* **Switched Multimegabit Data Service (SMDS)**
SMTP	*See* **Simple Mail Transport Protocol (SMTP)**
SNMP	*See* **Simple Network Management Protocol (SNMP)**
SONET	*See* **Synchronous Optical Network (SONET)**
STO	*See* **Security Through Obscurity (STO)**
TCP	*See* **Transmission Control Protocol (TCP)**
TCP/IP	*See* **Transmission Control Protocol (TCP), Internet Protocol (IP), TCP/IP**
TDM	*See* **Time Division Multiplexing (TDM)**
TFTP	*See* **Trivial File Transfer Protocol (TFTP)**
UA	*See* **User Agent (UA)**
UDP	*See* **User Datagram Protocol (UDP)**
URL	*See* **Universal Resource Locater (URL)**
UUCP	*See* **Unix-to-Unix Copy Program (UUCP)**
VPN	*See* **virtual private network (VPN)**
W3	*See* **World Wide Web (WWW)**
WAIS	*See* **Wide Area Information Server (WAIS)**
WAN	*See* **wide area network (WAN)**

WWW   *See* **World Wide Web (WWW)**

Abbreviation Finder

Internet people like to conserve network **bandwidth** by using abbreviations for commonly-used phrases, such as "in my humble opinion" (IMHO). (Even the word abbreviations is abbreviated—see **abbrev**.) If you've run across an abbreviation in a **Usenet** posting or an **electronic mail** message, look here for a quick definition.

AAMOF	As a Matter of Fact
AFAIK	As Far As I Know
BBL	Be Back Later
DIIK	Damned If I Know
EOT	End of Thread
FOTCL	Falling Off the Chair Laughing
FYA	For Your Amusement
FYI	For Your Information
GD&R	Grinning, Ducking, and Running
GLG	Goofy Little Grin
HHOJ	Ha Ha Only Joking
IAE	In Any Event
IANAL	I Am Not A Lawyer
IMCO	In My Considered Opinion
IMHO	In My Humble Opinion
IMO	In My Opinion
IOW	In Other Words

IWBNI	It Would Be Nice If
IYFEG	Insert Your Favorite Ethnic Group
JASE	Just Another System Error
KISS	Keep It Simple, Stupid
LOL	Laughing Out Loud
MORF	Male Or Female?
NRN	No Reply Necessary
OIC	Oh, I See
OTOH	On The Other Hand
PMJI	Pardon My Jumping In
ROTF	Rolling On The Floor
ROTFL	Rolling On the Floor Laughing
ROTM	Right On The Money
RSN	Real Soon Now (that is, maybe never)
RTFM	Read The Fucking Manual!
RUMOF	Are You Male Or Female?
SITD	Still In The Dark
TIA	Thanks In Advance
TIC	Tongue In Cheek
TTFN	Ta-Ta For Now
TTYL	Talk To You Later
YMMV	Your Mileage May Vary

Abbreviation for *abbreviation* (and thus a manifestation of the principle of **recursion** which is much loved among Internet people generally and **UNIX** people in particular; *compare* **Gnu's Not UNIX [GNU]**).

Abbreviations such as IMHO (In My Humble Opinion) or BCNU (Be seeing you) pop up very frequently in **real-time** chatting applications such as **Internet Relay Chat (IRC)**, and **Multi-User Dungeons (MUD)**. They are also common in **electronic mail** and **Usenet** postings. Using an abbreviation is a practical necessity in a real-time computer chatting application, in which you must type quickly and concisely if you want to be part of the action. Elsewhere, it's a sign of commitment to the fundamental Internet value of conserving **bandwidth.**

You'll frequently encounter abbrevs in **Usenet** postings:

```
Captain Delete wrote the following:
>IMHO, you're wasting money to get a Power PC
>just now—there isn't a lot of native software,
>and you don't get the performance gains if you
>try to run the software in emulation.
PMJI, but that's just not true. The Power PC's
emulation is lots better than previous
emulation platforms. But YMMV.
```

Here's what the abbrevs stand for: "In My Humble Opinion," "Pardon My Jumping In," and "Your Mileage May Vary." Check out the Acronym and Abbreviation Finder for a list of commonly-used abbrevs.

Like **smileys**, there are frequently used abbreviations—and then there are abbreviations created by people playing with the idea of making up abbreviations. These aren't in common use. Some examples:

AWGTHTGTTA	Are We Going To Have To Go Through This Again?
GOTFIA	Groaning On The Floor In Agony.
PMYMHMMFSWGAD	Pardon Me, You Must Have Mistaken Me For Someone Who Gives a Damn.

AberMUD

An early, combat-oriented **MUD** (a computerized, multi-user adventure game modeled on the famous Dungeons and Dragons role-playing games). AberMUDs take their name from the Welsh university (Aberstywyth) where Richard Bartle and Roy Trubishaw created the game in the late 1970s. Echoing the Dungeons and Dragons theme, characters can include clerics, warriors, magicians, and thieves.

Among many of AberMUD's innovations: **wizards** (adept players) are given the ability to build additional options into the game. Considered old hat, AberMUDs are eclipsed by newer MUDS that place more emphasis on cooperative social relations as well as combat (**DikuMUDs**), offer more extensive and imaginative environments (**LPMUDs**), eliminate combat altogether (**TinyMUDs**), or offer builders the opportunity to use sophisticated, object-oriented programming languages (**MOOs**). If you're looking for a MUD to play, check out the newer ones.

Abstract Syntax Notation One (ASN.1)

An **Open Systems Interconnection (OSI)** protocol for defining data types in a computer **database**. (A data type is a definition of the type of data—for example, an integer or a date—that can be inserted into one of the fields of the database. In a library card catalogue, for example, the field *date of publication* must contain a date.)

Why is something like ASN.1 needed? This isn't a problem with database programs, which contain proprietary methods for figuring out what kind of data is contained in a field. As the network offers more databases for public access, however, the specter arises that many different programs will be trying to access the same data. ASN.1 represents an attempt to define a protocol that identifies the data type for the **client** that is trying to access the data.

In the OSI scheme, called the **Open Systems Interconnection (OSI) Reference Model**, ASN.1 is one of the key elements of the **presentation layer**, where it would come into play any time a client tried to access information from a database. In the Internet, it plays a much more restricted role. A version of ASN.1 has been incorporated in **CMOT**, a protocol governing access to databases that equipment such as routers keep about their performance. This information is used by applications that help to automate the tedious tasks of network maintenance. *See* **Simple Network Management Protocol (SNMP).**

Here's an interesting point. The use of ASN.1 came from a sincere attempt by Internet professionals to try to make the Internet more compatible with the **Open Systems Interconnection (OSI) protocol suite,** a competing set of networking protocols that is much favored in Europe and Japan. While ASN.1 proved useful, it had to be modified. OSI was designed by a committee full of lots of executives of monopoly telephone companies, while the Internet's design stems from real-world experience with living, breathing computer networks.

| Acceptable Use Policy (AUP) |

A policy statement adopted by a **service provider** to indicate what kinds of network uses are permissible. A publicly-subsidized network may restrict network use so that commercial activities are excluded.

NSFNET's AUP expressly states that the purpose of the network is to advance research communication in and among U.S. research and educational institutions; business participation is restricted to non-proprietary uses carried out in a spirit of open scientific collaboration. The guidelines permit announcements of new products, but only if they pertain to research or instruction. Specifically excluded are uses motivated by profit or extensive use for private or personal business.

An organization called the **Commercial Internet Exchange (CIX)**, a consortium of regional **service providers**, provides an AUP-free alternative to the NSFNET **backbone.** These networks do not restrict commercial use and are expected to play a significant role in the growing use of the Internet for business purposes. *See* **privatization**.

What no one seems able to explain is how the heck you tell whether your message, if commercial in spirit, traverses the Internet or a CIX backbone. After all, you can't hit a key and choose an option called "Commercial Message, Do Not Send Via NSFNET." The NSFNET's AUP is increasingly little more than a convenient fiction, designed more to keep Congress off the backs of government bureaucrats than to regulate Internet usage. A case in point: NSFNET's **backbone**, which is provided by a non-profit **service provider** (ANS), also carries *commercial* traffic by a for-profit division of the same organization (CO+REN). The Internet isn't a public service financed by taxpayer dollars; it's *already* effectively privatized and commercialized. Fact: In 1993, there were almost as many sites in the **com** (business) domain as in the **edu** (university and research) domain.

A means of gaining entry to a computer system so that you can make use of its resources.

There are two basic methods of getting connected to the Internet: **indirect connection** and a **direct connection.**

In an indirect connection, you use a personal computer, and access a computer that has a direct connection to the Internet. By means of this remote access, you may be able to use all or most of the Internet applications, such as **electronic mail**, **FTP**, and the various **resource discovery tools**, such as **Gopher** and **World Wide Web (WWW)**. But there is an important drawback to an indirect connection: You are operating the directly-connected computer remotely. The mail, files, and other resources you retrieve from the Internet go to this remote computer, not to your PC. This is very inconvenient because if you wish to use these resources you must **download** them to your computer, a tedious and often time-consuming process.

If you have a personal computer, you can easily obtain a type of indirect connection called **dialup access** at costs as low as $9 per month for unlimited on-line connect time. **Service providers** such as **PSINet** are making dialup Internet access easily available throughout the U.S. and beyond. For people living in rural areas where local access numbers can't be dialed, some service providers make dialup access available through 800 numbers.

In some cities, you can get free or inexpensive dialup access to the Internet through a **freenet**. Often provided through libraries, freenets are designed to ensure public access to information resources.

If you work for a government agency, a university, or a corporation, you may already have free Internet access. Perhaps your organization makes dialup access available.

Another way to get indirect Internet access is through **online information services** such as **America Online**, **CompuServe**, **Delphi**, or **The Well**. These and other services either offer Internet access now or are planning to implement it.

The best Internet connection is a **direct connection**. In a direct connection, the information you get from the Internet comes directly to your computer. In general, direct connections are more expensive than indirect ones. **Dialup IP** using **SLIP** or **PPP** lets you achieve direct Internet connectivity with a personal computer and a high-speed **modem**, but this is difficult to implement at present and prices are considerably higher than ordinary dialup access. If your office computer is connected to a **local area network (LAN)**, you may already have direct Internet connectivity. To find out, check with the network administrator.

access control

A method of ensuring the **security** of an Internet **host** that is more restrictive than allowing all outside users to have full access to the system, but less restrictive than installing a **firewall**. In access control, a host checks outside access requests against an **access control list**, a file that specifies which outside systems may gain what kind of access. If the list contains information indicating that a certain system can gain access, then access is granted. *See* **Access Control List (ACL)**.

Access Control List (ACL)

A file that lists the services a **host** makes available and indicates which **remote hosts** may access those services.

An ACL provides a measure of security that's less effective than a **firewall**, but better than nothing: It lets a network

administrator provide full access to users from another
branch of the same organization, for example, while denying access to browsers from outside the organization.

---

access site

In **dialup access** and **dialup IP**, the **host** system that provides
Internet connectivity via telephone connections.

---

account

A formal, contractual arrangement between you, the user,
and a **service provider** that provides access to the computer system (here, the Internet). You must agree to honor
the provider's **Acceptable Use Policy (AUP)** and to pay the
charges for accessing the provider's computer resources. If
you're a student at a university or you work for a government
agency, university, or corporation, there may be no charge
for the access, but you still have an account and you're
bound by the organization's AUP.

---

acknowledgment (ACK)

In the **Transmission Control Protocol (TCP)**, the Internet
protocol (standard) that governs connection-oriented
data delivery, a message sent by the receiving host that
this **host** is ready to start receiving data. The data transfer
does not begin until the sending host receives this
acknowledgment.

---

acronym

A neologism (new word) that is made from the first or other
important letters in a descriptive phrase, often because the
phrase itself is full of polysyllabic words or is difficult to
remember: for example, EBCDIC (pronounced "ebb-see

dick") stands for Extended Binary Coded Decimal Interchange Code.

Acronyms are a twentieth-century innovation, according to linguist John Ciardi (of National Public Radio's popular program titled "A Word in your Ear"), and may be symptomatic of bureaucracy in the making: The first English acronyms stem from President Roosevelt's New Deal legislation. But by far the top generator of acronyms nowadays is the computer industry.

Some acronyms serve a legitimate purpose, in that they name things (such as **protocols**) that computer people really need convenient names for, such as TCP (Transmission Control Protocol). But it's also true that the computer industry is acronym-happy; just about any new computer phrase appears with its acronym in parentheses, as if providing the acronym dignifies the term or establishes its legitimacy.

An acronym may embark on a journey that results in its becoming a full-fledged word, a transition that's accompanied by the loss of capital letters. Thus SPOOL (Simultaneous Peripheral Operations On Line) becomes *spool*—and from there, one can speaking of *spooling* and *spoolers*. Hastening this process is the need to fit acronyms into a sentence; thus Internet users say that they've FTPed a file from Point A to Point B. This process may involve transforming the acronym's noun phrase into a verb, as this example attests. A regrettable tendency: making up an obviously-strained noun phrase just so that it will transform a common word or name into an acronym. The Internet tool called **Jughead**, for example, is supposed to stand for Jonzy's Universal Gopher Hierarchy Excavation And Display (JUGHEAD).

Computer people pronounce most acronyms by saying their letters—FTP is pronounced "F-T-P." But some acronyms contain vowels in such a way that makes them easy to pronounce, such as ANSI (an-see), CERT (sert), RISC (risk), and SONET (soh-net).

address

Within the Internet, the location of a computer or a computer resource. Each of the millions of **hosts** connected to the Internet has a unique **IP address**. In addition, Internet users have **electronic mail** addresses that allow people to direct messages to their **mailboxes**. To use these addresses, you type them according to the rules of the **domain name system.**

> **Tip**: Looking for someone's **electronic mail** address? You may be able to find it using a **knowbot**, which explores **white pages** on dozens or even hundreds of servers.

address depletion

A potential crisis for the Internet's future that is brought about by built-in limitations to the number of **hosts** that can be given a unique **IP address.** Because the Internet requires that every **host** have a unique address, the exhaustion of the available numbers could stop the growth of the network.

The original design specifications for **ARPANET** in 1973 and 1974 called for a maximum of 256 networks—a number that has been exceeded by more than 20,000. In recognition of the development of **local area networks (LAN)**, Internet addressing was subsequently modified by using a 32-bit address. This would have been enough to handle billions of hosts, but the 32-bit address was broken down into classes to reduce the processing burden on **IP routers**. This reduced the number of addresses available and led, ultimately, to the current problem. Only 128 **Class A networks** are permitted, but each Class A network can have millions of hosts. There can be thousands of **Class B networks**, and each can have thousands of hosts. There can be millions of **Class C networks**, but each can have no more than 254 hosts. At current rates of Internet growth, Class B network addresses—by far the most popular choice for networks seeking to link to the Internet—will be exhausted in a matter of months. This problem is currently being addressed by the **Internet Engineering Task Force (IETF)**.

address resolution

The process by which the addresses of **hosts** on a **local area network (LAN)** are translated into **IP addresses**. This translation is needed because LANs and the Internet handle addresses in very different ways. The translation is handled by the **Address Resolution Protocol (ARP)** for incoming **datagrams**, and the **Reverse Address Resolution Protocol (RARP)** for outgoing datagrams.

Address Resolution Protocol (ARP)

In **TCP/IP,** a **protocol** (standard) that translates **IP addresses** used on the Internet to the physical locations of computers on a **local area network (LAN)**, such as an **Ethernet** network, that is connected to the Internet. In addition, ARP dynamically discovers new nodes on a LAN; the network administrator can add new PCs and **workstations** without having to update translation tables manually. *Compare* **Reverse Address Resolution Protocol (RARP).**

ARP is necessary because most of the local area networks connected to the Internet use a different method for **addressing**, that is, directing a message to the correct computer. This protocol operates invisibly, taking care of the details of translating messages between various physical networks so that, from the user's perspective, the Internet is a single **logical network** (a system that appears to be homogeneous because all of its devices seem to operate in the same or much the same way).

addressing

In a computer network, the directing of a message to the correct destination computer. *See* **address, IP address**.

Advanced Research Projects Agency (ARPA)

An agency of the U.S. Department of Defense (DoD), renamed **Defense Advanced Research Projects Agency (DARPA)**, that funded early research in the late 1960s and early 1970s on the potential of new communications technologies for scientific and technical collaboration. Working with major universities and research centers, ARPA was responsible for creating the Internet's predecessor, **ARPANET.** Responsibility for ARPANET-related research was turned over to the Defense Communications Agency (DCA) in 1975.

advertising

In **distributed routing**, a dynamic and automatic method of distributing information about the routes a **router** can choose from to send a **packet** of data to its destination. These routes may change if a portion of the network fails or if new networks are added. Each router advertises the routing information it knows about to all the routers to which it is directly connected. These routers, in turn, are incorporating and relaying the information *they* have received. In this way, an accurate map of th network's current **topology** quickly propagates throughout the network. This process is called **convergence**.

agent

A computer program or process that operates on behalf of the system's users and performs a specific function. In contrast to a **daemon**, a simple computer program that constantly runs in a computer's memory and springs into action when needed, an agent possesses at least some capacity to make decisions and to react in different ways depending on the situation. In the **Simple Network Management Protocol (SNMP)**, for example, a **router's** network management agent exchanges information with other network management agents, and configures the routing device accordingly.

Alex

A **client** program that enables the most important function of a **Network File System (NFS)**: That is, it enables the user to **mount** a remote directory so that it appears to be part of the **host** system's file system. After mounting the files, the user may read them—but can not modify them in any way, unless explicit permission is given. By incorporating this restriction, Alex's designers address the concerns of network administrators who feared that granting remote access to NFS servers would lead to security problems. *Compare* **Andrew File System (AFS), Prospero**.

alias

An additional name for something. In **electronic mail**, for example, a system administrator can use aliases to set up alternate names (nicknames) for users, so that a message addressed to *skywalker@marine.com* will reach the user registered as *lbl@marine.com*. Aliases are also used to set up groups, such as *humanities-faculty@boondocks.edu*.

Tip: If your electronic mail address has lots of subdomains that are difficult to type, ask your system administrator to create an alias that will allow your correspondents to ignore subdomain names. For example, after creating such an alias, a message addressed to *skywalker-@marine.com* will reach *skywalker@babybyte.eng.-marine.com*).

aliasing

In **electronic mail**, the process of creating an **alias**, another name for a person or group.

alt

In **Usenet**, the foremost—and most controversial—of several **alternative newsgroup hierarchies** that are carried and propagated only by those Usenet sites that elect to do so (in contrast to **world newsgroups**, which are automatically fed to every Usenet subscriber). Reflecting the generally anti-establishment ethos of Internet, self-styled "Usenet anarchists" created the alt **newsgroups** to bypass the normal, stiff requirements for establishing newsgroups (*see* **Call For Votes [CFV]**). The name "alt" does not stand for "alternative perspectives," as is commonly assumed, but rather suggests an alternative to the rigid voting procedure required to create one of the world newsgroups. But according to one wag, "alt" stands for "Anarchists, Lunatics, and Terrorists."

Virtually anyone can establish an alt newsgroup, and in consequence, quality ranges widely. Some groups offer serious and valuable discussions of subjects such as archery, best-selling books, folklore, and meditation); others explore virtually every aspect of human sexuality, from the normal to the bizarre (including cross-dressing, diaper, and foot fetishes); still others are just plain silly (notably, alt.barney.dinosaur.die.die.die, for the Barney haters of the world). In general, alt newsgroups are noted for a low **signal-to-noise ratio**—they sometimes generate more heat than light.

> **Tip** Although anyone can create an alt newsgroup, system administrators are by no means obliged to carry the new group. To ensure that a new group gains acceptance, it's wise to propose it for discussion in alt.config, a newsgroup designed for this purpose. In addition, the group should be named so that it fits into the existing logical hierarchy of names in a consistent fashion: alt.norwegian.culture wouldn't fit very well if there's already a newsgroup class called alt.culture.* (the best name would be alt.culture.norwegian). It goes without saying that obscene, vengeful, shocking, or obscure names won't gain much acceptance.

alternative newsgroup hierarchies

In **Usenet**, newsgroup categories (such as **Alt**, **Biz**, and **Clari**) that bypass the normal procedures required to set up a new newsgroup. Not all sites carry the alternative newsgroup hierarchies.

AlterNet

A national Internet **backbone** network and service provider with headquarters in Falls Church, VA. One of the founding members of the **Commercial Internet Exchange (CIX)**, AlterNet provides Internet connectivity throughout the U.S. without imposing **acceptable use policies (AUP)** that forbid business activity.

American National Standards Institute (ANSI)

A U.S. non-profit organization, composed of technical and industrial manufacturers and business organizations that support the concept of **standardization**. ANSI is the U.S. representative to the **International Standards Organization (ISO)**.

American Standard Code for Information Interchange (ASCII)

A seven-bit code used for representing text, graphics, and control characters for use in the computer. There are a total of 128 character codes in the standard ASCII set, the first 32 of which are used to symbolize keyboard and printer operations, such as backspace, carriage return, and line break. The remainder represent the characters you find on any standard computer keyboard, including lowercase and uppercase letters, numbers, and punctuation marks. ASCII lacks the accented characters and ligatures (conjoined characters such as æ, common in Danish and Norwegian) that are widely used in European languages. The fact that the Internet assumes a 7-bit ASCII character set amounts to an implied bias against languages other than English. *Compare* **EBCDIC.**

Personal computers employ an **extended character set** that employs an additional 128 codes, for a total of 256. To represent the additional characters, these computers must encode characters using an 8-bit code. These codes are used to provide foreign language characters, mathematical and technical symbols, and graphics characters. However, extended character sets are not standardized. For example, the IBM PC's extended character set differs from that of the Macintosh. *Compare* **Kermit.**

analog

The representation of information by means of continu-ously-varied electrical properties, such as voltage, in such a way that the variations capture the patterns of the origi-nal information. For example, an analog telephone con-verts the intensities and frequencies of the human voice into electrical signals; the signal varies in proportion to the strength and frequency of the voice. *Compare* **digital**.

analog network

A communications network such as the local telephone system in which the changing electrical signals mimic the continuos variations of the source, such as a human voice. A telephone, for example, converts the sound of a voice into an electrical current whose strength and other char-acteristics parallel the changing sounds of the voice.

anchor

In a **hypertext** system such as the **World Wide Web (WWW)**, a word or phrase that is highlighted on the screen to serve as the starting point or ending point of a **link**. When the user selects the anchor, the system jumps to the document that contains the corresponding anchor, which is also high-lighted.

Andrew File System (AFS)

A **client** program that enables the user to **mount** a remote directory so that it appears to be part of the **host** system's file system. Unlike the **Network File System (NFS)**, AFS allows users to access only those files that have been linked to AFS. In this way, AFS addresses the concerns of network administrators who fear that granting remote access to

NFS servers will lead to security problems. AFS has additional advantages: It allows system administrators to allocate disk space on the fly, and a cache system reduces the file systems's demand on network **bandwidth**. *Compare* **Network File System (NFS), Prospero.**

---

animation

The simulation of natural movement by presenting a series of images on the computer screen in rapid succession, with each image—called a frame—showing one or more objects in a slightly altered position. A smooth animation, one that tricks the eye into thinking the movement is continuous—requires at least 15 frames per second (fps).

Animations are notorious guzzlers of network **bandwidth.** Because they must store a great deal of information, files containing animations tend to be very large—as much as 500K for less than a minute of animation. Animations may figure prominently in coming high-bandwidth networks (*see* **integrated services network).** Until then, efforts are underway to compress animations and other video images so that they require less disk space. A new multimedia standard called MPEG, short for **Motion Picture Experts Group (MPEG)**, enables Internet users to exchange low-resolution animations and video accompanied by high-quality stereo sound.

---

anonymity

In the Internet, the creation of an **electronic mail** message or **anonymous posting** in such a way that the link between the user's **identity** and the message is difficult—but probably not impossible—to recover. Anonymity is achieved, to the extent possible, by an **anonymous server,** a computer program that strips mail of identifying information.

| anonymous FTP |

The use of the **FTP** file-transfer program to **log on** to another computer system via the Internet to obtain files from a public-access **archive**. No **login name** or **password** is required to gain access to the computer system that contains the archive.

When you make contact with the remote system, you type *anonymous* in response to the prompt to supply your user name. When prompted for a password, you type your **electronic mail address**. This is normally just a courtesy; system administrators like to have a record of just who's been using the system. Increasingly, it's required to gain access to the system.

Typically, the files you'll want are stored in a **directory** called pub, or in one of its **subdirectories**. And that's where you'll wind up, since on most systems typing *anonymous* locks you into a restricted directory path. The following commands typify an FTP session:

```
ftp
```
Starts the FTP client

```
ftp>open ampere.land.tim.edu
```
Opens the FTP server

```
login name: anonymous
```
Log in as "anonymous"

```
password:wings-o@kleopatra.jcmu.edu
```
Your email address

```
ftp>cd pub
```
Switch to /pub

```
ftp>dir
```
View a file list

```
ftp>get index.txt - | more
```

Read index on-screen

```
ftp>get filename
```

Send the file to you

```
ftp>bye
```

End the FTP session

> **Tip**: If you can't gain access to a hot anonymous FTP site you've read or heard about, it's not necessarily your fault: anonymous FTP sites come and go. An anonymous FTP site depends on the good will of system administrators, as well as the time of the people who have volunteered to maintain it; if either good will or time runs out, the site may disappear.

> **Do** supply your **email address** when you log in via electronic mail, even if this is not required.

> **Don't** overuse an FTP site, try to explore the system outside the pub directory, or disobey the rules you see when you log on to the FTP site. Repeated abuse may result in the site's termination—and if that happens, everyone loses.

anonymous posting

In **Usenet**, a **posting** (public message) that has been contributed through an **anonymous server** to disguise the **identity** of the person who authored the message.

> **Do** disable your **signature** file—the file that, on most systems, automatically appends information about you to the bottom of your posting—if you plan to send an anonymous posting. Not all anonymous servers strip signatures.

> **Don't** assume that anonymous mail ensures your **privacy**—it can't. The anonymous server maintains records of its linking of anonymous and real addresses. An

unscrupulous system administrator or investigative agency could link the message with you.

anonymous server

A computer program based on an Internet host that allows a person to create an **anonymous posting** to **Usenet.** To use the anonymous service, you send electronic mail to the anonymous server, an automatic program located on an Internet host. The server then strips the mail of information that would identify its origins, and sends it on to its destination. (This term is also used to describe the software that enables **anonymous FTP**.)

ANS CO+RE

An Internet **backbone** and **service provider** that offers high-speed **(T1** and**T3)** Internet connectivity throughout the U.S. Operated by Advanced Networks and Services, the firm that operates the **NSFNET** backbone, ANS CO+RE also offers a variety of services to organizations and businesses seeking solutions in Internet networking. ANS CO+RE is a for-profit organization that actively encourages commercial Internet usage.

Because the CO+RE and NSFNET backbones are one and the same, is there a conflict with NSF's **Acceptable Use Policy (AUP)**, which forbids commercial use of the publicly-subsidized backbone? The agreement between CO+RE and NSF stipulates that any commercial traffic carried on CO+RE's lines must pay its full share and then some, with the remainder going to finance regional educational and research networks. A Congressional committee wasn't so sure, however, that this arrangement was in the taxpayer's best interest. An investigation concluded that the commercial traffic did not interfere with legitimate NSF uses.

.answers

In **Usenet**, a **moderated newsgroup** that is set aside for information about the Usenet in general, and about specific newsgroups in particular. These newsgroups are called news.answers, alt.answers, comp.answers, rec.answers, sci.answers, soc.answers, and talk.answers.

In .answers newsgroups, you will find **FAQs** (lists of frequently-asked questions, together with answers), and additional valuable information. A browse through the group comp.answers, for instance, may reveal treasures such as an extensive bibliography on computer music, lists of valuable MS-DOS programs available free via **FTP**, and an updated catalog of computer tools useful for a variety of professions.

> **TIP**: Before posting a message to a newsgroup asking whether a FAQ is available for the group, check out the corresponding .answers group. For example, if you're looking for a FAQ for rec.pets.cats, check out rec.answers. Chances are you'll find the FAQ posted there.

> **Do** browse through news.answers before posting your own messages to Usenet. New users should subscribe to net.announce.newusers, where you will find many useful postings, including "What is Usenet," "A Primer on How to Work With the Usenet Community," and "Answers to Frequently Asked Questions about Usenet."

Apocalypse of Two Elephants

A debacle, described and named by David Clark at the Massachusetts Institute of Technology (MIT), that ensues when **standards** are developed at the wrong time, that is, either before research is completed or after companies have managed to establish their **proprietary standards** as **de facto standards**.

The "two elephants" refer to activity peaks. The first peak of activity occurs when many researchers are investigating the properties of a new system. As research results accumulate and the system's properties become known, researchers lose interest, and move on to new things. Subsequently, companies launch a new upswing in activity as they try to implement the research in new products.

The appropriate timing for the creation of successful standards lies in the trough between the two "elephants": the research is complete, but companies haven't yet developed proprietary standards. If the research isn't complete, the technology may not be sufficiently understood and the standards will be poor. If companies have already made substantial capital investments in their proprietary standards, they will ignore the standards.

The **TCP/IP** protocols attest to the virtues of good timing. They were developed during several years of intensive research, using the **ARPANET** as a **testbed**. The standards reflected the wisdom gained from years of practical experience in internetworking and could be utilized anywhere to create an effective, functioning network. Only then were the standards formulated and made widely available. As more people implemented **TCP/IP** in a variety of organizational settings, a market for Internet products developed. This market has recently become one of the hottest in the computer industry, with companies manufacturing Internet **routers** experiencing very rapid growth. The story of the Internet's standards provides a textbook example of the enormous contributions effective standards can make to technological progress and economic development.

append

To place at the end of something. In the **file capture** utilities typically found in **communications programs**, each new segment of captured data is appended to the file that the utility creates.

AppleLink

A commercial **online information service** designed to serve the needs of Apple Computer's customers. A **gateway** is available so that AppleLink subscribers can exchange **electronic mail** with Internet users.

application

The use of a computer system for a purpose that benefits the user. Among the most common applications of the Internet are those that take full advantage of the net's world-wide scope, and allow users to access people and computer resources in distant locations. These include **electronic mail** and file transfer via **FTP.** In addition, several applications help the user navigate the Internet as if it were a massive **digital library** from which information may be retrieved; these include **Archie, Gopher, WAIS,** and **World Wide Web.** With the coming installation of **broadband networks,** applications that feature **multimedia** will become commonplace (*see* **composite imaging, interactive visualization, multimedia databases,** and **multimedia mail**). The **gigabit networks** of the future will permit applications to be divided among two or more geographically separated computing facilities (*see* **heterogeneous distributed computing [HDC]**).

application layer

In the **Open Systems Interconnection (OSI) Reference Model** of computer networks, the layer in which one finds **protocols** (standards) that can be used by application programs. Typically, these standards define **terminals**, handle **file transfer**, and specify the formats for **electronic mail**. For Internet protocols at this level, *see* **Telnet,** the Internet's **Network Virtual Terminal (NVT)** protocol; the **File Transfer Protocol (FTP)**; and the **Simple Mail Transport Protocol (SMTP)**.

application program

A computer program that performs a useful service for you, the user, in contrast to a **system utility** (such as a background mailing router program), which supports a given computer system function.

application program interface (API)

A program that performs a frequently-needed task, such as displaying text on the screen, that can be accessed and used by application programs. For example, Microsoft Windows has many **API** resources that application programs access for commonly-used processes such as displaying a window on the screen. To use the routine, the program issues a call and the operating system responds by supplying the needed information or performing the requested task.

Archie

A **resource discovery tool** that is designed to help you locate publicly-accessible file directories, as well as the

files that are available in them, by means of **anonymous FTP**
at more than 1,000 **archive sites** throughout the Internet.

A product of students and volunteers at the McGill University's
Department. of Computer Science, Archie is freely distributed worldwide. Once per month, McGill University tech-
nicians run a program that accesses every known FTP site
and compiles a list of directory and file names. When you use
an Archie **client**, the program searches this database and displays the results.

Suppose you're looking for a poker game you can run on your
computer. When you run Archie, you start the client and enter
a query using a command such as the following (UNIX
systems):

```
watt: /home/qxs$ archie poker
```

In response, you receive a list of all the archive sites that have
a file with this name:

```
Host plaza.aarnet.edu.au

  Location:/usenet/comp.sources.games/volume7
      DIRECTORY drwxr-xr-x 512 Apr 26 13:36 poker

Host krynn.efd.1th.se

  Location:/pub/hp-
          calc/educalc/horn_disk_7/games
    FILE -rwxrwxr-x    4666 Aug 19 1992 poker
  Location: /pub/hp-calc/games
    FILE -rwxrwxr-x    32087 Oct 7 1992 poker
```

Archie is most useful when you know the name of the file
you want to retrieve and just need to know where it's stored.
After discovering the location, you can download the file using
anonymous FTP. If you want to find out more about a file
whose name you've found, you may be able to do so using
the **whatis** option, which retrieves a short description of
the file (that is, if the system administrator or someone else

took the time to create one). To use whatis, you must contact an Archie **server**.

Tip: By default, Archie searches for an exact string match—which means that, if you search for "poker," the program displays only those file names that exactly match what you typed (including lowercase letters). It does not even show you file names in which the text you typed occurs as a substring (within additional text, as in *winpoker.zip*). For best results, learn the command that performs a case-insensitive substring search. With **UNIX** versions of Archie, you set this feature by using a switch, an additional part of the command that lets you choose an option. To perform a case-insensitive substring search, you type a space followed by a dash and the letter *s*:

```
archie -s poker
```

This retrieves many more items:

```
Host ftp.luth.se
  Location: /pub/amiga/game/misc
    FILE -rw-r-r-  184980  Jun 4 1993
    JBPoker10.lha
    FILE -rw-r-r-  242  Jun 4 1993
    JBPoker10.readme
    FILE -rw-r-r-  383398  Aug 7 1993
    Poker10.lha
    FILE -rw-r-r-  444  Aug 7 1993
    Poker10.readme
    FILE -rw-r-r-  22161  Aug 14 1993
    Poker10p1.lha
    FILE -rw-r-r-  247  Aug 14 1993
    Poker10p1.readme
```

Do use the Archie **client** if one is available on your **host** system rather than accessing an Archie server. Archie server sites are seriously overloaded with Archie requests.

architecture

In a computer network, the overall design of the network, as expressed in a list of the **protocols** that govern the network's operation at each **layer**. *See* **Open Systems Interconnection (OSI) Reference Model**.

archive

A repository of stored files, which are accessible by means of **anonymous FTP** (*see* **Archie**, **archive site**). This term is also used to describe a collection of files that has been grouped together (and sometimes compressed), and stored under one file name (*see* **file compression program**).

Files are combined and optionally compressed into an archive not only to economize on disk storage, but also to keep related files together. For example, as many as a dozen utilities for Microsoft Windows may be compressed and stored together in a file called windows-utils.tar. The **UNIX** utility that creates a .tar archive, tar, does not compress the files. Tar is short for "tape archive."

Tip: If you encounter a file archive with a resource discovery program such as **Gopher**, you'll find that the file has a one to three letter **extension** that specifies the program that was used to create the archive. To extract the files from the archive, you need to use the same program or a program that is compatible with the program that created the archive. A file archive with the extension .zoo has been archived and compressed with the zoo utility. The extensions .shar or .sh are used to name archives created (without compression) with shar, a UNIX utility. The .sit extension is used to name archives created with Stuffit, a popular Macintosh compression and archiving program. Frequently encountered is the extension .zip, which is used to name archives created with PKZIP or WINZIP, the most popular IBM PC and Microsoft Windows compression and archiving utilities. *See* **file compression program**.

archive site

A **host** that has devoted part of the available disk space to serve as a repository for files. You can retrieve these files via **FTP**.

 Tip: If you know the name of the file you're looking for, you can use **Archie**—one of the Internet's several **resource discovery tools**—to find an archive that contains the file.

ARPANET

A **Wide-Area Network (WAN)** created in 1969 by the **Advanced Projects Research Agency (ARPA),** (which is now called **Defense Advanced Projects Research Agency [DARPA]**), in tandem with major universities and research centers, for the specific goal of investigating the utility of high-speed data communication for scientific collaboration and military operations. ARPANET provided the staging ground for the development of the Internet's **protocol suite**, the roughly 100 protocols (standards) that enable dissimilar **physical networks** to exchange data.

ARPANET has its origins in late 1960s proposals. A firm called **Bolt, Beranak, and Newman (BBN)** was awarded the contract to construct the network. The firm designed and constructed the first **Interface Message Processors (IMPs)**—now called **routers**. These were installed in four sites—three California universities and the University of Utah—and, on September 2, 1969, they were connected via telephone lines, turned on, and the ARPANET was born.

The methods used to relay messages in the early ARPANET were not very effective. Early ARPANET research focused on this and other network problems. From this research emerged the concept of a **packet switching network**, and more specifically the **protocols** that make packet switching possible. The basic challenge of designing an efficient data communications system is that computer communications are inherently "bursty"—there's a lot of data for a minute, then nothing for an hour. If two linked computers tie up a telephone line without much happening, the system isn't very efficient. A packet switching network achieves great efficiency by breaking down the data from each computer into segments (packets), each of which contains a delivery address (just like a first-class letter). The system then combines these packets into a single, high-speed bit stream, and shoots this stream over the line as fast as the line can handle it. On the other end, routers figure out where the packets should go, and they're reassembled at their destination.

The engineers who created this design also created the **protocol suite** that is responsible for the current explosive growth of world-wide networking. (A protocol suite is a collection of standards by which the network operates.) Vincent G. Cerf and Robert E. Kahn first described these protocols to the wider engineering community in a 1974 paper published in *IEEE Transactions on Communication*. The first specification of the Internet protocols appeared as an **Internet Experiment Note** in December of that year.

The ARPANET's design was strongly shaped by military considerations. Interested in a network that could transmit messages across differing physical media (including radio and satellites), the military encouraged ARPANET engineers to develop **hardware-independent** protocols that were capable of **multivendor interoperability.** In addition, the military called for a network that could survive the destruction of significant proportions of the network, a possibility in a wartime situation, by means of **transparent adaptive routing** (the sending of information along whatever route is available and viable, without the need for direct intervention from the user). Their success was demonstrated with considerable technical panache in a 1978 test: A computer in a van traversing a freeway in California relayed data via **packet radio** to a nearby host site, which transmitted the data across the U.S. continent via ARPANET and then to a host in London, U.K., via a **communications satellite** network.

By 1980 it was obvious that the ARPANET was an extremely valuable tool for research collaboration. Although the system had been designed to facilitate file transfer, users demanded—and got—**electronic mail** and **mailing lists**, and it became clear early on that these applications would prove vital to scientific collaboration and progress. However, ARPANET could not fully link the research community because it was administered by the Department of Defense; universities and colleges that did not have DoD contracts were not permitted to use ARPANET. In recognition of this problem, the **National Science Foundation (NSF)** funded CSNET in the early 1980s to link computer science departments throughout the U.S.

In 1983, the U.S. Department of Defense (DoD) adopted the TCP/IP protocols as a **Military Standard (MIL STD)**. At the same time, DoD created the **Defense Data Network (DDN)** to serve as the central platform for the conversion of defense-related networkings to the Internet protocols. The adoption of this standard created a huge market for **TCP/IP**-capable hardware and is in large measure responsible for the Internet's phenomenal success. In the same year, the ARPANET was divided into two parts, MILNET (an unclassified military network) and ARPANET, devoted to research and development. By this time, an **internet** had emerged—a network of networks, employing ARPANET as its **backbone**, that could share data using **TCP/IP**. However, this system still had a military basis and could not serve as the foundation for college and university research coordination.

In the late 1980s, the **National Science Foundation (NSF)** introduced **NSFNET**, which was specifically intended to replace the military-funded ARPANET with an NSF-funded **backbone**, thereby freeing the network for use by researchers not affiliated with universities under DoD contract. The ARPANET was phased out in 1990.

| article |

In **Usenet,** a contribution posted to a **newsgroup** by an Internet user. An article is essentially an electronic mail message that has been directed to the group, where it is publicly accessible to anyone who wishes to read it.

| article selector |

In a **newsreader** client for reading **Usenet** postings, the level or mode in which you can read the text of posted **articles**. When you "read" the article (defined as paging through the entire posting to the end), the newsreader marks it as read and it no longer appears in the **subject selector** or **thread selector**. In addition to providing the means to page through the article as you read it, most newsreaders provide commands that let you junk the article (mark it as read even though you haven't paged all the way through it), forward the article to an **electronic mail** address, save the article to a file, or **kill** the author so his or her postings do not appear in future lists. *Compare* **newsgroup selector, subject selector,** and **thread selector.**

| ASCII |

See **American Standard Code for Information Interchange (ASCII).**

ASCII art

A drawing or picture that is composed of nothing but the standard **ASCII** characters that are found on the standard computer keyboard.

Given that the ASCII character set is the lowest common denominator of data interchange in the Internet, graphics are difficult to exchange and display. But that hasn't stopped the net's would-be artists. ASCII art can be found everywhere on the Internet; it is considered fashionable, for example, to include a few lines of ASCII art as part of the **signature** at the bottom of one's **email** messages or **postings** to **Usenet**.

ASCII art isn't high-brow art by any means. Still, it's amusing to see how people have transcended the severe limitations of the keyboard as a means of artistic expression. Characters such as X and H can be used to express dark areas, shading into Is and apostrophes to express lighter tones. One can stand back some distance from the best ASCII art and, suddenly, the image makes sense and even appears to have gently gradated shading.

Tip: Like to see the latest ASCII art? The newsgroup alt.ascii.art carries the artistic creations of ASCII artists from around the globe.

ASCII file

A file containing nothing but the standard ASCII text and control characters. Such files include the **text files** created by **text editors** such as **EMACS**, as well as the **source code** of computer programs, **uuencoded** graphics files, and **PostScript** files.

ASCII text

ASCII text

Synonymous with **ASCII file**; a file containing nothing but the standard ASCII text and control characters.

asynchronous

Not timed or synchronized by a timing mechanism; characterized by the transmission of units of data that occupy varying units of time. In asynchronous data transmission, some method must be employed to demarcate the beginning and the end of a unit of data. A personal computer's serial port does this by adding a start and stop bit at the end of each eight-bit character. *Compare* **synchronous.**

asynchronous communication

A method for solving the chief problem in **serial communication**: How to demarcate the beginning and the end of a unit of transmitted data. In asynchronous communication, the method used is simpler than that of **synchronous communication**, which involves the use of a timing signals to synchronize the arrival of units of data. Instead, the beginning of each unit is marked with a start bit—which says, in effect, "Here comes a unit of data." And the end of the unit is marked with a stop bit, which says, "That's the end of the data." In PC data communications, the start and stop bits are added to each eight-bit unit (**byte**) of transmitted data. This means that each character, normally one byte (eight bits) in length, requires the transmission of 10 bits of data.

> **Tip:** If your new modem doesn't seem to be performing up to its full potential, remember that the modem must transfer ten bits of information for every character. For this reason, a 14,400 bps modem probably won't manage to transfer 1800 characters per second; you'll be lucky to get 1,400. (Most **communications programs**

show you how many bits or characters per second your modem is transferring while a file transfer is in progress.) To get the maximum performance out of your modem, consult your modem's and communication program's documentation to learn how to establish a synchronous connection using an **error correction** protocol such as **V.42**.

Asynchronous Digital Subscriber Loop (ADSL)

A telephone protocol for forthcoming local **digital** telephone systems, capable of a 1.5 Mbps **data transfer rate**, that will enable the delivery of a single high-quality compressed video signal in addition to a noise-free digital voice channel.

Asynchronous Transfer Mode (ATM)

A high-speed **packet switching network** that employs **cell relay** techniques. ATM uses small **frames** of fixed size and super-fast switching devices to achieve data transfer rates of up to 622 Mbps. ATM is a **network layer** and **data link layer** design that is independent of **physical media,** but its full potential requires **fiber optic** lines that are compatible with **Synchronous Digital Hierarchy (SDH)** standards. This network design has nothing to do with automatic teller machines, also known as **ATMs**.

ATM directly addresses the challenge of advanced telecommunications: namely, the need to handle **multimedia**, which combines interactive, high-resolution video (which can tolerate some data loss but no delay) with massive flows of computer data (which can tolerate some delay but no data loss). Neither of today's existing network technologies, **circuit switching networks** such as the telephone system or **packet switching networks** such as the Internet, handle multimedia well. Because they establish and maintain a single physical connection between two points, circuit switching networks are notoriously inefficient for computer data, which tends to come in bursts followed by periods of silence. But packet switching networks, which are subject to transmission delays when a line becomes overloaded (*see* **net lag**), are far from ideal for voice or video.

Like the Internet, ATM is envisioned as a packet switching network, one that divides up each message into **packets** (fixed-length units of data). But ATM is a **connection-oriented protocol**: it establishes a **virtual** circuit and transmits the packets in a high-speed burst. In addition, ATM uses sophisticated statistical procedures to parcel out **bandwidth** and to assign priority levels to specific streams of data. This ensures that voice and video packets would get high priority, preventing delays. In sum, ATM seems to offer the best of both worlds: high-bandwidth data transmission coupled with the ability to transmit **real-time** voice and video.

Just how ATM would co-exist with **TCP/IP** (the protocols that form the basis of the **Internet**), are among the several technical issues concerning ATM that await resolution. But it is already clear from trials that ATM can handle high-speed access to computer on-line services as well as **video-on-demand**, and ATM is widely expected to become one of the major players among the technologies that will form **integrated services networks.** Several federal agencies have selected Sprint to create an ATM-based network capable of 622 Mbps speeds for their **interagency networks**.

AT command set

A command language that enables you (or your **communications program**) to tell a modem what to do. Originated by Hayes Microcomputer Products, Inc., the AT command set has become a de facto industry standard. A modem that responds to the AT command set is said to be Hayes-compatible.

attached document

In an **electronic mail** message, a file that has been linked to the message so that it is delivered to the message's recipient.

It's easy to attach a text file to a mail message, but it's another matter to attach a **binary file**. Unfortunately, the standard Internet mail software, the **Simple Mail Transport-Protocol (SMTP)**, can't handle any of the graphics or control characters included in binary files. To send a binary file with your mail, then, you must first encode the file using a program such as **BinHex** or the **UNIX** program called **uuencode**; the recipient must then decode the file using the matching decoder (such as **uudecode**). The purpose of the encoding process is to transform the binary file into a coded file containing nothing but the standard **ASCII** characters; this file can be transmitted via Internet links without difficulty. The decoding process retranslates the text file into an exact duplicate of the binary original. The better electronic mail programs handle the coding and decoding processes automatically when the program detects that your message includes a binary file.

attenuation

A decrease in the amplitude (power) of a signal conveyed through a **physical medium** such as **twisted pair**. In **DIX Ethernet** networks, for example, the attenuation of carrier signals prevents the networks from extending more than 2.5 km.

AUP

See **Acceptable Use Policy (AUP).**

AUP-free

Not restricted by the **National Science Foundation (NSF) Acceptable User Policies (AUP)** which restrict commercial activity on the **NSFNET backbone;** able to provide services to commercial firms for commercial purposes.

Australian Academic and Research Network (AARNet)

An Internet member network of some 70,000 **hosts** that serves universities, government organizations, companies, and research organizations. AARNet uses the AU **domain name**.

authentication

The process of attempting to assure that the person using a computer system and performing tasks such as sending **electronic mail messages**, is one and the same as the person in whose name his or her **account** is registered. The only means of authentication in most networks is the provision of a **password**, but this doesn't guarantee that the person using the system is the person to whom the password was given. In busy campus computing labs, **crackers** can observe students typing their passwords, or sit down at terminals that students have thoughtlessly left without logging off.

One of the challenges currently facing the Internet is to provide a more effective means of authentication. One current proposal: the use of a password **encryption** system that would require the user to possess not only the password but also the **key** required to decode it.

automagically

Automatically, but employing a process so complicated that it would take too much time, in the present context, to explain it: for example, "The router automagically sends the datagram to its destination."

automated newspaper

A networking **application** in which individuals can design a custom newspaper by selecting just those topics for which they would like to receive news. This is already feasible because the major news organizations, such as Reuters, disseminate news stories topically in what amounts to **electronic mail** messages.

Tip: If your **Usenet** site receives **Clari** postings, you can create your own automated newspaper (albeit with text only). The Clari hierarchy consists of **moderated newsgroups** categorized by topic; for example, clari.news.disasters sums up the day's tragedies, including a remarkable 1993 event in which an overheated water heater "shot like a rocket" through the roof of a two-story house. Other categories include everything from world political news to sex crimes. By **subscribing** to just the Clari newsgroups in which you've an interest, you can create an automated newspaper today.

autonomous computer

A computer that is not forcibly controlled or operated by some other computer. An automated teller machine (ATM) is not an autonomous computer; it is controlled by a central computer at the bank's office. Autonomous computers are the basic building blocks of a **computer network**.

Autonomous System (AS)

Synonymous with **routing domain**. A portion of the Internet in which a set of **routers** is under the control of a single administrative organization. The system may consist of one or more **physical networks**, but the chief point is that within the system, the administrating organization possesses the right to organize and define the network as it pleases. At a typical large university, for example, the AS may consist of as many as a dozen **local area networks (LAN)** that are all linked in a local **internet** by means of routers.

An Autonomous System consists of one or more networks that are connected by a backbone. Think of an Autonomous System as if it were made up of several small towns in a county. The streets within this town (a local area network) connect the houses (hosts). A country road—corresponding to an AS's backbone—links the towns. Within the Autonomous System, networks are linked to the backbone by means of border routers. These routers use an **Interior Gateway Protocol (IGP),** the most popular of which is **Routing Information Protocol (RIP)**. A new and better protocol for this purpose is the **Open Shortest Path First (OSPF)** protocol.

The backbone is in turn linked to the wider world of the Internet by means of **boundary routers**. Boundary routers use the **Exterior Gateway Protocol (EGP)**.

backbone

A high-speed physical network that is designed to span hundreds or thousands of miles, and in so doing to provide the means to connect **regional networks** with each other. The current Internet backbone is provided by **NSFNET**. It spans the continental U.S. with speeds of 45 Mbps, using **T3** lines leased from commercial **service providers**.

backbone site

In **Usenet,** a major computing facility that has agreed to serve as a major relay station for Usenet messages. When a backbone site receives a Usenet message, its software immediately relays the message to other backbone sites, so that the message propagates throughout the Usenet system within a few hours. Backbone sites also serve as feed stations for major geographical subregions; the *enea* backbone station in Sweden, for instance, feeds Usenet postings to all the **downstream sites** within that country that have subscribed to Usenet.

Bake-Off

A method of testing the Internet's **interoperability** by trying to shoot **kamikaze packets** through the network. (A kamikaze packet is an Internet **datagram** that has every possible option enabled, thus putting a router's Internet compatibility to the test.)

bandwidth

A measure of the amount of information that can be transmitted via a given physical transmission line in a given period of time. Bandwidth is usually measured in **bits per second (bps)**.

The Internet was designed to link computers that worked with ordinary **(ASCII)** text and numerical data. But it's now linking computers that have high-resolution monitors capable of displaying graphics, animations, and video—and users are demanding that the Internet deliver more than text and numbers. That's going to require substantially more bandwidth than the Internet currently offers.

How much bandwidth is enough? If the future of the Internet lies in the model of **distributed computing**, in which the network's resources would seem like a seamless extension of one's own computer, a reasonable yardstick emerges: The network should have at least as much bandwidth as a disk drive directly attached to your computer. By this yardstick, seemingly huge numbers—such as 64 Kbps (64,000 bits per second), the bandwidth of a digital telephone line employing **ISDN**—take on new perspective. 64 Kbps is slower than the data transfer rates of most floppy disk drives, which most computer users would not consider a workable disk storage system for everyday use. Users of computer CD-ROM drives have found that the original 150 Kbps specification in Microsoft Corporations Multimedia Personal Computer (MPC) standards is too slow for **multimedia** applications; animations and videos were laughably jerky. The current MPC-II standards call for 300 Kbps data transfer rates, but "triple-speed drives" capable of 450 Kbps data transfer rates are considered necessary to animate even the relatively crude, low-resolution videos and animations offered in current multimedia applications. A good PC hard disk can achieve a data transfer rate of 10Mbps, which coincidentally is considered a minimal data transfer rate for **local area networks (LANs)**.

bang

An exclamation point (!). *See* **bang path**.

bang path

An **electronic mail** address that is used to reach someone through **UUCP**. The addresses use exclamation points (**bangs**) and, in the reverse of the Internet's **domain name system**, the site that is assumed to be reachable is listed first, followed in sequence by each **hop** the message must take to reach the user. For example, *!biggie!foonix!tom* directs the message to BIGGIE, a site accessible to everyone, and from there to FOONIX (a machine known to BIGGIE), and finally to Tom.

baseband

At the **data link layer** of a network, a method of conveying signals that does not employ **multiplexing**, so that only one channel is available at a time. Most **local area networks (LANs)** employ baseband transmission techniques.

Basic Encoding Rules (BER)

A set of rules, defined by the **International Standards Organization (ISO)**, that can be used to encode data so that it is easily accessible to other network users. BER is intended to be used with **Abstract Syntax Notation One (ASN.1)**, a compatible standard that specifies the type of data to be encoded using BER. With the exception of the databases maintained by the **Simple Network Management Protocol**

(SNMP), BER isn't widely used to specify the format of Internet databases; it is more commonly used on systems conforming to the **Open Systems Interconnection (OSI) protocol suite**.

| baud rate |

In computer **modems**, a measurement of the rate by which the modem modulates the computer's signals (converts them into sounds that can be sent over the **analog** telephone system). This is not necessarily the same as the modem's **data transfer rate**, which is measured in **bits per second** (bps), because advanced modems can send more than one bit of information for each modulation event. A "1200 baud" modem is actually a 600 baud modem that employs an advanced technique to send two bits of information for each event, resulting in a data transfer rate of 1200 bps. A "9600 baud" modem is actually a 2400 baud modem that encodes 4 bits per event, for a data transfer rate of 9600 bps. Use **bits per second (bps)**, not baud, to describe a modem's transmission speed.

| Bay Area Regional Research Network (BARRNet) |

A regional branch of **NSFNET** and a **service provider** serving the San Francisco Bay Area region. Headquartered in Stanford, CA, the network connects nearly 200 organizations including universities, research laboratories, schools, and most of Silicon Valley's hardware and software firms. In addition to Internet connectivity, the organization offers Internet installation and network consulting services.

| Because It's Time Network (BITNET) |

A **wide area network (WAN)** that links IBM-based mainframe computer systems at approximately 2,500 universities and research institutes in North America, Europe, and Japan. BITNET does not use the **TCP/IP protocols** but can exchange **electronic mail** with the Internet. BITNET is operated by the **Corporation for Research and Educational Networking (CREN)**, with headquarters in Washington, D.C. BITNET and linked networks such as **NetNorth** and **EARN** employ IBM's **Network Job Entry (NJE)** protocols.

BITNET propagates in the following way: To become a member of the network, an organization must pay for a **leased line** that connects to the nearest existing BITNET site— and it must also agree to let another institution connect with this line in the future.

BBS

See **bulletin board system (BBS)**.

Bell protocols

A set of protocols for **modems** that was developed by AT&T's Bell Laboratories during the 1970s. Although these standards were once widely used in North America, they conflicted with the international transmission standards developed by the **CCITT**. The use of the Bell protocols made North American-made modems inoperable in most of the rest of the world. But this is no longer true because newer North American modems, which are capable of **data transfer rates** in excess of 1200 bits per second (bps), now adhere to the CCITT standards.

Berkeley Software Distribution (BSD)

A version of the **UNIX** operating system that was developed, distributed, and supported by the University of California, Berkeley. BSD played a key role in fostering the growth of the Internet: BSD UNIX incorporated the TCP/IP code created under a U.S. government contract by **Bolt, Beranak, and Newman (BBN)**. This software—with internetworking capability built in—was subsequently distributed to hundreds of colleges and universities. Berkeley no longer supports the development and support of UNIX, but its innovative features—including **sockets**—are now part of standard UNIX offerings from providers such as the Open Software Foundation and AT&T

big endian

A computer system (such as an IBM mainframe) designed to store data with the most significant bit at the beginning of a unit of data, in contrast to **little endian** computers, in which the least significant bit comes first. A design distinction that launched a **holy war**, it can cause problems when data is shared across a network. The terminology comes from *Gulliver's Travels*, in which wars were fought over whether boiled eggs should be broken at the little end or the big end.

big iron

Slang term for **mainframe computer**: "The computer companies are having a tough time selling big iron these days—everyone wants PCs linked in local area networks."

bin

An abbreviation for **binary file**. In **archive sites**, this abbreviation is often used to name **directories** that contain programs you can obtain via **FTP** and use on your computer.

binary file

A file that contains characters other than the standard **ASCII** characters. You can't read binary files directly on-screen (unless, that is, you like looking at thousands of what appear to be "garbage characters"). These files include **executable programs**, the files created by many application programs (such as spreadsheet and database management programs), and most compressed files. A file that contains nothing but the standard ASCII characters is called an **ASCII file** or a **text file**.

Tip If you're trying to transfer a binary file via **FTP**, you must first type *binary* and press *Enter* to switch FTP to the binary file transfer mode.

BinHex

In Macintosh computing, a method of encoding **binary files** so that they consist only of **ASCII text**. The encoding is necessary so that the file can be transmitted via **electronic mail**; Internet mail can only handle ASCII text files. To read a BINHEX-encoded message, you need a program that can convert the BINHEX code back to binary. Files encoded with BinHex are saved with the .Hqx extension. *Compare* **uuencode/uudecode**.

bionet

In Usenet, one of several **alternative newsgroup hierarchies** that are carried and propagated only by those Usenet sites that elect to do so (in contrast to **world newsgroups**, which are automatically fed to every Usenet subscriber). The Bionet **newsgroups** offer valuable discussions of biological and ecological topics and issues, including agroforestry, tropical biology, the Human Genome Project, molecular biology, neuroscience, software for biology, and the status of women in biology.

bit

The fundamental unit of information in a **digital** computer or communications system; short for *binary digit*. A bit has just two possible states, a 1 or a 0. The reason digital computers can be so highly accurate is that these two states are clearly and unambiguously represented electronically; for example, a high voltage can be used to represent a 1, while a low or zero voltage can be used to represent a 0. The probability of confusing the two signals is very low. To make up meaningful units of information, bits are combined in longer units called **data words** (*see* **octet**). Digital encoding has many advantages when computers work with numbers and words, which can be precisely and economically represented by patterns of bits. For sounds and graphics, however, a serious problem arises: In comparison to **analog** encoding techniques, high-quality digital sound and video require huge amounts of disk space when stored, and equally huge amounts of network **bandwidth** when transmitted. A typical graphics file, for instance, may consume as much as 250KB of disk storage space, and a three minute sound file can eat up 1.5MB or more. By using fewer bits to encode pictures and sounds, it is possible to reduce the bulk of these files, but at the cost of reduced quality. Much research is now underway to improve the compression of computer-transmitted graphics and sound; *see* **Motion Picture Experts Group (MPEG)**.

bit hierarchy

In Usenet, one of several **alternative newsgroup hierarchies** that are carried and propagated only by those Usenet sites that elect to do so (in contrast to **world newsgroups**, which are automatically fed to every Usenet subscriber). The bit **newsgroups** echo the most popular **LISTSERV** mailing lists from the **BITNET** network (which links colleges and universities). The highly varied topics include Down's Syndrome, Dutch literature, 18th century history, electronic music, ethics in computing, and technical writing. But it's not all deadly serious, as the existence of Romance Reader's Anonymous (bit.listserve.rra-1) amply suggests.

BITNET

See **Because It's Time Network (BITNET).**

bit stuffing

At the **data link layer** in a computer network, a method used to fill up a **frame**—a unit of transmitted data—if there isn't enough data to do so. The **Xmodem** file transfer protocol, for example, uses bit stuffing to make sure that all the transmitted data fits into blocks of exactly 128 bits. The filler bits are discarded when the data is received.

bits per second (bps)

A measurement of the **data transfer rate** of a computer network that specifies the number of **bits** (yes-no units of information) that the system can transmit per second. A computer **modem** enables you to transfer as many as 28.8 thousand bits per second (Kbps, an abbreviation for kilobits per second) via the telephone system. Many existing computer networks can transmit millions of bits per second (Mbps, an abbreviation for megabits per second) or even billions of bits per second (Gbps, an abbreviation for gigabits per second). If these transfer rates sound impressive, remember that a bit doesn't amount to much: It takes seven or eight bits to represent a single letter or number, and **overhead** (additional information that is required to send the message correctly) may add as many as two bits for each character.

In computer modems, data transfer rates measured in bps are often confused with an obsolete measurement called the **baud rate**. The baud rate specifies nothing more than the number of switching operations that the modem can perform per second. Today's modems can send four or more bits of information with each switching operation, so the baud rate is no longer identical (as it once was) to the bps rate.

> **Don't** refer to a modem's **data transfer rate** using the term baud. Today's modems employ clever techniques that allow them to convey more than one bit of data for each change in the signal; a modem capable of transferring 2400 bits per second, for example, operates at 600 baud.

> **Do** use the term **bits per second (bps)** to describe a modem's data transfer rate. This measurement is more closely related to a modem's actual performance and enables you to compare the performance of two modems meaningfully.

| biz |

In Usenet, one of several **alternative Usenet hierarchies** that are carried and propagated only by those Usenet sites that elect to do so (in contrast to **world newsgroups**, which are automatically fed to every Usenet subscriber). The biz **newsgroups** offer announcements of business (and particularly computer) products and services.

| blind courtesy copy (BCC) |

In **electronic mail**, a copy of a message that is sent without the knowledge of the primary recipients and any copy recipients.

bogus newsgroup

In Usenet, a **newsgroup** that has been deleted from the official list of active newsgroups, even though it still appears on the list of the newsgroups (kept in a file called .newsrc) to which you have **subscribed**. A newsgroup may be deleted for one of several possible reasons: it may have been replaced by one or more new newsgroups, or it may have been completely inactive for a lengthy period of time.

If one of your subscribed newsgroups has been deleted from the active list, you will discover this when you start your **newsreader**, the program that allows you to read Usenet newsgroups. Every time you start a newsreader such as **rn** or **nn**, the program compares the newsgroup names in your **.newsrc** file to the official list of active newsgroups. If there is a discrepancy, you'll be asked whether you want to delete the bogus newsgroup.

Tip: Always respond **Y** (yes) when you're asked whether you want to remove a bogus newsgroup from your .newsrc file. If you respond **N** (no), you'll just see the same message about removing the bogus group the next time you start the newsreader.

Bolt, Beranak, and Newman (BBN)

A Cambridge, MA company that has a long history of U.S. government contracts concerning the development of Internet technologies.

BBN developed the first **routers** for the now-defunct **ARPANET,** the Internet's predecessor. In 1983, BBN was asked to implement the newly standardized **TCP/IP** protocols in **UNIX**, thus beginning the close association between UNIX and the Internet.

In most **Gopher** clients, the location of an item buried deep within a tree of menus, which you've marked so that you can later return to it without having to traverse the menu tree all over again.

Boolean operator

A word (AND, OR, or NOT) that helps you refine the scope of a **key word search.** In the Internet, you can use Boolean operators with **Veronica, Jughead**, and some versions of **WAIS**.

Boolean operators are named after George Boole, a nineteenth-century Scots mathematician whose logical algebra remained a curiosity until computers were invented. Using Boolean operators, you can widen or narrow the scope of a search.

The OR operator widens a search because it retrieves any items that contain *either* of the key words linked with OR. For example, a search for Finland OR Sweden finds items that contain "Finland," items that contain "Sweden," and items that contain *both* "Finland" and "Sweden."

The AND operator narrows a search because it retrieves only those documents that contain *both* of the search terms. For example, a search for Finland AND Sweden finds only those items that contain *both* "Finland" and "Sweden." Documents that contain only "Finland" or only "Sweden" are rejected.

The NOT operator also narrows a search by excluding those documents that contain an unwanted term. For example, a search for Finland NOT Sweden finds any item that contains "Finland," but it rejects the ones that contain *both* "Finland" and "Sweden."

Border Gateway Protocol (BGP)

A **routing protocol** designed to handle the routing of **datagrams** from one **Autonomous System** (a collection of networks under the control of a single administrative agency, such as a university or corporation) to another.

BGP defines a new routing model that emerged as Internet engineers came to understand the limitations of the former reliance on a single **core** network with gateways to external systems. Because this system relied on the core to make routing decisions, it forced every datagram to traverse the core and placed heavy demands on the core's processing capabilities. This model also required new networks to be connected to the core. With the rise of regional **backbones** and alternative national backbones, a datagram did not necessarily have to be routed through the core to get to its destination. So the Internet was reconceptualized as a limitless series of network domains, each of which borders on one or more adjacent networks. The Border Gateway Protocol provides the means of distributing routing decision capability to each of these domains.

border router

In an **Autonomous System (AS)** linked to the Internet (a collection of networks under the control of a single administrative agency, such as a university or corporation), the routers used to connect the physical networks to the system's **backbone**. *Compare* **boundary router**.

bot

In a **MUD** (a computerized, multi-user role-playing game) or **Internet Relay Chat (IRC)**, an on-screen personality whose actions and expressions are the result of a computer program rather than a human being. MUDs involve the interaction of numerous human players, each of whom controls an on-screen character, while in Internet Relay Chat, the words you see on-screen presumably stem from a human typing something. Bots are user-created programs that mimic the actions of human players, for such purposes as greeting new entrants to a virtual "room." Some can seem like a human-controlled character to the uninitiated. One famous MUD bot, named Julia, seems to have passed a modified version of the Turing Test of artificial intelligence: Many players in Julia's MUD are said to have believed that she was controlled by a human player.

bounce

To return after a failed delivery attempt. If an **electronic mail** message cannot reach its destination, the **postmaster** returns it to the **mailbox** of the person who sent the message. The message's header now includes several additional lines— sometimes a dozen or more—explaining where the message had gone and what went awry.

boundary router

In an **Autonomous System (AS)**, a collection of networks under the control of a single administrative agency, a router on the system's **backbone** that handles the system's connection with other autonomous systems.

bps

See **bits per second (bps).**

bridge

A device used to connect two or more **local area networks (LANs)** that use the same **Medium Access Control (MAC)** protocol. Bridges can be used to divide a LAN that has grown so large that its performance degrades. Two bridges connected by a **wide area network (WAN)** can be used to connect geographically separated LANs.

broadband

At the **data link layer** in a computer network, a transmission technique that employs **multiplexing** to combine analog signals from more than one source into a single cable. The two most common multiplexing techniques are called **frequency-division multiplexing (FDM)** and **time-division multiplexing (TDM)**. More generally, the term is used to mean "high **bandwidth**" (*compare* **broadband network**, **narrowband network**).

broadband coaxial cable

A type of **coaxial cable** that is designed to carry **analog** signals, such as analog television signals.

Chances are good that you've got broadband coaxial cable in your home, in the form of a cable TV line. According to cable TV industry figures, coaxial cable has been extended within reach of 97% of all U.S. homes, just one percent shy of the penetration of **narrowband** telephone services. Some 62% of U.S. households subscribe to cable television service, at a cost of approximately US$20 billion annually. With this degree of penetration, cable TV industry officials argue that the cable TV system offers the solution to the **last mile problem** for the emerging **National Information Infrastructure (NII)**—the problem of how to link homes, schools, and offices to high-bandwidth **integrated service networks**.

Broadband ISDN (BISDN)

An international standard, established by **CCITT**, that provides the blueprint for the mid-21st century development of an **Integrated Services Digital Network (ISDN)** capable of delivering 155 Mbps or 622 Mbps **fiber optic** access links to homes, schools, and offices. CCITT has chosen **Asynchronous Transfer Mode (ATM)** as the foundation for Broadband ISDN, which would be capable of carrying voice and **full-motion video** as well as computer data and text. Because it does not work with the **twisted pair** telephone lines currently connected to 98% of U.S. homes, Broadband ISDN differs significantly from the ISDN standards for twisted-pair transmission (which are often called **narrowband ISDN** to emphasize the contrast). *See* **Integrated Services Digital Network (ISDN)**.

broadband network

In **local area networks (LANs)**, a network that uses **frequency-division multiplexing (FDM)** to combine many signals on a single analog line at high speeds. More generally, this term is used to describe any computer network that has high bandwidth—roughly, 100 Mbps or more. *Compare* **narrowband network**.

The Internet isn't a broadband network—yet. The current Internet **backbone**, called **NSFNET**, operates at 45 Mbps, but many of the **regional networks** and local **service providers** that connect you to NSFNET operate at much lower speeds—as low as 56 Kbps (56,000 bits per second).

broadcast

To send a message to every **host** on a network. **IP address** definitions include the capability to route a **datagram** to every host on the Internet but most **routers** are programmed to intercept and discard such messages. *Compare* **multicast**.

broadcast address

In **IP addresses**, an address that has all or part of the address numbers set to a "wild card" number (such as 255 or 0), so that the message will go to all the hosts in a **domain**. A message addressed to 128.58.255.255, for example, will be sent to every **host** on the network numbered 128.58.

broadcast model

In the plans now being formulated for the **National Information Infrastructure (NII)**, a conception of the system's design that emphasizes the broadcasting of high-quality programming to paying subscribers. *Compare* **community model**.

The broadcast model is enshrined in the U.S. public's imagination, thanks to a series of devastatingly funny editorial cartoons that play off the theme "500 channels and there's still nothing on." But the implications aren't very funny. Service providers working with the broadcast model in mind could very well construct local delivery systems that allocate very little **bandwidth** to upstream communications (messages that originate from the home). This would effectively prevent individuals from becoming the originators of information as well as consumers.

broadcast network

A computer network, such as a **local area network (LAN)** or a **metropolitan area network (MAN)**, in which all the messages relayed by the system reach every computer that is connected to the network. Computers other than the one or ones to which a given message is directed just ignore the message. *See* **Medium Access Control (MAC) Sublayer**.

browser

An **application program** that provides tools for exploring information. The browser acts on your behalf as a **client**. It helps you extract information from **servers** (matching or compatible programs on other computers that can provide information). Examples of widely-used Internet browsers are **Gopher** and **Mosaic**. These programs provide easy-to-use tools for locating and retrieving files, tasks that would otherwise be performed with the less approachable **Archie** and **FTP**.

browsing

A **resource** discovery method that involves the use of a **client** program, called a **browser**, to explore the resources that are available to that client on Internet **servers** throughout the world. The two predominant browsing techniques in common Internet use are tunneling with **Gopher** (finding and "going down" into the subordinate Gopher menus of remote Gopher servers) and exploring hypertext links with the **World Wide Web (WWW)**.

brute force

In **cryptography** and other mathematical fields, a problem-solving technique that employs a computer programmed to perform a simple task over and over, in the hope of finding the answer. Because the computer can perform these tasks very rapidly, brute force techniques can sometimes work.

Crackers employ brute-force programs that try to find a user's **password** by running through every conceivable combination of letters.

Computer processing speed is increasing very rapidly, calling the security of many **encryption** methods into question. A team of 600 cryptographers, linked by the Internet, recently cracked a 17-year-old code that mathematicians once said would take "trillions of years" to break. The code, with a **key** 129 letters long, was used to encrypt the words, "The magic words are squeamish ossifrage." The solution of the problem renewed fears that high-performance computer systems have undermined the reliability of the **Data Encryption Standard (DES)**, which employs a 56-letter **key**.

buffer

A temporary storage location in a computer's memory or disk storage area that is used to store information that is being transferred. In the Internet, **routers** store **datagrams** in a buffer while the router is waiting for the line to clear.

bug

An error in a computer program. Non-destructive bugs may cause odd things to happen, such as leaving a "ghost" of the mouse pointer on the screen momentarily. More severe bugs can cause a program to "crash," potentially resulting in lost work.

Very few Internet **resource discovery tools** are completely bug-free. That's because they're created by volunteers who may lack the time to test them exhaustively before making them available; the test comes with widespread use. It's considered appropriate to make available a program that is "reasonably stable" (meaning that it has several known bugs in program areas that aren't accessed very often).

bulletin board system (BBS)

A do-it-yourself on-line computer information system that is created with a personal computer, a **modem**, and BBS software. Usually operated on a volunteer basis by computer hobbyists, BBS systems typically offer hundreds or even thousands of programs and graphics files to **download**, local **electronic mail**, games, and—increasingly—access to the Internet. Most levy a modest fee, such as $35 for one year of unlimited access. Several hundred of the estimated BBS systems now in existence offer limited Internet connectivity such as electronic mail and **Usenet**. In light of recent dramatic price declines in the cost of 56 Kbps **leased lines** and the growing availability of **SLIP/PPP** connections, many are contemplating full Internet connectivity. It is likely that BBS systems will play a valuable role in providing public Internet access at low cost.

byte

In personal computing, a sequence of eight **bits** that constitutes the smallest addressable unit in the computer (a **data word**). This term is avoided in the Internet context, in preference to **octet,** because some of the computers linked to the Internet use data words of different sizes.

byte stream

In **serial communication**, the flow of information in the form of a continuous stream of characters (bytes). Ideally, this flow would occur at very rapid speeds, without the need for the addition of **overhead** information (information needed to synchronize or demarcate the data so that the receiving station knows how to handle it). To resolve the byte stream into meaningful units of information, two methods are used: **asynchronous communication** and **synchronous communication**.

cable television (CATV)

The subscription-based provision of television services to residences by means of **coaxial cable**. CATV systems are emerging as an important potential solution to the **last mile problem** (bringing internetworking connectivity to homes, schools, and offices). A 1992 court decision cleared the way for CATV companies to offer information services, and substantial development is expected in this area. Note: Some industry experts insist that the acronym CATV applies properly to community antenna television, but in common usage the acronym is synonymous with cable television.

According to cable TV industry figures, coaxial cable has been extended within reach of 97% of all U.S. homes. Some 62% of U.S. households currently subscribe to cable television service. Relatively unregulated, the CATV industry is moving fast to shed its image of being parochial, isolated content providers with no connections to international telephone or data networks. Most current systems, however, have a technical flaw when it comes to Internet connectivity:

Technically, they are heavily biased towards the provision of **downstream bandwidth**, which is not surprising considering the CATV industry's history as content providers, and provide only enough **upstream bandwidth** to facilitate the user's origination of control and content selection messages. If CATV systems are to compete effectively for the provision of Internet connectivity, they must take advantage of technical innovations that balance the bandwidth disparity. And such innovations are underway. A project jointly carried out by a major West Coast cable TV firm and Arizona State Univ. demonstrated the feasibility of multiplexing Ethernet connectivity via CATV systems, providing 10 Mbps Internet access.

In the first joint venture of its kind, a cable TV company (Continental Cablevision Inc.) and an Internet **service provider** (Performance Systems International Inc.) announced plans to offer Internet access services via CATV. From the subscriber's viewpoint, connecting to the Internet will be as simple as connecting an office computer to an Ethernet **local area network (LAN)** that has full Internet connectivity. The service is planned initially for Eastern Massachusetts.

| California Education and Research Federation Network (CERFnet) |

A regional Internet network and service provider that offers Internet connectivity for both educational organizations and businesses throughout southern California. One of the founding members of the **Commercial Internet Exchange (CIX)**, CERFnet encourages business connectivity and bypasses the **National Science Foundation (NSF) Acceptable Use Policy (AUP)** that restricts business use of NSFNET. CERFnet continues its commitment to education with programs such as Global School House and is one of the first Internet service providers to offer **dialup access** with an 800 number.

California State University Network (CSUnet)

A state Internet network that was originally designed to link California's twenty state university campuses with high-speed **T1** connectivity, CSUnet has expanded its mission. It now seeks to provide Internet connectivity to all of California's K–12 schools, community colleges, and libraries.

Call For Votes (CFV)

In **Usenet**, a posting to the newsgroup news.announce-.newgroups that invites votes concerning the creation of a previously-proposed new newsgroup (*see* **Request for Discussion [RFD]**). During the voting period (which lasts from 21 to 31 days), voters send **electronic mail** messages to a volunteer, who keeps track of the votes. To pass, a newsgroup must receive 100 more YES votes than NO votes, and the total number of YES votes must amount to at least two-thirds of the total. If the proposed group does not pass, six months must elapse before the group can be proposed again.

These rules apply only to the **world newsgroups**; anyone can create an **alt** newsgroup without votes. (That's why the alt hierarchy was created.)

Campus-Wide Information System (CWIS)

A computer information system that has been developed to make information about a college or university easily accessible to students and to the public. Ideally, a good CWIS integrates many different kinds of information—for example, a **white pages** phone book of faculty and staff, a list of course offerings, and the college library's catalog. Moreover, it does so by providing the same, easy commands for browsing or searching each of the different kinds of information. A University of Minnesota CWIS development program led to the creation of **Gopher**, which functions as a CWIS at

C

many colleges and universities worldwide as well as serving as one of the Internet's most accessible and widely-used **resource discovery tools**.

Canadian Network (CA*NET)

The national **backbone** network of Canada providing Internet connectivity to research and educational organizations.

capture

See **file capture**.

capture file

In **communication programs**, the file that is created by the program's **file capture** feature, which lets you record incoming, on-screen data to a disk file.

carpet bomb

To post a bogus "get-rich-quick" scheme, electronic chain letter, commercial advertisement, or a deliberately offensive message to numerous **newsgroups** or **Usenet** in violation of the Internet's **Acceptable Use Policy (AUP)** and the Usenet community's social values.

Most carpet bombs are pranks (*see* **trolling**); others may stem from misguided advertising experiments. But all are **flame bait**. In a much-discussed April, 1994 carpet-bombing, a law firm posted an advertisement to all of the nearly 5,000 newsgroups available on the system that handled their account. As the **posting** propagated throughout the network and outrage grew, this system was inundated by an estimated 100 megabytes of **email** largely critical of the posting, causing the system to overload and crash. (100 megabytes corresponds to roughly 50,000 one-page letters.) A spokesman for the law firm subsequently told a *New York Times* reporter that the firm had done nothing illegal, and that he was planning to write a book on how to advertise on Usenet.

Don't flame carpet bombers or post messages critical of their actions. You're giving them exactly what they crave: Attention. They want to see **threads** in lots of newsgroups, with their own juvenile, immoral, or self-serving actions front and center. Conserve network **bandwidth** by ignoring carpet bombers, and you'll deprive them of the one thing they're after.

Do crosspost a Usenet message to more than one group if doing so makes good sense; a message posted to rec.aquaria (a newsgroup devoted to discussion of tropical fish) might also prove of interest to readers of sci.aquaria.

carrier

In computer **modems**, a continuous signal that carries information through the telephone system by changes in its amplitude, frequency, or phase. Each shift transmits 2 bits of information.

Carrier Sense Multiple Access with Collision Detection (CSMA/CD)

In a **local area network (LAN)**, a commonly-used **protocol** (standard) that deals with the problem of resolving **contention** (the attempt by more than one **workstation** to access the network at the same time). This protocol resolves the problem of contention by equipping each workstation with the ability to detect whether other workstations are using the channel. If two stations start broadcasting at exactly the same time, they both withdraw from the network and wait for a period determined by a random number generator. This assures that the collision will not occur again. **Ethernet**, a commonly-used LAN standard that is widely used on LANs connected to the Internet, uses CSMA/CD, and it forms a key part of the **IEEE Standard 802** protocols for local area networks.

| cascade |

The accretion of quotation markers in **Usenet** postings that occurs when an original **posting** is quoted by several or even dozens of additional **follow-up postings**.

Cascading is a **bandwidth**-wasting game, the juvenile objective being to have the last word on a subject:

```
>>>>>>>>Forget I ever said it.
>>>>>>>No, I won't.
>>>>>>Oh, please do.
>>>>>You first.
>>>>Who started this, anyway?
>>>Not me.
>>And who will end it?
>Me. I win.
```

```
No, you don't.
```

And so it goes on, wasting previous network resources.

> **Don't** flame cascaders; you might find yourself on the wrong end of a **mail bombing** attack. Ignore them. Or, better yet, set up a **kill file** to exclude future postings on this subject.

| case sensitive |

Able to distinguish between uppercase (capital) and lowercase letters.

> **Tip:** If you're used to using MS-DOS, using a **UNIX host** may cause a number of minor difficulties, not the

least of which is the fact that UNIX file names are case sensitive. The name *Information-highway* is *not* the same as *information-highway*. To perform operations on UNIX files, you must type the capitalization pattern correctly.

cat

One of the essential **UNIX** commands for Internet users, cat displays a text file's contents on-screen. This is very useful if you're using **dialup access** to the Internet: You can avoid **downloading** the file by "capturing" the displayed text (that is, recording it) in a **capture file** on your computer's disk. Most **communications programs** can capture text in this way.

Tip: To read a file on-screen, pipe the cat output to the more command, which enables you to press a key before the system displays the next screenful of text. To display the file *readme.txt* with cat and more, you type the following: ***cat readme.txt / more*** (the more command is preceded by a vertical line character.)

catenet

A collection of physically distinct networks—in other words, an **internet**—which can nevertheless exchange data and permit users to access remote resources via intercomputer communication. Even though a message may travel through several physically distinct networks as it makes its way to its destination, this is invisible (**transparent**) to the user. This word was used early in the **ARPANET**'s development in an attempt to capture its design philosophy. Today, **internet** is much more common.

catch up

In **Usenet**, to use a command that marks all the articles in a **newsgroup** as read—even if you have not actually read them—so that they don't appear on the **thread selector** or **article selector** the next time you access the **newsreader** program.

> **Tip:** Catching up is worth doing if you've scanned the subjects and found nothing of interest. The next time you start the newsreader, you'll only see the articles that have come in since the last time you read the news.

cd

One of the essential **UNIX** commands for Internet users, cd changes the current **directory**. To switch to the **subdirectory** /pub/docs, for example, you type the following and press **Enter**:

```
cd /pub/docs
```

To move up one directory in the directory hierarchy, you type the following and press **Enter** (note the space between "cd" and the two dots):

```
cd ..
```

> **Tip:** If you're used to MS-DOS, note that UNIX uses a forward slash (/) to indicate directories—unlike DOS, which uses a backwards slash (\).

cell relay

A type of **packet switching network**, now just appearing in its first commercial versions, that achieves very high speeds by using small packets of fixed size and super-fast switching devices (see **fast packet switching**). *See* **Asynchronous Transfer Mode (ATM)**.

CERN

See **European Laboratory for Particle Physics (CERN)**.

chain letter

An illegal pyramid scheme, generally a hoax, that promises that you will receive a great deal of money if you participate by duplicating the message and sending it on to others. Chain letters appear frequently on **Usenet**, where they can become notorious wasters of network **bandwidth**; most systems forbid participation in them and will terminate the accounts of those who respond.

checksum

A simple **error correction** technique that involves performing a calculation to see whether a block of data was transmitted accurately. The checksum involves performing an arithmetic operation on the bit values contained in the block, resulting in a value. This value is calculated before transmission and afterward. If the two values don't agree, the error-checking software assumes that an error occurred during transmission, discards the block, and requests a retransmission.

 Tip: If you receive a checksum error after **extracting** or **downloading** a file, it's probably **corrupt**.

ciphertext

A message that has been encrypted so that it can be read only by the intended recipient, who possesses the **key**. *See* **encryption**.

circuit switching network

A network, such as the telephone system, that works by establishing a direct connection between the originator and the receiver of a message. An end-to-end path must be set up before the message is sent, and during the transmission the entire line is devoted to the link (even if it's disused for a period of time). *Compare* **packet switching network**.

Although circuit switching networks are used to set up **leased lines** (permanently switched lines that connect **hosts** to an Internet **backbone**), it is inefficient for computer communications, which tend to be "bursty." Imagine that you're retrieving a file with **FTP**: for a brief period of time, you're receiving a great deal of information at high speed. But then you read it on-screen to see if it's valuable; for several minutes there's practically no activity at all. A packet switching network solves this problem by combining the messages from many computers into **packets** (segments that contain information about where the packet should be delivered), and sending the segments through a dynamically-switched system in which routing equipment can examine each packet and choose the best route for its delivery.

clari

In Usenet, one of several **alternative newsgroup hierarchies** that are carried and propagated only by those Usenet sites that elect to do so (in contrast to **world newsgroups**, which are automatically fed to every Usenet subscriber). The Clari **newsgroups** carry the moderated postings of **ClariNet**, a for-profit provider of current news stories from national and international wire services, including United Press International (UPI), Newsbytes (news related to the computer industry), and TechWire (news related to a variety of technical, scientific, and industrial areas). A site must pay a fee and sign a license to carry the ClariNet newsgroups. With the exception of clari.news.talk, all the ClariNet newsgroups are moderated and accept postings only from qualified news organizations.

In the hundreds of ClariNet newsgroups, you'll find gems galore: hourly Associated Press newsbriefs, news on movies and filmaking, daily gold prices, the Dow Jones averages, TechWire stock reports, insiders' stock market analyses, interest rates, airline news, reports of mergers and acquisitions, legal news, fashion stories, human interest stories, unusual or funny news stories, consumer news, Today in History, TV news, news from all of the 50 states organized by state, Internet coverage in detail, Newsbytes (an award-winning computer industry newswire), crime and disaster coverage, world news from every world region, sports coverage organized by sport (basketball, football, etc.), industrial news organized by industry (telecommunications, nuclear power, etc.)—and much, much, more.

Tip: If your Usenet site carries ClariNet, you can create your own custom daily newspaper by subscribing to just those newsgroups that fit your interests. My favorites: clari.biz.economy (where the economy's headed), clari.biz.tip (top business news), clari.biz.urgent (even hotter business news), clari.feature.dave-barry (the humorist's column), clari.nb.top (the hottest and latest news about computers), clari.news.goodnews (stories about the few good things that actually do happen from time to time), and clari.news.top (the day's top news stories).

Don't forward or redistribute ClariNet postings; they're copyrighted with no right of redistribution.

Class A network

An Internet-connected network that can define up to 16,777,215 **hosts**. Current **IP addressing** limitations specify a maximum of 128 Class A networks, of which there were 74 in January, 1994. Class A networks are allocated to large universities and government agencies.

> **Tip:** Curious about the class of a network? Examine its numerical IP address (such as 126.31.235.67). If the first number is in the range 0 to 127, it's a Class A network. If this number falls in the range 128 to 191, it's a **Class B** network. If it's in the range 192 to 221, it's a **Class C** network.

Class B network

An Internet-connected network that can define up to 65,535 hosts. Current **IP addressing** limitations limit the number of Class B networks to 16,384; in January, 1994, there were 4,043 Class B networks. Class B networks are allocated to corporations and other organizations with the capacity for growth.

Class C network

An Internet-connected network that can define only 256 **hosts**. **IP addressing** permits up to 2,097,152 Class C networks. In January, 1994, there were 16,422 Class C networks. Class C networks are allocated to small businesses, schools, Bulletin Board Systems (BBS), and individuals with direct Internet connections.

Class 1

A standard for **fax modems** that specifies the extensions to the **AT command set** needed to handle the sending and receiving of faxes. The job of processing the fax data—for example, of digitizing the image—is left to fax software. The Class 1 standard was jointly developed by the Electronics Industry Association and the Telecommunications Industry Association. *Compare* **Class 2**.

Tip: If you're shopping for a modem, Class 1 isn't a liability compared to Class 2. Today's high-powered personal computers can handle fax processing easily. Just be sure to equip your computer with a Class 1-capable fax program.

Class 2

A standard for **fax modems** that, like **Class 1**, specifies the extensions to the **AT command set** needed to handle the sending and receiving of faxes. The difference lies in the fact that Class 2 transfers most of the processing operations, such as digitizing and compression, to the modem. The Class 2 standard was jointly developed by the Electronics Industry Association and the Telecommunications Industry Association. *Compare* **Class 1**.

The theory underlying the Class 2 standard is that underpowered personal computers need assistance handling the complex processing operations needed to send and receive faxes, such as digitization and compression. With a Class 2 modem, fax operations could run in the background without making demands on your computer's microprocessor.

Like all too many nice theories, the one underlying Class 2 hasn't worked out in practice. First, it's not really necessary. Today's "underpowered" personal computers aren't so underpowered anymore. Even a 386SX-25 can handle Class 1 fax operations. There's no compelling need to transfer the processing to Class 2 fax modems, which are much more expensive than Class 1 modems because they must include additional processing circuitry.

The second reason Class 2 hasn't worked out well lies in the development of conflicting Class 2 standards. The Class 2 specification was published in 1992, but only after several fax modems appeared that followed a provisional Class 2 specification, which differed in some respects. To distinguish the two, the published (official) version of the protocol is called Class 2.0, while the interim version is simply called Class 2. Most of the "Class 2" modems on the marked observe the interim (Class 2) protocol. As if this isn't confusing enough, modem manufacturers introduced their own proprietary discrepancies between their implementation of the interim protocol and the final, published version (2.0). As a result, Class 2 is not a uniform standard.

> **Don't** spend money on Class 2 fax compatibility—arguably, you'll be throwing money away needlessly. Although a modem with Class 1 compatibility requires your computer's processor to handle digitization, compression, and other fax-processing operations, most of today's standard systems (486 and higher) can handle these tasks quite well, even while you're running other applications.

| client |

An **application program** that works on your behalf to contact a compatible information source, called a **server**, elsewhere on the network. Think of a client as if it were a librarian working for you. You need some information; your client, the librarian, goes out and gets it. One of the most popular clients on UNIX systems is **Gopher**; you can use Gopher to contact Gopher servers all over the world. Increasing in popularity are **Mosaic** (a client for the World Wide Web) and **Eudora** (an electronic mail client), both of which offer **graphical user interfaces (GUI's)**.

client-server model

In a computer network, a philosophy of network organization in which each user's computer is equipped with a **client** program, an application that works on your behalf to find information or resources. The client program contacts a **server** program, probably (but not necessarily) on a **remote host**, that is designed to provide a certain type of information or service to clients. The client-server model has many advantages, but chief among them is the way it distributes processing demands among the computers linked to the network. Consider a situation in which several hundred people, all over the world, are all trying to access files available on one server. If all of these people were to log on to the server machine and use the client software located there, the server would be overwhelmed with the demand. By distributing the client programs to hosts everywhere, the client-server reduces the burden on central server sites: With a local client, much of the processing is done on the user's host; the remote server is contacted only when it is necessary to exchange data. The **resource discovery tools** in widespread use on the Internet (**Archie**, **Gopher**, **WAIS**, and **WWW**) employ the client-server model.

Clipper Chip

A low-cost **encryption** (message coding) device that the U.S. federal government proposes to make available for public use. The device would allow private persons and businesses to send confidential messages, while at the same time allowing government investigative agencies to intercept and decode the messages if criminal activities were suspected.

Already in existence are several **encryption algorithms** (techniques for coding messages so that only the intended recipient, who alone possesses the decoding key, can understand the message) that can effectively scramble telephone and digital messages. And that worries U.S. government security agencies, such as the Federal Bureau of Investigation (FBI).

In the past, court-authorized wiretapping of telephone conversations has proven invaluable in detecting the activities of organized crime. Now that most communications can be encrypted easily and cheaply, it is possible for a drug dealer to make a telephone call from Miami to New York knowing that the conversation can be understood only by the intended recipient. This is what law enforcement agencies call the "two-edged sword" of encryption technology: At the same time that it provides U.S. software firms with a promising new market and gives law-abiding citizens a way to ensure the confidentiality of their messages, it also shields the communications of criminals and terrorists. The proposed Clipper chip would "blunt" the two-edged sword of encryption technology by providing law-abiding citizens with secure encryption while at the same time allowing investigators to tap the conversations of criminals.

U.S. government defenders of the Clipper initiative deny that it represents a new level of government intrusiveness in public communications. The key to decoding Clipper messages would be held in "escrow" by independent agencies, which would release the key to the agencies only when directed to do so by a court order.

Civil libertarians aren't so sure. Why would criminals use Clipper technology if they could use alternative encryption techniques that could not be intercepted? Clipper would work only if the U.S. government outlawed the use of other encryption technologies, which would harm the U.S. software industry, ruin some companies completely, and create in effect a government monopoly. Puzzlingly, U.S. government agencies have repeatedly denied that this is their intention. If this is so, however, what conceivable motivation could criminals have to use Clipper in favor of some other encryption algorithm? Clipper will succeed only in luring law-abiding citizens into making themselves susceptible to government investigations. Critics also maintain that the Clipper initiative does not include adequate safeguards against abuse; unscrupulous government agencies could, conceivably, obtain the key and use it to snoop on an administration's political opponents.

Although the U.S. government has repeatedly stated that it does not intend to outlaw competing encryption technologies, it may be relying cynically on export regulations to deter U.S. software firms from developing programs with encryption capabilities. According to these regulations, encryption features fall into the category of "munitions," and require special export licenses. In consequence most U.S. software publishers have dropped encryption features, which could prevent their programs from being exportable—despite the fact that the encryption algorithms they would have included are commonly available overseas.

The Clipper initiative has met opposition from several civil liberties advocacy groups, including the American Civil Liberties Association (ACLU) and the **Electronic Frontier Foundation (EFF)**. Perhaps the greatest threat to Clipper, however, comes from an amorphous group of some of the software industry's most brilliant programmers and product developers, who call themselves **cypherpunks**. They are working to develop, and freely distribute, encryption technologies that will assure the right of any person to send a message that can't be cracked by snoops.

Clipper may be its own worst enemy. In 1994, Matthew Blaze, a researcher at AT&T's Bell Laboratories, reportedly discovered a potentially fatal flaw in the Clipper chip's encoding scheme: a computer expert can use the chip to encode a message that security agents wouldn't be able to read. AT&T subsequently denied that this discovery had occurred, amid reports of a fierce internal debate concerning the release of this information.

Coalition for Network Information (CNI)

A non-profit organization founded in 1990 to assist in the development of computer networking as a resource for advancing scholarship and increasing the richness of intellectual resources. The 192 member organizations reflect a cross section of the knowledge production sector, including universities, libraries, book publishers, and network service providers. The organization is concerned with questions concerning networking and intellectual property, navigation tools for scholarly researchers, the improvement of network bibliographic standards, equity of access to networked resources, and educational applications of networking technology.

coaxial cable

A rigid copper wire that is surrounded by insulating material, which is in turn encased in a second conductor made from a braided copper mesh. The second conductor is protected by an outer layer of plastic covering. In contrast to **twisted pair** telephone wires, coaxial cables offer much higher **bandwidth** (data transmission capacity) while at the same time providing greater protection from noise and interference. Two types of coaxial cable are in common use, **baseband coaxial cable** (used for **local area networks [LAN]**), and **broadband coaxial cable** (used for cable television systems).

codec

A program that provides a suite of tools for working with multimedia files, including utilities for **file compression** with ratios of up to 200:1. Codec is an abbreviation of compression/-decompression.

collaboratory

A shared scientific work space, consisting of facilities for research collaboration such as **federated databases, tele-conferencing**, and **tele-experimentation**, that is made possible by computer networking.

Most of the major problems in science today—the **grand challenges**—are so complex that they require researchers to pool and share information. There's no question of trying to go it alone. By making research tools widely available and creating a shared space for scientific collaboration, the Internet is contributing to a new mode of scientific investigation in which dozens or even hundreds of researchers are all working on various angles of a large problem and sharing their results.

com

In the **domain name system**, a **top-level domain** name that is assigned to a corporation or business. The top-level domain name follows the last period in the site's domain name (such as safety.com).

Comité Consultif International de Télégraphique et Téléphonique (CCITT)

An international standards organization, headquartered in Switzerland, that maintains the standards that enable you to pick up a telephone and place a call virtually anywhere in the world. In the 1970s, CCITT expanded its scope to include international data communications. More than 160 nations belong to CCITT and send representatives to its conferences. CCITT's parent organization is the International Telecommunication Union, a United Nations agency that also deals with international radio broadcasting. Among the CCITT standards relevant to the Internet are the standards employed by **public data networks** (called **X.25**) and standards for **modems**. In a recent reorganization, CCITT was renamed International Telecommunications Union – Telecommunications Standardization Sector (ITU-TSS), but the acronym CCITT is still commonly used to refer to this organization. *See* **International Standards Organization (ISO)**.

CCITT standards are published every four years in volumes called *fascicles*, with the color of the covers varying by year. But don't look for **electronic text** versions with **Archie**; because these volumes are copyrighted, they're not available on-line.

command line interface

An early design for handling the interaction between the user and the computer that requires the user to type commands one line at a time. Command line interfaces stem from the early years of computing, prior to the development of video displays; users interacted with the computer by typing commands at teletype keyboards and reading the replies that the system typed back. Although difficult to learn and at times tedious to use, command line interfaces are still in common use because they operate quickly and make low demands on system memory. Examples of command line interfaces include the MS-DOS operating system for PCs as well as several UNIX-based Internet utilities, including **Archie**, **FTP**, **Ping**, and **Telnet**. Most of these utilities can be accessed by means of programs employing easier interfaces, such as **menu-driven interfaces** (used in **Gopher**) and **graphical user interfaces (GUIs)** (used in **Mosaic**).

Commercial Internet Exchange (CIX)

A corporation formed by regional Internet **service providers** with the express purpose of promoting commercial use of the Internet. Such use is forbidden by **NSFNET** and its **Acceptable Use Policies (AUP)** that forbid the use of the Internet for business purposes, so one of the goals of this organization is to promote the development of an alternative to the NSFNET **backbone**. The commercial market for Internet services is currently estimated to be growing at 50% per year, and is expected to approach US$500 million by the end of the century.

| commercialization |

The transformation of the Internet from a publicly-funded research and educational network, in which business use is limited by **Acceptable Use Policies (AUP),** into a commercial communications medium in which business use is both accepted and widespread.

The Internet's federally-subsidized backbone communications system, as well as many of the state-funded university computer systems that number significantly among Internet host systems, maintain **Acceptable Use Policies (AUP)** that forbid commercial use of the network. In practice, it has proven exceptionally difficult to draw meaningful lines between acceptable or unacceptable uses. For example, do university researchers benefit from being able to purchase research-related software and receive technical support by means of Internet connections?

To bypass acceptable use policies, several regional **service providers** joined forces in 1991 to form the **Commercial Internet Exchange Association (CIX),** with the express purpose of forming an Internet **backbone** to bypass **NSFNET** and its acceptable use policies. In 1992, Sprint, a long-distance carrier with significant investment in a **fiber optic** backbone, created **SprintLink** for precisely the same reason. And in 1993, regional service providers joined forces with MCI Communications Corporation, another long-distance carrier that specializes in microwave transmission, to form **CoREN** (**Corporation for Regional and Enterprise Networking**). By providing alternative back-bones through which commercial traffic can be routed, these services allow private sector enterprises to use the Internet without fear of violating NSFNET's acceptable use policies.

Current National Science Foundation plans call for the complete **privatization** of NSFNET, beginning in 1994. This transformation will be hardly noticeable. In fact, the current level of U.S. government subsidy for NSFNET operations is minor, an estimated 10%. The bulk of NSFNET's operating costs are recovered from flat-fee charges to regional and other service providers, who in turn pass these costs on to subscribing organizations. The NSFNET backbone itself is not a U.S. government asset; it is leased from commercial service providers. When privatization is complete, the former NSFNET acceptable use policies will not apply even to the Internet backbone.

In short, the commercialization of the Internet is very nearly an established fact. What is far less clear is how this transformation will affect the Internet. Many Internet users worry that commercialization will destroy the very characteristics that have made the network so successful, namely, the way the net facilitates the coming together of knowledgeable users, who collaborate democratically and disinterestedly in the creation of knowledge for public use (*see* **community model**). For example, unscrupulous advertising, particularly by means of **carpet bombing** hundreds or even thousands of **newsgroups** with unwanted solicitations, could destroy the value of **Usenet**. Virtually the only control against such solicitations is the anger of the Usenet community, whose outraged replies to such solicitations overload the offenders' mailboxes to the point of bringing down the advertisers' **host** system.

Most Internet users accept and even welcome a passive model of commercialization, in which Internet-accessible commercial services reside on non-subsidized host systems. A user interested in such services can contact the private host system, obtain the desired services, and pay the necessary fees. Some passive Internet businesses have experienced rapid growth by means of unsolicited "word of mouth" email testimonials from satisfied customers.

Another concern of Internet users: commercialization may bring with it **time-based billing**, in which every transaction—such as a successfully relayed **electronic mail** message or **FTP** file transfer—would be billed at a certain rate. Many Internet users view this as nothing short of a catastrophe, but they frequently do not realize that Internet services are *not* provided for free. Somebody, somewhere, is paying for the network connectivity millions of people now enjoy. It is clear that, in the future, users will have to shoulder more of the burden.

Committee on Institutional Cooperation Network (CICNet)

A regional Internet network and **service provider** specializing in the Midwest (Minnesota, Wisconsin, Iowa, Indiana, Illinois, Michigan, Ohio) that offers its own **T1 backbone**. A non-profit organization launched by the universities of the Big Ten football league, CICNet now offers connectivity to other colleges and universities, k–12 schools, and businesses.

common carrier

A company that provides communications services, such as telephone and data communications, to the public. *See* **Public Data Network (PDN)**.

Common Management Information Services and Protocol over TCP/IP (CMOT)

A **protocol** for the automatic management of network devices such as **routers** that implements a version of the **Open Systems Interconnection (OSI)**-developed Common Management Information Services/Common Management Information Protocol (CMIS/CMIP) for use on Internet systems. This protocol is designed to replace the current **Simple Network Management Protocol (SMNP)**, and in so doing bring Internet-linked networks into conformity with OSI's network management model.

communications program

In personal computing, a program that is necessary to link your computer to the Internet via **dialup access**. This program transforms your PC into a **remote terminal** (a keyboard and screen that are linked to another computer located elsewhere), linked to an Internet **host** system via a computer accessory called a **modem**.

The **terminal emulation** capabilities of most communications programs allow your computer to mimic several different kinds of terminals, but by far the most useful is the **VT-100** terminal emulation that is recognized by most Internet **hosts**. In addition to emulating specific terminals, communications programs typically provide **file transfer protocols** that allow you to **upload** to the host system and **download** files stored there; you will find that the **Kermit** protocol is useful for exchanging files with the large computer systems used by hosts that provide dialup access. Another popular feature of communications programs is a screen capture utility that lets you save incoming screens to a disk file.

communications satellite

A satellite in a stationary orbit that can function as a microwave repeater for data communications. The satellite's receiver detects incoming signals, amplifies them, and beams them back to earth, where they can be received by inexpensive rooftop antennas. A network formed of two such antennas mediated by a communications satellite can bypass the telephone system entirely and achieve a **data transfer rate** of 50 Mbps.

The potential of communications satellites to serve as gateways for Internet data communications took on new meaning in 1994, when high-tech CEO entrepreneurs Craig McCaw and Bill Gates announced plans for a $9 billion satellite project, slated for operation in 2001. The plan calls for a total of 840 communications satellites that would saturate the Earth with high-**bandwidth** communications links for interactive television, electronic mail, cellular telephone service, and Internet access.

community model

In the plans now being formulated for the **National Information Infrastructure (NII)**, a conception of the system's design that emphasizes the value of allowing individual subscribers to originate information as well as consume information produced by others. *Compare* **broadcast model**.

Of the several reasons for the Internet's phenomenal growth, the importance of Internet users' ability to make information available should not be discounted. This information is not produced accordant to professional standards, but that has not stopped millions of people from going on-line to try to retrieve it. These information resources contain invaluable information for people working in specific fields—information that may prove vital to resolving a business or technical problem. They have also proven invaluable for individuals looking for information and assistance with matters of personal or social concern, such as information about ways to reduce the consumption of energy by computing equipment. It is unlikely that professional content providers would have much interest in developing such materials because they could not be sold on-line in sufficient quantities to repay their investment. An NII infrastructure biased against the capacity of users to originate information would work profoundly against public interest.

comp hierarchy

One of the seven categories of **world newsgroups** in Usenet, the comp newsgroups cover hundreds of aspects of computer development and use. Not merely of interest to computer professionals, comp newsgroups include those that appeal to users of computer applications (such as comp.database.paradox), specific computer brands (such as comp.sys.atari.st), and the social issues of computing (such as comp.org.eff.news, the newsgroups of the **Electronic Frontier Foundation**, and the several comp.society newsgroups). There is even a newsgroup, called comp.ai.philosophy, of interest to philosophers interested in the implications of artificial intelligence.

compatible

Able to work with. A networking device that is compatible with the **TCP/IP** protocols can be incorporated into an Internet-connected network and function correctly (for example, as a **host** or a **router**). *Compare* **incompatible**.

compress

A **UNIX** utility for file **compression,** as well as for decompressing files that have been compressed with this utility. A file compressed with this program has the .Z extension (for example, *information-highway.Z* is a compressed version of the file *information-highway*). You will commonly encounter compressed files when you use **resource discovery tools** such as **Archie**, **FTP**, and **Gopher**.

compression

The reduction of a file's size through the use of a compression algorithm. Many of the files you will access on the Internet have been compressed. There are two types of compression techniques: **lossless compression**, used with text and program files, and **lossy compression**, used with graphics, video, and voice files. To compress a file, you use a **file compression program**.

An example of a compression algorithm is Huffman coding, which takes advantage of the fact that in any symbol system some symbols occur more frequently than others. In English, for example, the letter "e" occurs about 100 times more frequently than the letter "q." This suggests that text could be compressed through a coding scheme in which frequently-used letters such as "e" have a short code, while infrequently-used letters such as "q" have a longer one. This compression method does not destroy any of the data because, during decompression, all of the original text can be recovered with no errors.

 Tip: For the latest information on compression, see the Usenet newsgroups comp.compression (an unmoderated discussion group) and comp.compression.research (a moderated group for researchers in this field). The group's four-part FAQ is a treasure-trove of information about compression techniques and problems.

Computer Emergency Response Team (CERT)

An organization formed by the **Defense Advanced Research Projects Agency (DARPA)** in 1988 to assist Internet users with their security concerns. Formed in response to the **Internet Worm** incident, the organization tracks Internet security violations and maintains resources of interest to Internet system administrators.

Computer Fraud and Abuse Act of 1984

A U.S. federal law that addresses the abuse of U.S. government computers or computer systems that cross state boundaries. The act criminalizes unauthorized access to U.S. government computer systems with the willful intent to obtain information that would aid foreign governments. It also forbids unauthorized access to a financial institution's computers in order to obtain confidential credit information and to U.S. government computers with the intent to defraud, gain something of value, or commit sabotage. Violation of these laws is a felony with sentences up to 10 years in prison and a $10,000 fine. In the famous **Internet Worm** incident, computer science graduate student Robert Morris was convicted under this act, even though he claimed that he did not have the intent to cause damage. His conviction was upheld by an appeals court.

computer network

A collection of **autonomous computers** that have been connected to share resources, enhance human communication, improve information system reliability, and save money.

A mainframe computer is linked via communications cables to terminals, but it is not a network because the workstations are not autonomous—they are forcibly controlled by the mainframe computer. The concept of networking suggests a democracy of computation, in which each **workstation** offers users the option of controlling the nature and extent of network involvement.

A major goal of computer networking is **resource sharing** (making geographically distant computer resources instantaneously available to every user of the network). Enhancing human communication through media such as **electronic mail**, a second goal, is succeeding. The volume of interpersonal messages carried by computer networks already exceeds the number of first-class letters delivered to U.S. households, and by a wide margin. A third goal, improving information system reliability, is achieved by creating robust systems that can survive the breakdown or destruction of some of the connected computers; networking achieves this goal by distributing processing among hundreds, thousands, or even millions of geographically dispersed computers. Networks also save money by allowing organizations to deliver computational resources in the form of inexpensive personal computers, which are as much as 100 times more cost-efficient than centralized mainframe computer systems.

Computer Professionals for Social Responsibility (CPSR)

A public-interest alliance of computer scientists, computer educators, and interested citizens who are broadly concerned with the social issues raised by computerization, including worker health and safety and electronic civil liberties. Headquartered in Palo Alto, CA, the group has offices in Washington, D.C., and Cambridge, MA, and has 21 local chapters. The organization's activities include lobbying, litigation, conferences, and publications.

CPSR has its origins in a 1981 mailing list circulated around Palo Alto, CA, the home of Stanford University, the Xerox Palo Alto Research Center (PARC), and other institutions that have played vital roles in the advancement of computer technology. Broadly rejecting the notion that technological systems are infallible, or that technology alone can solve social problems, CPSR draws on the expertise of the computer industry's leading professional practitioners to highlight the possibilities and risks of computing and computerization. The group is by no means anti-technology; on the contrary, its members hold that informed public choice is the key to producing computer systems that will make human life more democratic and more enjoyable.

Areas of CPSR concern include computer system reliability (such as the dangers of "autonomous" weapons systems), civil liberties and privacy issues raised by computer systems (such as the growing use of credit database information by government agencies and private firms), workplace issues (such as worker health and safety in computerized office settings), and the 21st Century Project, which attempts to envision new, peaceful roles for science and technology in the aftermath of the Cold War's ending.

The group is involved in litigation in an attempt to force U.S. and other government agencies to declassify information related to issues such as **Operation Sundevil** (the abortive "hacker crackdown") and the alleged interference of federal security agencies in issues related to **cryptography**. The organization sponsors conferences on social issues related to computing and publishes a newsletter, *CPSR Alert*.

CONCERT

A state Internet network and **service provider** in North Carolina that operates a high-speed **backbone** spanning the state. CONCERT links businesses, research organizations, universities, and colleges throughout North Carolina.

conditioning

In **twisted pair** telephone wiring, the improvement of a telephone line so that it is ready to carry high-bandwidth digital signals. For example, **ISDN**'s basic services can make use of twisted pair wires, but they must first be conditioned.

congestion

A delay in network response owing to the overloading of **routers** on one or more **hops** (transmission segments). *See* **net lag**.

connection

A physical, end-to-end link between two computers on a computer network, in which both computers are ready to exchange data. A connection results from a successful **handshake** (exchange of control information). In the Internet, **connection-oriented protocols** such as **FTP** handle the tasks of making physical connections and providing for applications such as file transfer.

connection-oriented protocol

A set of rules (a **protocol**) that govern the physical **connection** between two computers. This involves three stages: establishing the communication by means of a **handshake** (an exchange of control information), the transfer of data, and the close of the connection. An example of a connection-oriented protocol is **X.25**, the protocol used by many **public data networks (PDN)**. The Internet, in contrast, is a **connectionless network**.

connectionless

Able to communicate despite the lack of a direct physical connection and the exchange of control information (**hand-
shaking**). *See* **connectionless network, connectionless
protocol.**

connectionless network

A **packet-switching network** such as the Internet in which
it is not necessary for the two linked systems to **handshake**
(exchange control information) before data exchange can
occur. The opposite of a connectionless network is a **circuit-
switching network** such as the telephone system, which
establishes a physical circuit between the sending and
receiving stations.

The system works by dividing data into units called **packets**, each of which contains the destination address together with information about how the packets should be
reassembled at their destination. The packets make their way
via any open route, so that the individual packets of a message may travel via different physical connections and
arrive out of order. If a packet fails to arrive due to an error,
the system automatically resends it. All this is invisible to the
user, who receives the message—for example, an **electronic mail** message—without realizing that it has been
chopped up into pieces and reassembled at the destination.

connectionless protocol

A networking protocol (standard) that permits the exchange
of data between two computer systems despite the lack of
a direct physical connection between them. In the Internet's
protocol suite, the **Internet Protocol (IP)** is a connectionless
protocol.

connector conspiracy

A computer manufacturer's scheme, embodied in a **proprietary standard** for connecting the firm's networking devices, that locks its customers into buying that firm's equipment and no others. Some computers, for example, are manufactured using secret proprietary techniques for connecting them with peripheral devices, such as disk drives. This prevents the firm's competitors from marketing **compatible** products. But it may impose a burden on the firm's customers if the cost of these peripherals is higher than the industry average, or if these peripherals become unavailable. *Compare* **open systems computing**.

contention

In a **local area network (LAN)**, the attempt by more than one workstation to access the network at the same time. This problem must be resolved by **protocols** (standards) at the **Medium Access Control (MAC) sublayer**. A popular contention-control protocol is **Carrier Sense Multiple Access with Collision Detection (CSMA/CD)**.

convergence

In integrated routing, in which the **routers** of a **packet switching network** can dynamically exchange information about network **topology**, an automatic process of table-building that takes place during the operation of the network. Each router gradually builds an accurate table of the various routes by which packets may be sent to their destinations, and uses this table to decide the route by which packets are sent. Disturbances to the network—for example, a failure of one of the communication links or the addition of a new network to the topology—set off a new process of convergence.

A copyright that permits the free distribution and copying of a work for non-commercial purposes.

Anti-commercial in intent, copyleft derives from one of the core premises of the Hacker Ethic, as memorably described by Stephen Levy in *Hackers* (1984): Information is the property of the human community and all access to information should therefore be free.

The copyleft concept originated in a software license, called the General Public License (GPL). This license was adopted by the **Free Software Foundation**, which is dedicated to eliminating restrictions on the copying, redistribution, understanding, and modification of computer programs. This organization developed several copylefted software tools, including GNU EMACS (a text editor), that are in widespread use on UNIX systems. Users of this software are specifically invited to distribute the software freely and to change the underlying program instructions as they please.

With the rise of Internet document-accessing tools such as **anonymous FTP**, **Gopher**, and **World Wide Web**, the copyleft concept has been extended to works other than software, such as **electronic texts**. In this extension, the concept has changed: Gone is the endorsement of user modification. As applied to documents, the purpose of the copyleft is to preserve the document's integrity while at the same time ensuring free access. A typical copyleft statement specifies that no changes should be made to the work without the express permission of the original author:

```
Copyright (c) 199x by <The Author>. All rights
reserved.

You may freely redistribute verbatim copies of
this document for non-commercial purposes by
any means, provided that this copyright notice
is not removed. This work may not be sold for
profit, included within commercial works, or
```

```
altered or changed in any way without the
express written permission of the author.
Permission is expressly granted for this work
to be made available in public computer
retrieval and file transfer systems offering
unrestricted anonymous public access.
```

Copyleft has never been tested in a court of law. It is far from certain whether a notice of this type could successfully impede some third party from incorporating a copylefted work into a commercial product. What compliance there is stems from the shared and internalized moral values of the inter-networking community rather than the threat of prosecution.

core

In **ARPANET** and the early Internet, the ARPANET back-bone that carried the long-distance traffic. The core was con-nected to external networks, called **Autonomous Systems (AS)**, by **core gateways**. An AS is a collection of networks under the control of a single administrative agency, such as a university or corporation.

This structure was appropriate back in the days when the ARPANET was the Internet's only **backbone**. Now that alternative regional and national backbones exist, howev-er, there is no longer any justification for forcing every datagram to traverse the core. The solution was to recon-ceptualize the Internet as a collection of autonomous rout-ing domains, with borders between adjacent ones. *Compare* **Border Gateway Protocol (BGP)**.

core gateway

In the original Internet **architecture**, a centrally managed link between the Internet **core (backbone)** and one of the sev-eral external **Autonomous Systems** connected to the core. The core gateways chose the best route for the **datagram** to take. *Compare* **Border Gateway Protocol (BGP)**.

core model

An outmoded model of internetworking in which the network is composed of a single, high-speed **backbone** that connects a number of much smaller, autonomous systems such as **local area networks (LAN)**. The Internet is now conceptualized as a series of **Autonomous Systems (AS)** that can exchange information.

Corporation for Regional and Enterprise Networking (CoREN)

A national Internet **service provider** and **backbone** formed in 1992 by regional service providers and MCI Communications Corporation, a long-distance carrier that specializes in microwave transmission, to form **CoREN**. A member of the **Commercial Internet Exchange (CIX)**, CoREN provides an alternative backbones through which commercial traffic can be routed.

Corporation for Research and Educational Networking (CREN)

A non-profit organization formed in 1987 to manage the **BITNET** network. CREN is funded exclusively by contributions from member organizations.

courtesy copy (CC)

In **electronic mail**, a "carbon copy" of a message that is indicated on the Copy line, so that the message's recipient knows to whom the copy is sent. *Compare* **blind courtesy copy (BCC).**

cp

One of the essential **UNIX** commands for Internet users, cp copies a file. To make a copy of the file *information-glut* so that the copy has the name *information-paradise*, you type the following and press **Enter**:

```
cp information-glut information-paradise
```

cracker

A computer hobbyist who finds amusement in gaining unauthorized, illegal access to ostensibly secure computer systems. Often, this is done just for the sheer thrill of thwarting carefully-planned defenses and gaining knowledge of interesting, advanced systems, but some crackers have a malicious streak and destroy system resources. *Compare* **hacker**.

crossspost

In **Usenet**, to **post** a message to more than one **newsgroup**. When you compose a Usenet posting, you may list more than one destination newsgroup on the message's **header**. But be careful: crossposting to too many unrelated groups transforms your message into **flame bait**. And this has a very unfortunate consequence for network **bandwidth**: the people flaming you will no doubt unthinkingly duplicate your crossposting list, sending *their* messages to all the groups to which you sent yours.

Do crosspost when doing so makes sense. For example, a message posted to rec.aquaria might also prove of interest to readers of sci.aquaria. When replying to an existing posting by composing a **followup posting**, be aware that your reply will go to all of the newsgroups listed in the original posting's destination list. If the crossposting list doesn't make sense in the original message, it won't make sense in yours—and you could find yourself the object of the same flames the original poster received.

Don't crosspost to a collection of unrelated newsgroups; this is called **carpet bombing**, and it's a serious breach of Usenet **netiquette**.

The science, theoretical and applied, of coding messages so that they cannot be read by any person other than the intended recipient. A related science, cryptoanalysis, is devoted to trying to break coded messages when the key to the coding is not known.

An early, and perhaps the first, application of cryptography dates back to ancient Rome. Caesar didn't trust his own messengers, so he shifted every letter alphabetically by 3 (in effect, "M" would become "P," and so on). This made the message incomprehensible to anyone who did not realize that the letters could be decoded by shifting the letters back three places in the alphabet.

The process of coding the message is called **encryption**, and it uses a procedure known as a **key**. (The key to Caesar's method is the "shift-by-3" rule.) In **decryption**, the intended recipient employs the key to decode the message.

The ease with which computers can encrypt messages that are virtually impregnable to cryptoanalysis has government agencies worried: They fear that terrorists, drug dealers, and organized crime will be able to send and receive messages that cannot be intercepted. For this reason, the various security agencies of the U.S. federal government have proposed outlawing all computer-based encryption technology save one, called **Clipper**, which enables government security agencies (but not the public) to intercept and decode encrypted messages. This proposal is opposed by computer rights advocacy organizations such as the **Electronic**

Frontier Foundation (EFF), Computer Professionals for Social Responsibility (CPSR), as well as a loose confederation of computer programmers and system designers who call themselves **cypherpunks**.

CSO name server

A **white pages** directory service for looking up the telephone numbers and electronic mail addresses of people who belong to or work for a specific organization. The acronym CSO stands for Computing Service Office, the unit of the University of Illinois, Urbana-Champaign, that originally developed the name server software.

You may encounter a CSO name server while browsing the **Gopher** of a **Campus-Wide Information System (CWIS)**; if so, you'll *see* the <CSO> tag at the end of the Gopher item, as in the following example:

```
8.  Green Valley College Faculty and
    Students <CSO>
```

When you choose this item, you're connected to the CSO name server, and you can type the name you're looking for.

Cuckoo's Egg

The title of a book by Clifford Stoll, an astronomer and computer system administrator at the University of California's Lawrence Berkeley Laboratory (LBL), describing his experiences in the mid-1980s tracking down a particularly persistent **cracker**. The book is an important contribution to network **security** and should be read by anyone with Internet system administration responsibilities.

It's a good story, too. Stoll first became aware of the cracker's activities when he encountered a minor discrepancy in a computerized grant account. Trying to track the cracker's activities and figure out what the cracker was up to, Stoll became obsessed with the intruder and at one point carried around a pager that would tell him when the cracker logged on to the system. At first, it was something of a game: Stoll was determined to set up a trap that would reveal the cracker's identity. The story took a more sinister side, however, when Stoll realized that the cracker was using the LBL access to hunt for military-related information. Attempts to trace the cracker's calls revealed that they originated from West Germany, suggesting that the cracker might be engaged in espionage. When finally apprehended, the cracker turned out to be a young German named Markus Hess who, with several cracker friends, had developed an ill-considered plan to obtain Western military secrets and advanced Western military software and then offer these items for sale to the KGB. The trial concluded that, although Hess and his friends had gained unauthorized access to U.S. military computers, they had not obtained any particularly sensitive information. Hess was given a suspended sentence and a fine.

curses client

In **UNIX** systems, an Internet **client** program that employs the default UNIX utility programs, collectively called curses, for displaying characters on-screen. A commonly-used curses client is the **Gopher** client widely found on **Campus-Wide Information Systems (CWIS)**.

cybernaut

An Internet user who is an experienced and knowledgeable traverser of the Internet's **cyberspace**, composed of its myriad network pathways and interconnections. *See* **net surfing**.

cybersex

A new form of human sexuality made possible by computer networking, in which two users—engaged in **real-time** conversation—stimulate each other by exchanging sexually explicit messages. The principle technical limitation of cybersex is the difficulty of typing with one hand.

Do bear in mind that it's possible to get hurt by engaging in cybersex; in some sense, it's "real." A cybersex relationship that's cut off abruptly can hurt almost as much as the termination of a real relationship. Bear in mind, too, that there are malicious users out there who try to lure you into cybersex, only to post an embarrassing transcript of your messages to a Usenet newsgroup.

Don't harass women who use the Internet by making unwanted computer "advances" to them in inappropriate contexts. This is a form of sexual harassment that is as unwanted and possibly illegal as sexual harassment in other contexts, such as the workplace. Many female users report that sexual harassment is rampant on the Internet and creates a negative environment for women—so much so, in fact, that several "women-only" networks have been set up in an effort to avoid on-line harassment.

cyberspace

The electronic space created by a computer system or a computer network, which the user can explore at will.

This term has its origins in a pioneering science fiction novel by William Gibson, *Neuromancer*, which defined the cyberspace of a future world-wide network as a "consensual hallucination." The sensation of cyberspace, of being inside a virtual space that has been created by a computer system, is most powerful in virtual reality games and applications. Yet one has a sense of cyberspace when exploring the Internet as well. Linking millions of computers worldwide, the Internet collapses the geography that divides them with its near-instantaneous links, and constructs in its place a chaotic wilderness rich in hidden treasures (such as new **Gopher** and **World Wide Web** sites).

cyborg

A hybrid of human and machine. Typified by the Borg, the extensively modified and murderous half-men, half-robots of *Star Trek: The Next Generation*, future cyborgs would stem from the marriage of machines and meat.

Arguably, cyborgs already exist, and not merely where prostheses assist the disabled. To the extent that technology comes to mediate between individuals and their social worlds, we may be cyborgs already. In the form of telephones and electronic mail, for instance, technology increasingly interposes itself between ourselves and our consociates. In **MUDs**, cyborgs are "clones" of your character that you program to perform specific tasks, such as greeting new people who enter a room you're in (or dealing with the constant barrage of questions from clueless newbies).

Cyclic Redundancy Code (CRC)

A commonly-used method of checking for errors in a data transmission. Before a data **frame** is transmitted, a utility program performs a complex computation on the data contained in the frame and produces a **checksum**. If even a single bit of the frame has been altered or lost in the transmission, the receiving station will be able to detect the loss and discard the corrupted frame.

cypherpunk

A computer amateur or professional—a hobbyist, programmer or system designer—who strongly believes that ordinary people should possess the right to **encrypt** (code) their everyday communications so that nobody besides the intended recipient can read it. They are working to develop secure encryption programs, place them in the public domain, and make them widely available as a technological defense against government surveillance.

Software engineer and peace activist Philip Zimmerman is the author of Pretty Good Privacy (PGP), a virtually unbreakable encryption program that lets Internet users ensure the **privacy** of their **electronic mail** messages. Zimmerman placed the program on the Internet for free redistribution.

daemon

In **UNIX**, a program that constantly runs in the background, ready to spring into action and perform a specific task when needed. An example of a daemon is biff, which lets you know when mail arrives.

Data Circuit-Terminating Equipment (DCE)

In the **X.25** protocols for **wide area networks (WANs)**, a device—called a **modem**—that transforms the computer's digital signals so that they can be transmitted over the telephone system.

Data Encryption Standard (DES)

An **encryption** method, developed by IBM, that the U.S. government certified in 1977 as the official encryption technique for unclassified information. Decertified in 1988, DES is still in widespread use and remains controversial.

The circumstances surrounding DES's adoption left some cryptography researchers speculating about the government's motives. According to critics, U.S. security agencies have acted as if the only encryption scheme they like is one that they think they can break. DES's **key** size, for example, is 56 bits, which, according to some crytographers, would enable a government agency equipped with a supercomputer to decrypt a message using a brute force technique. The original DES proposal called for a key size of 128 bits, which would have made brute force decryption very unlikely. *Compare* **Clipper Chip**.

data link layer

In the **Open Systems Interconnection (OSI) Reference Model** of computer networks, the layer that deals with the transmission of data across a given point-to-point line so that it comes across as data, not gibberish, on the other end. The **TCP/IP protocols** are not concerned with this level. The **Internet Protocol (IP)** installed in a router, for example, shoots the **datagrams** out as fast as it can to the next router down the "line," which may in fact involve several completely different data links and physical media. The challenge of figuring out how to get the Internet datagrams across a given point-to-point data link has been solved in many different ways.

From the standpoint of the physical media, what's traversing the point-to-point link is a stream of **bits**. But there's no guarantee that all the bits will arrive intact. Noise—produced by lightning, telephone system signaling tones, crosstalk between lines, and many other sources—can cause errors. The most popular approach to this problem is to divide the data into **frames**, which aren't the same things as the datagrams created by **TCP/IP**. The frame may be as short as one **octet** (8 bits) or several thousand bits. To see whether the data arrived safely, most data link protocols employ a **checksum** at the beginning and at the end of the transmission. If the two values do not agree, an error is presumed to have occurred and the frame is retransmitted.

There are no universally-accepted **protocols** at the data link layer. Personal computer users who transfer files via a **modem** are familiar with a number of **file transfer protocols** such as **Xmodem, Ymodem, Zmodem**, and **Kermit**. For transmission across analog telephone lines, **SLIP** and **PPP** can deliver IP datagrams over analog telephone lines. The High-level Data Link Control (HDLC) protocol, an international **ISO** standard, has many variations, including one used on **X.25 networks**. **T1** and **T3** digital telephone trunk lines, which form the bulk of the current Internet's **backbones**, have their own methods of dividing the data into frames.

Data Terminal Equipment (DTE)

In the **CCITT's** terminology for **asynchronous communication** via **modems**, a remote **terminal** that can be hooked up to a telephone line.

data transfer rate

The speed at which a point-to-point transmission line can convey data, measured in **bits per second (bps)**.

Data transfer rates are commonly expressed with the abbreviations Kbps (one thousand bits per second), Mbps (one million bits per second), and Gbps (one billion bits per second). Commonly-used modems, for example, can transfer data via telephone lines at a speed of 14.4 Kbps. To put these terms in perspective, a **modem** running at 14.4 Kbps would require about 5 minutes to transfer a 50-page essay, but a **gigabit network** running at 2 Gbps could transfer the entire text of the *Encyclopedia Britannica* in less than a second.

data word

The smallest addressable unit of information in a computer of a given design. In personal computers, the data word is eight **bits** long (one byte)—indeed, for PCs, the terms data word and byte are all but synonymous. But some of the computers linked to the Internet use data words of differing lengths. In deference to this fact Internet computer professionals prefer to use the term **octet** to describe a data unit eight bits in length.

database

A collection of information on a single topic or a group of related topics that has been organized in a way that facilitates retrieval by the computer.

More formal definitions of this term are possible, but they wouldn't be true to the database resources available on the Internet through database servers such as **WAIS**. These databases are sometimes little more than an index to a collection of text files in a directory.

datagram

In the **Internet Protocol (IP)**, the standard format for a **packet** of data that is routed through the network for delivery to a specific **destination address**. This format includes standards for preparing the **header**, the first 6 32-bit **data words** of the message. The header includes the **source address**, the destination address, **routing**, and other information.

The terms *packet* and *datagram* are not synonymous; **packet** refers to the physical unit of data that is transmitted over the network, while **datagram** refers specifically to the **Internet Protocol (IP)** rules for organizing the information within the packet. If a datagram encounters a network that requires an even smaller **maximum transmission unit (MTU)**, it can be broken into smaller datagrams in a process called **fragmentation**. When the datagram reaches its destination, **reassembly** unites the disparate parts of the message.

de facto standard

In computer networking, a **standard** that has won widespread acceptance without the benefit of rational planning or the creation of international **de jure standards**. (The word "de facto" means "from the fact" in Latin.)

For example, **UNIX** provides the basic platform for Internet networking because the Internet protocols were first implemented on a UNIX computer and AT&T permitted the UNIX operating system to be distributed at low cost to colleges and universities. De facto standards can also arise when a company's **proprietary standard** gains widespread acceptance. They can also arise when an **open standard** gains widespread acceptance, despite the fact that they have not been recommended by an international standards organization. The **TCP/IP** protocols have become de facto standards for internetworking. *Compare* **de jure standard**.

de jure standard

In computer networking, a **standard** that has been imposed by a nationally or internationally recognized standardization organization, such as the **ISO** or **CCITT**. An example of de jure standards in internetworking is supplied by the **Open Systems Interconnection (OSI) protocol suite**. *Compare* **de facto standard**.

declarative markup language

A **markup language** for coding a text document for computer use. Unlike a procedural markup language, a declarative markup language merely indicates ("declares") the parts of the document, such as the title and abstract. The program that displays the received document, called a **parser**, formats these document parts with distinctive fonts, indentations, and spacing. A procedural language includes instructions that tell the computer exactly how to display the document, including all specifications for such matters as fonts, indents, and spacing.

decryption

In **cryptography**, the process by which the recipient of a coded message employs a **key** to decode and read the message.

dedicated access

A method of connecting to the Internet that permits a large computer system or an extensive **local area network (LAN)** to become an Internet **host**, with a unique **IP address**. Although expensive (installation costs and monthly fees run as high as several thousand dollars), dedicated connections provide sufficient **bandwidth** that dozens or even hundreds of users can access the Internet simultaneously.

Required for direct connections are a **router** linked to a high-speed data transmission line such as a **leased line**.

A computer linked to the Internet by means of a direct connection is typically left on 24 hours per day, so that anyone using the system can access the Internet at any time. Available speeds range from 56 Kbps (56,000 bits per second) to nearly 45 Mbps (45 million bits per second).

Do consider other, less costly Internet access options for personal computer users, including **dialup access** (in which you use the dialup host system as your base of operations) and **dialup IP** (in which your computer temporarily becomes a full-fledged Internet **host**).

dedicated connection

A permanent connection to an Internet **service provider** by means of a **leased line** or direct high-bandwidth cabling. At an estimated $2,000 to $5,000 per month, dedicated connections to the Internet are too expensive for individuals, but they're affordable for medium- to large-sized organizations.

dedicated line

Synonymous with **leased line;** a telephone cable or a cable provided by a **Public Data Network (PDN)** that provides a permanent, non-switched connection between an Internet **host** and a regional or national **backbone**.

default editor

In a **UNIX** system, the **text editor** that the system automatically starts by default when you (or a program, such as an electronic mail **client**) requires a text editor's services. In virtually all UNIX systems, the default text editor is **vi**.

Tip: If you're unhappy with vi (and who isn't?), you can change your default text editor by making a change to one of the configuration files in your **home directory**. Contact your system administrator to find out whether more capable text editors (such as JOVE or EMACS) are available, and if so, how to change your default editor.

| default route |

In a **routing table,** the route that the router will automatically choose unless there is some problem with that connection.

Defense Advanced Research Projects Agency (DARPA)

A U.S. military research funding agency, the successor to the **Advanced Research Projects Agency (ARPA)** that funded the Internet's predecessor, the **ARPANET.** Among DARPA's recent Internet-related activities is the formation of the **Computer Emergency Response Team (CERT)**, an organization formed in the aftermath of the Internet Worm event to monitor Internet security. DARPA is currently a member of the **High Performance Computing and Communications Program (HPCC)**, a consortium of U.S. government agencies that is developing the **National Research and Educational Network (NREN)**.

Defense Data Network (DDN)

One of several **interagency networks** in the U.S. federal government that is part of the Internet. DDN was created in 1990 to meet the networking needs of the U.S. Department of Defense (DoD).

Defense Data Network Information Center (DDN NIC)

A **Network Information Center (NIC)** maintained by the **Defense Data Network (DDN)**. Sometimes called "The NIC," this is the chief NIC; there are regional NICs, too, but "The NIC" is responsible for the all-important task of assigning new network numbers, such as **IP addresses** (*see* **registered host**). It's also responsible for maintaining an authoritative collection of documents (such as **For Your Information [FYI]** and **Request for Comments [RFC]**) about Internet protocols.

delete/write access

In **file ownership**, a setting that allows a user to delete or alter a file. *Compare* **read only access**.

delurk

In a **Usenet** newsgroup, particularly one that deals with a controversial topic such as alternative sexual lifestyles, to post a message identifying oneself as a regular reader of the group. A delurk posting may be the prelude to **real life (RL)** meetings with others who share the same proclivities.

demodulation

The process of transforming an incoming audio signal, in which varying tones signify information, into digital information that a computer can process. *Compare* **modulation, modem**.

demultiplexing

The process of breaking down an incoming **byte stream**, which contains data from many sources, so that the data can be sent to the correct **transport protocol** and **application**. Numbers contained in each **datagram**, called the **port address** and the **protocol address**, make this possible. *Compare* **multiplexing**.

destination address

In the **header** part of a **datagram** (a **packet** format defined by the **Internet Protocol [IP]**), the **IP address** of the message's destination.

dialup access

A method of connecting to the Internet by means of a personal computer equipped with a **modem** and a **communications program**. You use your computer and modem to call into an Internet **host** system that has high-speed, **dedicated access**. By far the simplest and cheapest method of Internet access, this is also the slowest and least capable (for example, you will not be able to run graphical **front ends** such as **Eudora** or **Mosaic** at tolerable speeds). Using your computer and communications program, you dial a connection to an Internet **host**. Once this connection is established after the **logon** procedure, your computer becomes a **remote terminal** of the host system. **Dedicated access** is preferable for full access to the Internet's capabilities.

To contact the Internet by means of dialup access, you must have an account on an Internet-connected host system, such as a university's central computing system. If your organization does not offer dialup access to an Internet host, you may be able to obtain dialup access by means of a **freenet**, an Internet-linked **bulletin board system (BBS)**, or a commercial dialup access provider such as Performance Systems International (PSI), located in Herndon, Virginia. Commercial on-line services that are accessible by means of dialup access, such as CompuServe, also offer limited Internet access.

With dialup access, your personal computer isn't really connected to the Internet. The host system is, though. Depending on the host's resources, you can use standard Internet applications such as **electronic mail, FTP, Usenet**, and **Gopher**. However, the slow speed of the telephone link ensures that you must use only the text-based clients available on the host system.

Do ask your organization's computer center whether Internet dialup access is available.

Don't subscribe to a commercial access provider or online service without first finding out just which Internet services are available. Many systems that advertise "Internet access" provide only electronic mail.

dialup IP

A method of Internet access that allows computer users to establish a temporary but direct Internet connection by means of a high-speed **modem** and the telephone system. Requiring special software both on your computer and on the Internet host you contact, dialup IP works by presenting your computer to the Internet as if it were a **node** (workstation) on a **local area network (LAN)** with a unique **IP address**. As a result, Internet **packets** can go directly to your computer (this is not possible with ordinary **dialup access**). The programs required to implement dialup IP are governed by two protocols called **SLIP** and **PPP**.

Dialup IP has a number of advantages over **dialup access**. Because the data packets can travel directly to your computer, you can use **FTP** to obtain files without the tedious, intermediary step of downloading them from the host system (which is required when you use dialup access). Unlike **dialup access**, dialup IP allows you to run **clients** such as Eudora and Mosaic on your computer system, and has other advantages such as convenient file transfer (files obtained through **FTP**, for example, go directly to your computer's hard disk instead of being stored temporarily on a minicomputer or mainframe computer host system).

Dialup IP is still something of an art; much of the required software is in the public domain and is, in consequence, poorly documented. With the growing availability of high-speed (9600 bps and 14.4 Kbps) modems, dialup IP is certain to become more widely used, and more user-friendly products are sure to emerge. For other access options, see **dedicated access**, **leased lines**, and **local area network (LAN)**.

dialup site

A computer, such as an individual's personal computer, a computer **bulletin board system (BBS)**, or a network in a developing country, that accesses the Internet by means of **dialup access**. Lacking full Internet connectivity, these sites can nevertheless exchange **electronic mail** and **Usenet** postings with Internet users by means of **UUCP**.

dictionary flame

In **Usenet**, a message that sidetracks a debate by focusing in a pointless or pedantic way on the meaning of terms.

digest

In **Usenet**, a **moderated newsgroup** in which the postings consist of periodic summaries of contributions made to a mailing list. The digest includes information about how to obtain the full text of these contributions, if you wish. An example: comp.dcom.telecom.

digital

The representation of information by means of discrete digits (units), which can be absolutely and unambiguously distinguished from each other (like the fingers on your hand). In computers, information is represented by low and high currents, which represent the basic units of binary encoding (0 and 1). Within the computer, information is represented using digital techniques, but this information must be transformed (through a process called **modulation**) before it can be sent via the telephone system. *Compare* **analog**; *see* **modem**.

digital library

The library of knowledge accessible via the Internet, consisting of a diverse and uncatalogued mixture of publicly-available materials (such as **electronic texts**) as well as indexes of copyrighted or rare materials that are kept in special collections. The virtual "shelves" of the digital library contain reference materials (such as the *CIA-KGB World Fact Book*), the full text of non-copyrighted classics of science and literature, publicly-accessible databases accessible through **WAIS**, **hypertext** documents accessible through **World Wide Web**, telephone directories, sound and voice recordings, images, video clips, and collections of statistics and scientific data. Compare **virtual library**.

The Internet appears on the verge of making the dream of a universal, publicly accessible library come true—but if so, the dream has some nightmarish elements. A key problem: conceptualized as a digital library, the resources of the Internet are very rich—but it's very difficult to *find* these resources.

The difficulty of locating materials on the Internet is addressed with only partial success by information retrieval **clients** such as **Gopher**, **WAIS**, and **World Wide Web (WWW)**. None of these can guarantee that you'll find what you're looking for. To be accessible, someone must have deliberately made the information publicly available by means of a corresponding **server** program on an Internet host system. In addition, the navigation and search tools provided by these applications are extremely primitive. At best, you can search for words that appear in the titles of files indexed by these servers. But most of the files that are publicly accessible via Internet applications are named so oddly or cryptically that the file names do not describe the files' contents. Your best bet currently is to use **WWW**, since the **hypertext** documents that provide **links** to electronic texts usually include at least some descriptive text about these resources.

The National Science Foundation's Digital Library Initiative, announced in 1993, seeks to address these and other problems by investigating new ways of making materials available in digital form, generating searchable indexes of digital library resources, and helping users locate materials with new, more sophisticated search clients.

A **network** that transmits data that has been represented in the form of **bits** (high or low voltages, which correspond to 1s or 0s). The opposite of a digital network is an **analog network**, such as the local telephone system, which converts the sound of a voice into an electrical current whose strength and other characteristics mimic the changing sounds of the voice. Digital networks are required for computer data, which must be transmitted with perfect accuracy. But digital networks are also capable of handling voice and video. What is more, they can do so more cleanly than analog networks; noise and distortion, for example, all but disappear. Today, digital networks handle computer data, while analog networks handle voice and video. But tomorrow's **integrated services networks** will make high-speed computer networking, voice, and video communications available to homes, schools, and offices.

Digital Telephony Act

A legislative act proposed by the U.S. Federal Bureau of Investigation (FBI) that would require providers of **electronic mail** and **Private Branch Exchange (PBX)** systems to permit government investigators to intercept private communications. The proposed legislation would further empower the U.S. Department of Justice to prohibit the development of computers systems, peripherals, and software that would enable private persons to escape FBI surveillance.

Underlying the Digital Telephony Act is concern that **encrypted** (coded) digital communications could allow terrorists, drug dealers, and organized crime to evade the wiretapping that has proven so effective in the past. Successfully opposing the legislation was a consortium of civil rights advocacy organizations, including the American Civil Liberties Union (ACLU), the **Electronic Frontier Foundation (EFF)**, and **Computer Professionals for Social Responsibility (CPSR)**. These organizations argued that the legislation overstepped legitimate law enforcement needs and would have resulted in a severe erosion of civil liberties as private communication increasingly moves to digital media.

DikuMUD

A combat-oriented **MUD** (a computerized, multi-user role-playing game) that emulates the characters, actions, and settings of Advanced Dungeons and Dragons. Originating in the Deptartment of Computer Science at the University of Copenhagen (Datalogisk Institute ved Køpenhavns Universitet—or DIKU for short), the first DikuMUD server was completed in 1990.

An improvement on the Dungeons and Dragons emulation introduced in the first MUDs, such as AberMUD, DikuMUD allows for social interaction and cooperation while still retaining the emphasis on combat, action, and adventure. The game does not include a programming language (as does another popular combat-oriented MUD, **LPMUD**), and includes limited facilities for user modification of the perceived environment (as do **TinyMUDs** and their many variants).

directory

In **UNIX** and other operating systems that organize files hierarchically, a catalog for the files stored on a disk that provides a way of organizing the files so that related ones can be grouped together. On a large UNIX system, for example, there may be hundreds of thousands of files, but these are grouped into directories so that the list of them does not overwhelm the user. *See* **home directory**.

Directories are organized hierarchically using a tree-like structure. The top-level directory, called the root directory, contains many subdirectories. Each subdirectory, in turn, may contain subdirectories. The term subdirectory is a relational concept; it's used when you're talking about the relationship of one directory to another.

directory of servers

In **WAIS**, a database that contains information about all the known WAIS databases, and that allows you to search for databases in fields of interest to you. You can type in search terms that describe the subject in which you're interested, and WAIS displays the databases—if any—that correspond to your interests.

diskless workstation

In a computer network, a **workstation** or **personal computer** that has its own processing unit and memory, but does not contain a hard disk or floppy disk drives. In place of local disk drives, a diskless workstation makes use of files on a server computer, located elsewhere on the network. In UNIX systems, file access is enabled by the **Network File System (NFS)**. At the beginning of each operating session, the workstation lacks software, so necessary files must be transferred to the workstation using the **Trivial File Transfer Protocol (TFTP)**.

Why set up diskless workstations? Doing so ensures the maintenance of single, centralized repository for information (on the server), while at the same time relieving the server of much of the processing that it would otherwise have to do (the processor inside the workstation takes care of this job).

distance-vector routing algorithm

A **routing algorithm**, embodied in a computer program running on a **router**, that computes the best route through the network for a given **datagram** by finding the shortest possible route. A router that uses distance-vector techniques builds a map of the network by communicating with other routers. Each router **advertises** the information it possesses about routes to the router one hop away; this router, in turn, has received information from the router one additional hop down the line, and relays this back to the first router. In this way, information about route availability spreads throughout the network in a process called **convergence**. An Internet **Interior Gateway Protocol (IGP)**

that embodies a distance-vector routing algorithm is called
Routing Information Protocol (RIP).

| distributed |

Made widely available, especially so that processing bur-
dens can be spread around the network equitably. Distributing an automatically updated database of Internet
resources to hundreds or even thousands of **hosts** helps to
free up the system that formerly held the only copy of the
database.

| distributed computing |

A mode of computing in which computer resources are
geographically distributed in a physical sense among the various **nodes** of a **computer network**, but in such a way that
the user is unaware of the geographical dispersal of these
resources: So far as you know when you are using a distributed computer system, all the resources are available
seamlessly, and without regard to their actual physical
location, from your **workstation**. The networking software
handles the task of accessing the resources, without your
having to determine physical locations or give commands
that include references to such locations.

Does the Internet offer distributed computing? If you're
using **FTP**, **Archie**, or **Telnet**, the answer is "Not really"—
you're concerned with specific locations. Among contemporary Internet applications, it's the **World Wide Web
(WWW)** that will give you a glimpse of the future world
distributed computing network. When you select one of
the **hypertext** links in a WWW document, WWW operates invisibly in the background to establish the connection
to the computer that houses the information you've requested. As you navigate WWW documents by means of these

links, you may have—without realizing it—accessed computer resources in Finland, Australia, Mexico, and Taiwan.

distributed routing

In a **packet switching network** such as the Internet, the distribution throughout the network of **integrated routers** that contain the microprocessors, memories, and disk drives needed to run a **routing algorithm** (a program capable of making routing decisions). In older networks, routing decisions had to be made by centralized routers, but this does not **scale well**—as the network experiences rapid growth, centralized routers quickly become overburdened. By distributing routing tasks to every router in the network, the network can continue to grow indefinitely without suffering degraded performance.

distribution

In **Usenet**, the geographic region to which a Usenet **posting** will be broadcast. The default distribution in most systems is world (world-wide distribution), but you can limit your posting to smaller regions by using the appropriate geographic or institutional distribution code. Examples are *can* (Canada), *fl* (Florida), *ba* (San Francisco Bay Area), and *uva* (University of Virginia).

Do limit the distribution of your Usenet posting to the smallest geographic region that will serve your purpose. For example, if you are trying to sell an old PC in Ann Arbor, Michigan, use the *aa* code to restrict your posting to that city alone. Posting a Usenet message for world distribution places an additional load on already hard-pressed Internet resources and may run up hundreds of dollars of indirect costs.

Don't worry about distribution if you're using a **local newsgroup**, such as uva.news.basketball. By default these newsgroups limit distribution to a specific institution or region.

Tip: Because of the way Usenet postings propagate throughout the Internet, there are restrictions on the use of distribution codes. To use a distribution code, you must be using a computer that is *within* the area or institution to which the code applies. For example, a San Francisco user can use the *ba* (San Francisco Bay Area), *ca* (California), or *usa* (United States) distributions. But she cannot use the *la* (Los Angeles), *fl* (Florida), or *no* (Norway) distributions. Postings originating from her with these distributions will be ignored.

DIX Ethernet

A standard for **local area networks (LANs)** that was jointly published in 1982 (with a 1984 revision) by Digital Equipment Corporation, Intel Corporation, and Xerox Corporation. The DIX specifications call for a 10 Mbps network constructed from **baseband coaxial cable**. Subsequently, these specifications—somewhat modified—served as the basis for the widely-accepted **IEEE 802 network** protocols. Networks constructed according to the IEEE protocols differ from earlier Ethernets, but the term **Ethernet** is widely used for both. To distinguish between the two, LAN experts prefer to speak of "DIX Ethernets" and "IEEE 802 networks."

domain

In the **domain name system**, a single word or abbreviation that describes a level of responsibility for naming subordinate groups or hosts. For example, within the domain *ucsd* (University of California, San Diego), the system administrator may create as many groups (such as *med-school.ucsd*) or subhost names (such as *maxwell.ucsd*) as she wishes, without fear of duplicating names chosen by administrators at other sites. A domain isn't necessarily, or even often, equivalent to a physical network; the domain *medschool* at *ucsd*, for example, may comprise faculty and administration who have accounts on several distinct **local area networks (LAN)**.

domain name

In the **domain name system**, a name that uniquely identifies an Internet **host**. People can use domain names, such as bioprofs.maxwell.ucsd.edu,to describe the source or destination of an Internet link; the Internet's software takes care of translating the domain name into the exact **IP address** that's needed to deliver the messages to their correct destination. *See* **Domain Name Service (DNS).**

Domain Name Service (DNS)

A program that runs on Internet **hosts** or **routers**, and provides the important function of resolving **domain names** (such as wobbly@spunky.safety.com) into the **IP addresses** needed to deliver the data. *Compare* **domain name system** (the system of **domain names**).

For every **domain** within the Internet, there is an authoritative server that maintains up-to-the-minute information about how to deliver messages within that domain. If a router doesn't know how to deliver a message within an unknown domain, it contacts the authoritative server for the needed information. Subsequently, the router stores this information. In this way, knowledge of domain names and their relation to IP addresses diffuses throughout the Internet.

| domain name system |

A method of naming Internet hosts that allows a system administrator to choose **host names** without fear of duplicating a name already in use at another site.

The need for the domain name system became apparent when the **Network Information Center (NIC)** found that it could no longer deal with the deluge of host name registrations. Each new host had to have a unique name. Delays in registering new hosts, coupled with difficulties in finding new, unique names, led to domain name system. It distributes the responsibility of finding unique names to the system administrator of each host, who may choose names for groups and subordinate hosts without fear of duplicating the name choices made by administrators of other systems.

To read a domain name such as *bioprofs.maxwell.ucsd.-edu*, you go from right to left. Think of the domains as if they were Chinese boxes, one within the other. A domain name begins (at the right) with the biggest box, a **top-level domain**; here, it's *edu*, which stands for educational institution. The next level is a subdomain, a box within the biggest box—here, *ucsd*, which stands for University of California, San Diego (an educational institution). The third level, *maxwell*, refers to a specific host computer within the ucsd box. The final level, *bioprofs*, refers to a group of users with accounts on Maxwell.

The virtue of domain name system is that a system administrator at another site could name a group *bioprofs-.maxwell.uva.edu* without conflicting with the San Diego administrator's name choice. As far as the Internet is concerned, the names *bioprofs.maxwell.ucsd.edu* and *bioprofs-.maxwell.uva.edu* are completely different. To understand why, think of the directions you might give for driving somewhere. You want someone to drive to 1609 10th St. in Peoria, Illinois. Lots of cities have houses numbered 1609, and streets named 10th Street, but there's only one 1609 10th

St. in Peoria, Illinois. As long as your friend gets on the freeway and drives to Peoria, there's nothing to worry about. Similarly, an electronic mail message addressed to *jsmith@bioprofs.maxwell.ucsd.edu* won't wind up at *uva*, since the message first goes to ucsd and only then starts looking for *maxwell*, *bioprofs*, and *jsmith*—in that order.

What can you tell about a domain name by looking at it? Within the United States, the **top level domain** provides clues to the nature of the organization (for example, *com* refers to a business organization, while *gov* indicates a governmental organization of some kind). Outside the U.S., the top-level domain indicates the country in which the host is located (such as *ca* [Canada] or *se* [Sweden]). The next subdomain usually tells you the name of the organization, albeit cryptically (*uu* in *uu.se*, for instance, is the none-too-obvious domain name for Uppsala University). Beyond this point, it's hard to tell what the subordinate domains mean; they might refer to specific host computers (*maxwell.ucsd.-edu*), groups set up by the system administrator (*bioprofs.-maxwell.ucsd.edu*) or even programs (*archie.unr.edu*).

| dot address |

See **IP address.**

| dot file |

In **UNIX** systems, a file in the user's **home directory** that contains the user's configuration settings. The file name is preceded by a period and does not appear in default directory listings. For example, if you create a file called .signature, most **electronic mail clients** will automatically append a **signature** to each email message you send. If you create a file called .plan, people who **finger** you will receive this file automatically.

dot quad

Synonymous with **dotted decimal notation.**

dotted decimal notation

A method of writing down a 32-bit binary number using four base 10 numbers separated by dots (for example, 128.68.44.11). This method is often used to describe **IP addresses**.

down

Inoperable, comatose, not operating. "The network is down."

download

To transfer a file from another computer to your computer by means of a modem and a telephone line. *Compare* **upload**.

Downloading is one of the hassles of **dialup access.** Suppose you're using **FTP**, and you've retrieved several useful files. But you haven't retrieved them to *your* computer—you've retrieved them to the host your accessing. To get the files to your computer, you must download them at speeds very much slower than FTP file transfers.

To download a file from your host, you must use a **file transfer protocol** which assures that the transmission is free from errors. The file transfer protocol of choice for computer **bulletin board systems (BBS)** is **Zmodem**. If you're accessing a **UNIX** host, you're more likely to use **Kermit**. Most popular **communications programs** can transfer files with either of these protocols.

downstream bandwidth

In a network designed to provide Internet connectivity to homes, schools, and offices, the part of the delivered connectivity that carries content to information consumers. One of the technical options currently envisioned for the emerging **National Information Infrastructure (NII), cable television (CATV)**, is at present heavily biased toward downstream bandwidth; upstream bandwidth is sharply restricted and permits the user to do little more than originate content selection or control messages. An information infrastructure based on current CATV technologies would bring with it a technical bias towards the **broadcast model** rather than the **community model** of connectivity. Technical innovation in the CATV industry may alter this picture substantially in the coming years.

downstream site

A **host** system that has only one means of connection with the Internet. In **Usenet**, a downstream site's newsgroup repertoire may be limited by upstream decisions to delete certain unwanted newsgroups.

EBCDIC

See **Extended Binary Coded Decimal Interchange Code (EBCDIC)**.

| edu |

In the **domain name system**, a **top-level domain** name that is assigned to colleges and universities, mainly in North America. The top-level domain name follows the last period in the site's domain name (such as virginia.edu).

Electronic Communications Privacy Act (ECPA)

A U.S. federal law that criminalizes **unauthorized access** to any computer system in which private communications are transmitted. An amendment to previous wiretapping legislation, the ECPA was principally aimed at U.S. federal agencies, which are now required to obtain a court order to access electronic communications for investigative purposes. It also forbids unauthorized access to computer systems with the intention of reading someone's private communications. The act focuses on data in transit or in interim storage (up to 180 days) and does not protect messages stored permanently on computer disks.

It is obvious that the framers of this act knew very little about computer backup procedures, in which virtually all transactions are archived on computer tapes that may be kept for several years. In effect, an investigative agency can easily bypass the act by issuing a simple subpoena for communications more than 180 days old that are stored on backup tapes.

> **Don't** assume that your **electronic mail** has **privacy** protection. It doesn't. ECPA expressly allows system operators to read your mail in the course of normal "system maintenance" procedures.

Electronic Frontier Foundation (EFF)

A public advocacy organization dedicated to extending the American traditions of privacy, free information access, and civil liberties to the new realms of electronically-mediated communication, such as **electronic mail**. Founded in 1990 by ex-Lotus Software founder Mitchell Kapor and John Barlow, lyricist for the Grateful Dead, the organization seeks to "civilize" the emerging electronic frontier by extending **common carrier** principles to digital communications systems. Common carrier principles require a communications system to carry all speech, regardless of controversial content, and to provide equitable, non-discriminatory access.

EFF publishes a biweekly electronic newsletter, *EFFector Online*, as well as a quarterly newsletter titled *Networks & Policy*. EFF is a funder and organizer of the annual Computers, Freedom and Privacy conference. The organization also provides legal defense funds in cases involving computer communications that raise significant civil liberties issues.

An EFF lobbying focus concerns the need to amend U.S. federal legislation concerning computers, which from the point of view of people knowledgeable about computers contains numerous deficiencies. For example, *see* **Electronic Communications Privacy Act (ECPA)**, **Freedom of Information Act (FOIA)**.

electronic mail (email)

A means of computer-based communication in which you send an electronic "letter" to one or more recipients, who do not receive your message until they **log on** to their computer system and start their electronic mail **client** (such as **Pine** or **Eudora**). This client then notifies them that they've received mail. The recipient of your message then may read your message and, optionally, reply to it, delete it, or forward it to another computer user. Commonly abbreviated as email.

By far the most popular Internet application, electronic mail may well be responsible for the Internet's very existence. The Internet's predecessor, the **ARPANET**, was designed to facilitate **remote login** and **file transfer**. But it was the development of electronic mail services that convinced people throughout the U.S. government and military that ARPANET was indispensable. Electronic mail usage is currently growing very quickly, spreading out from the government and university communities to the population at large, and providing an alternative means of communication and a greatly esteemed method of communication for millions of people. For many, including Microsoft CEO Bill Gates, electronic mail is their most frequently-used application. Gates told a California audience that he reads all his mail, and uses his electronic mail program five times more often than other applications.

In comparison to its chief competitors, the telephone and **snail mail** (the postal system), electronic mail has both advantages and disadvantages. A major advantage is that you can avoid "telephone tag" (a game in which two people try to reach each other unsuccessfully for days). That's because electronic mail is a store-and-forward messaging system; your message remains on your recipients' systems until they log on. But that's where one problem arises—what if they don't log on? Unless you know that your recipient checks his or her electronic mail at regular intervals, it might be safer to write or phone. Although not as fast as a (successful) telephone call, electronic mail is much faster than snail mail; typically, a message from one Internet user to another can reach its destination in a matter of minutes.

One of the chief reasons for the Internet's explosive growth is that it has become the world's de facto electronic mail system. Thanks to the **domain name system**, electronic mail messages can traverse not only the Internet but also non-Internet networks that offer only partial Internet connectivity, such as **BITNET**, commercial on-line services such as Prodigy and CompuServe, and thousands of **bulletin board systems (BBS)**.

An Internet **electronic mail address** has two basic parts: the **mailbox name** (which might be the name of a group of people or an organization or an individual), and the **host name** (the name of the Internet **host** on which the mailbox has been created). The two parts are separated by an @ sign (pronounced "at sign"), as follows:

```
mailbox-name@host-name
```

In the **domain name system,** host names often have several parts, separated by dots, as in the following example:

```
esmith@scasss.uu.se
```

If you need to tell someone an email address over the telephone, pronounce it like this: "esmith at scasss-dot-uu-dot-se." (You'll need to spell out the "esmith" and "scasss" parts too.) Case (uppercase and lowercase letters) doesn't matter in email addresses.

An electronic mail message has two parts: the **originator header** (which contains information about the message's author, host of origin, and subject), and the **message body**, which contains the text, as in the following example:

```
To:      Lisa Anderson
         <landerson@holt.twomoons.com>
Cc:      John Twilling
         <jtwilling@troll.underground.com>
From:    Danielle Worthy
         <dworthy@troll.underground.com>
Date:    May 21, 1994
Subject:   April summary report


Lisa, thanks for sending me the report. It was
just what we needed and I've forwarded it to
John for review.

Regards, Danielle
```

Depending on the capabilities of the email **client** you are using, you may be able to take advantage of advanced features such as an **alias**, **attached documents**, **blind carbon copies**, **carbon copies**, **mailing lists**, **multimedia**, **receipt notification**, and a **signature**. The basic mechanics of dealing with Internet mail are usually handled by the **Simple Mail Transport Protocol (SMTP)**, which unfortunately includes no safeguards for the **privacy** of email messages. Proposed extensions to the SMTP protocol, such as **privacy enhanced mail (PEM)**, would add data encryption and other privacy protection measures.

Do show consideration for the recipient of your message. Many systems break up lines longer than 65 characters, so keep the lines shorter than that. And keep your message short—chances are, if you don't get your point across in the first screen of text, you never will. Use mixed upper and lower case letters; ALL CAPITAL LETTERS COMES ACROSS AS "SHOUTING."

Don't say anything in an electronic mail message that you wouldn't want to find on your boss's desk the next morning. What the sender thinks is simply a joke or a sarcastic remark might be taken by the recipient as fighting words. Worse, you can't assure the security of an electronic mail message. Someone other than the recipient might read it (for example, a coworker or secretary might be covering the boss's mail during vacation), and it's very easy to forward a message to someone else, perhaps with a note that says something like, "You see what a jerk this person is?" If you're hot under the collar, don't send the message until you've had a chance to cool off—once you choose the *Send* command, there's no way you can get your message back. Above all else, be very careful about responding to a message that has been addressed to a group of users that includes yourself—your response will go to everyone in the group, and could severely damage your career.

electronic mail address

A series of characters (such as tanya@fantasy.ivy.edu) that uniquely identifies the **mailbox** of a person who can receive and send **electronic mail**. The address includes the person's mailbox name ("tanya," in the above example) followed by an @ (pronounced "at") and a **Fully-Qualified Domain Name (FQDN)**, which precisely identifies the **host** on which this person's electronic mail account is registered. Finding someone's electronic mail address is a task increasingly assisted by Internet-accessible tools and directories; *see* **CSO name server, Knowbot Information Service, Netfind, white pages**.

Tip: If this person's system administrator has established an **alias**, it may not be necessary to type all the subdomains; tanya@ivy.edu will do. Check with the recipient of your messages to find out whether aliases have been established for their accounts.

electronic mail terrorism

A form of harassment that involves bombarding a person's electronic **mailbox** with huge numbers of meaningless messages or **flames**. This offense could result in the suspension of your Internet privileges. Synonymous with **mail bombing**.

electronic text (etext)

A computer-accessible version of a published or unpublished literary or reference work, such as the plays of Shakespeare and the *Oxford English Dictionary*. Many electronic texts (also known as *e-texts*) are directly accessible via Internet links and can be downloaded to your system via **anonymous FTP** or **Gopher**.

Not every computer-accessible body of text is electronic text, properly speaking; the term suggests a computerized reproduction of a published or unpublished work of more than passing significance. Reproducing such a text in computer-accessible form is an expensive and tedious process, involving optical-character recognition (OCR) scanning. The scanned texts must be hand-corrected for 100% accuracy.

Many electronic texts are available in **ASCII** format, meaning that you can easily display and read them on your computer. However, some electronic text archives annotate their texts with a **markup language**, such as **SGML**. The purpose of the markup language is to describe the various functional parts of the text, such as headings and indents, as well as to facilitate computer searches of the material. The markup language **SGML** is frequently chosen for this purpose because it represents a good compromise between functional markup (which allows you to print the document) and markup for searching purposes (which allows you, for example, to search for all the occurrences of the archaic verb *heist* in the plays of Shakespeare). You can still read a marked-up text on your computer, if you're willing to put up with lots of ugly-looking codes. You'll need a program called a **parser** to display and search marked-up text.

An electronic text involves a very considerable investment of time and money. The result is a significant, publicly-accessible resource for reading, analysis, and scholarship. Examples of such resources include the works of Lewis Carroll, *CIA/KGB World Fact Book,* the complete works of Charles Darwin, the Bible, the Koran, the U.S. *Federal Register,* and the Norse sagas. Despite the often considerable investment required to produce electronic texts, many are placed in the **public domain** or are **copylefted** and are, in consequence, **freely redistributable**. Electronic texts thus make up a significant proportion of the **freelore** that is increasingly available via Internet access. Note, however, that some electronic texts are copyrighted and cannot be accessed without first arranging permission from the on-line archive.

Tip: Project Gutenberg seeks to make 10,000 electronic texts available in ASCII format by the year 2001. To see an index of the works currently available, use **Veronica** and search for ***Project Gutenberg***. Among the many entries you'll find are explanations of the project, lists of available works, and even facilities for searching certain texts for key words. You can also retrieve the texts through **anonymous FTP** as follows:

```
ftp mrcnext.cso.uiuc.edu
login: anonymous
password: (type your email address) cd etext
dir (to see the available files and
     directories)
get filename
```

EMACS

A **text editor** commonly found on **UNIX** systems. Not often esteemed by beginning users, EMACS is beloved by computer hackers because it is constructed entirely from LISP, a language initially developed to create artificial intelligence systems. Many beginning users come face to face with EMACS unwillingly: In some UNIX systems, EMACS is the default text editor.

Tip: If EMACS gives you fits, you may be able to use an easier text editor. Call your computer center's help desk to find out if there's another, simpler text editor available.

---

email

See **electronic mail.**

| emoticon |

Synonymous with **smiley.**

| emulation |

The transformation of one computer hardware device by means of a computer program so that it is able to imitate all or most of the functions of a device made by a different manufacturer. Using a **communications program**, for example, you can transform your personal computer into a **VT100** terminal that facilitates **dialup access** to the Internet.

| encapsulation |

In the Internet **protocol stack**, the process by which each protocol adds **header** information to a **datagram** as it moves "down" the stack. For example, when an application passes data to the **Transmission Control Protocol (TCP)**, this protocol divides it into datagrams and adds header information regarding the message's source and destination. When TCP passes this datagram to **IP**, IP in turn adds more header information concerning the message's route. At the receiving end of the transmission, the matching protocols on the receiving **host** strip off the headers in a reverse of the encapsulation process. *See* **Open Systems Interconnection (OSI) Reference Model**.

| encryption |

The process of converting a **plaintext** message (a message that could be read by anyone) into a **ciphertext**, by means of a **key** (a method of transforming the message so that it appears to be gibberish). Ideally, the message can be read only by the intended recipient, who possesses the key and uses it (in a process called **decryption**) to make the text readable again.

A simple encryption technique used in **Usenet** postings is **rot-13**, which works by "rotating" letters 13 characters to the right in the alphabet (this is the **key**). What appears on-screen looks like gibberish. Since the key is widely known, any reasonably knowledgeable person can decrypt it; in fact, there's a command that does this automatically. The purpose of rot-13 encryption is to hide potentially offensive or erotic postings from the eyes of those who would prefer not to have such things thrown in their face.

Bankers and diplomats have long used encryption to ensure the secrecy of messages, but the problem lies in how to get the key safely to its intended recipient. (The recipient needs the key in order to decode and read the message.) Traditionally, this has been done by courier. A new crypto-gaphic method called **public key cryptography** eliminates the need to deliver the key, and raises the possibility that people who have never previously exchanged messages could send encrypted messages to each other. *See* **Privacy Enhanced Mail (PEM)**.

encryption algorithm

A technique for coding a message so that only the intended recipient, who alone possesses the decoding key, can decode and read the message. *See* **Clipper Chip, cryptography, encryption, public key cryptography**.

enterprise-wide computing

The linkage of all the computers and computer networks in an organization, regardless of their geographical location.

In any large, geographically dispersed company or organization, an enterprise-wide computer network is neither a

local area network (LAN) or a **wide area network (WAN)**—
it's a mixture of the two, but one that's focused squarely on
the organization's needs. Within each regional office, LANs
handle local computing needs—but WANs are needed to link
these networks together for such crucial operations as
updating records and exchanging documents. In the past,
X.25 networks have handled long-distance data exchanges
for enterprise computing, but the Internet is expected to play
an increasing role in this area. *See* **Commercial Internet
Exchange (CIX)**.

| error checking |

A technique, embodied in an error-checking **protocol** (standard) as well as in error-checking software that follows
these protocols, to ensure that the data transmitted by
means of a computer network arrives intact and free from
errors introduced by **line noise**. To enable error correction,
both the sending and receiving computers must conform to
the same error correction protocol. In the Internet, error
checking is provided by the **Transmission Control Protocol (TCP)**, which employs a **checksum** technique to make
sure that every **datagram** that arrives has not been corrupted by transmission errors.

| error correction |

The use of a verification technique of some kind to make sure
that line noise does not introduce errors during the transmission of data. Most computer modems employ a simple
checksum technique. More advanced modems, and **file
transfer protocols** such as **Kermit**, use more accurate error
correction methods such as **MNP-5** and **Cyclic Redundancy Code (CRC)**.

escape character

In **Telnet,** a character sequence, such as Ctrl-[(you hold down the Ctrl key and type a right bracket character) that lets you interrupt communications with the remote server and talk to Telnet directly. In this mode, you can obtain status information, cancel lengthy processes, or find out it the remote server is still alive.

escape sequence

A series of characters that you type to engage the modem's command mode, in which you can type commands directly. The escape sequence for modems conforming to the popular Hayes command set is +++(three plusses).

Ethernet

A widely-used standard for **local area networks (LANs),** originally developed at Xerox Corporation's Palo Alto Research Center (PARC) and published as a specification for a 10 Mbps LAN by Digital Equipment Corporation, Intel Corporation, and Xerox Corporation (*see* **DIX Ethernet**). At the **physical layer**, the network employs **baseband coaxial cable,** an inexpensive physical medium that allows **data transfer rates** of 10 Mbps. At the **Medium Access Control (MAC) layer,** it employs **Carrier Sense Multiple Access with Collision Detection (CSMA/CD).** *Compare* **IEEE 802 network.**

Xerox's PARC is responsible for a large slice of the technology we use (and take for granted) every day: the **graphical user interface (GUI)**, the computer mouse, laser printers, and on-screen fonts. Yet another contribution: Ethernet. The name is derived from "luminiferous ether," a mysterious universal medium that 19th-century scientists mistakenly believed was required for light waves to propagate through space.

Ethernet technology provided the basis for an **IEEE** specification (IEEE 802), which was subsequently adopted by the **American National Standards Institute (ANSI)** and the **International Standards Organization (ISO)**, albeit in slightly different form. Networks constructed in conformity with these standards are also called **Ethernets**, even though they are not directly compatible with the older **DIX Ethernet** specifications. LAN experts prefer to distinguish between DIX Ethernets and **IEEE 802 networks,** but this distinction hasn't found its way into everyday usage.

> **Tip**: If you're thinking of setting up a LAN and linking the LAN to the Internet, an Ethernet network is an excellent choice. The necessary hardware (such as **routers**) and software (such as the Internet's **Address Resolution Protocol**) have been in widespread use for more than a decade—which means that all the kinks have been ironed out! *See* **toasternet**.

A **client** program for Internet electronic mail users that runs on a wide variety of computers, including **UNIX** workstations, Macintoshes, and IBM PCs and compatibles. The program extends the functionality of Internet electronic mail by adding support for **multimedia** (voice, full-motion video, and animation) and **encryption** (the coding of messages so that they can be read only by the intended recipient).

Today, most Internet electronic mail users access the Internet from a personal computer or workstation that is connected, either directly or through a dialup connection, to an Internet host system. To receive and send electronic mail, they use the electronic mail program (such as Pine) that they find available for their use on the host system. Although millions of users find this approach valuable, it has its drawbacks. Because the mail is received and sent from the host system rather than the user's PC or workstation, for example, printing and file transfer become complicated operations. To include a file with an electronic mail message, for example, it is necessary to **upload** the file to the host system, where it can then be incorporated into the electronic mail message. Printing an incoming electronic mail message is a protracted hassle; you must **capture** the file, open it with a word processing program, adjust the formats, and print.

Eudora solves this and other problems by distributing the electronic mail **client** software to each workstation or PC. The Eudora client communicates automatically with an electronic mail **server**, called **POP**, that is housed on the host system. The server stores incoming messages until the user logs on with Eudora, which then automatically downloads all the messages to your PC or workstation.

Moving the client to your workstation or PC has many advantages. Because you are preparing your message on the same workstation where you store your files, no intermediary steps are required if you want to include files with the email messages you send. Printing is simple, fast, and easy. In addition, the **Microsoft Windows**, **X Windows,** and Macintosh versions of Eudora feature an easy-to-use **graphical user interface (GUI)**, a major improvement over the character-based interfaces characteristic of UNIX electronic mail clients. This allows you to prepare your message using the same familiar editing techniques your current GUI word processing program uses.

Steve Dorner at the University of Illinois began developing Eudora in 1989, and made the code openly available on Internet-based servers. Dorner named the program after Eudora Welty, the author of the popular short story "Why I Live at the P.O." Since then, Eudora clients have been developed for most of the computers that are commonly connected to the Internet. Although previous **freeware** versions of

Eudora remain available, the newest versions are available commercially from Qualcomm, which is offering the low-cost program as a universal mass market electronic mail client.

EUnet

A major network and service provider that is building Internet connectivity throughout Europe. The network currently connects over 4,000 sites and networks in 25 European countries. A cooperative network funded by subscriptions from participating organizations, the network emphasizes educational services and research collaboration.

European Academic and Research Network (EARN)

An academic network, essentially the European branch of **BITNET**, that links more than 500 universities and research institutions in 27 countries throughout Europe, the Middle East, and Africa. EARN users can exchange **electronic mail** with Internet users by means of a **gateway**. Like BITNET, the EARN network uses IBM's **Network Job Entry (NJE)** protocols.

European Backbone Network (EBONE)

A **multi-protocol backbone** service that is intended to encourage the development of research, educational, and commercial networking throughout Europe. Many European networks that are linked to the Internet use EBONE as a European regional backbone.

European Laboratory for Particle Physics (CERN)

A major European center for advanced research in particle and nuclear physics, located in Geneva, Switzerland. The acronym CERN stands for the center's previous name, Conseil Européen pour la Recherche Nucléaire. To Internet users, CERN is famed as the birthplace of the **World Wide Web (WWW)**, which was initially intended to aid scientific communication in the physics community. In 1994, CERN joined the Massachusetts Institute of Technology (MIT) to develop international standards for Web security, privacy, and commercial use.

even parity

A type of **parity checking** in which the parity bit, a bit in each transmitted byte of data that is set aside for error-correction purposes, is set so that the number of 1 bits in the transmitted byte always adds up to an even number. If the number turns out to be odd when the byte is received, the receiving modem concludes that an error has occurred, discards the byte, and requests a retransmission. *Compare* **odd parity**.

executable program

A program, contained in a **binary file**, that is ready to run on the computer system for which it was intended.

expired article

In **Usenet**, an article that the system has automatically deleted, even if you haven't read it, because it is older than a period of time specified in the article's **header** (such as two weeks).

 Tip: If you're following a **newsgroup** that contains information you've found very valuable, be sure to read it at least every few days; otherwise, you may miss articles that expire before you get a chance to read them. Only a few of the newsgroups maintain archives of expired postings.

Extended Binary Coded Decimal Interchange Code (EBCDIC)

An eight-bit code used for representing text, graphics, and control characters for use in the computer. EBCDIC (pronounced "ebseedic") is mainly employed in IBM mainframe computers. Its incompatibility with **ASCII** provided **ARPANET** designers with one of their first internetworking challenges.

extended character set

An extension to the core, 128-character **ASCII** character set that allows a computer system to represent foreign language, technical, and graphics characters. Personal computers employ an extended character set with an additional 128 characters, for a total of 256. Unfortunately, there's no universally-observed standard for extended characters; the IBM PC's extended character set, for example, differs from the Macintoshes. This is one of the chief reasons that the Internet's ASCII text transfer modes cannot handle foreign languages and other special characters.

extension

A series of characters (usually one to three) that are added after a period at the end of a file name to clarify the type of information contained in a file. A file with the extension .zip, for example, has been compressed by the program PKZIP.

Exterior Gateway Protocol (EGP)

A **routing protocol** that is designed to handle the routing of **datagrams** between an **Autonomous System** (a collection of networks under the control of a single administrative agency, such as a university or corporation) and the wider Internet. EGP enables a **boundary router**, a router designed to link an AS with the Internet, to find out which networks can be reached by other boundary routers on the Internet. The router then uses this information to route datagrams to their destinations.

The EGP protocol stems from the days when the Internet could be conceptualized using the **core model** (a single **backbone** connecting many Autonomous Systems). The protocol is not well suited to the current situation, in which there are many regional backbones and several national and international ones. A protocol that addresses EGP's short-comings is the **Border Gateway Protocol (BGP)**.

F2F

Face to face; a meeting in **real life** by people who had pre-viously "met" only in **cyberspace**.

fall back

In a **modem**, to revert to a slower **protocol** if the receiving modem cannot handle the faster rate. A modem capable of transmitting data at 14.4 Kbps, for instance, can fall back to 9600, 4800, 2400, and 1200 bps. This ensures compatibili-ty with systems that have not upgraded their modems to the fastest available speed.

false drop

In a computerized information retrieval system, the retrieval of an item or a document that proves to be unrelated to the searcher's topic of interest. False drops are inevitable in any computerized retrieval system, including the **resource discovery tools** employed on the Internet.

FAQ

See **Frequently-Asked Questions (FAQ)**.

fast packet switching network

A **packet switching network** that achieves high **data transfer rates** (at least 1.544 Mbps). Packet switching networks that can achieve such speeds include **frame relay** (already in widespread use) and **cell relay**. *See* **Asynchronous Transfer Mode (ATM)**.

fax

A communication medium that employs the telephone system and point-to-point communications to convey digitized images. At both ends, there must be a fax machine or computers equipped with **fax modems**.

Can you send—and receive—faxes via the Internet? Several firms offer fax services for a fee, billable to a credit card. To send a fax, you send electronic mail—or, with some services, you upload a **PostScript** file—and they subsequently print it and fax it to its destination. This makes sense only if you're trying to reach someone to whom you can't send electronic mail.

fax modem

A modem that can send and receive faxes as well as computer data. You need a fax program, such as WinFax Pro (Delrina Corporation), to make use of your modem's fax capabilities.

Like data communications, faxing benefits from the widespread adoption of international standards (called **protocols**) that govern the transmission of fax data. The standards relevant to fax modems are **Class 1, Group 3, V.17, V.27ter, V.29,** and **V.34**. Your fax modem should be able to communicate with most fax machines if it is compatible with the Class 1 and Group 3 standards.

Tip: Faxing from your computer, rather than a fax machine, has both advantages and disadvantages. In computer faxing, your incoming faxes are more secure than they would be if they arrived at a fax machine used by many people. You can also store copies of all your faxes (the ones you've received as well as the ones you've sent) on your computer's hard disk, and retrieve them when you please. Fax programs include many more features than fax machines do, such as a phone book that lets you select a destination number just by choosing an item from a list. On the down side, you can only send faxes that you've created with your computer, such as word processing documents or graphics files. If you want to fax something that's already printed on paper, you'll need a scanner—an expensive peripheral—which might cost more than a good fax machine.

federated database

A network-accessible database for computerized scientific collaboration—in short, a **collaboratory**—that presents itself to the user as a single database rich in resources, when in reality it consists of several linked databases with overlapping subject coverage. A database of gene maps, for example, contains links to a database of bibliographic citations. Federated databases are under development at several network-accessible research institutes in the U.S. and Europe. They may contribute significantly to the solution of a series of unsolved scientific problems called the **Grand Challenges**, which are too complex for a single researcher or research team to tackle without large-scale collaboration and the creation of shared knowledge resources.

Fiber Distributed Data Interface (FDDI)

A standard for the use of **fiber optic** cables in **local area networks (LANs)** and **metropolitan area networks (MANs)**. With FDDI, a **token ring** network can connect 1000 workstations, achieve **data transfer rates** of 100 Mbps, and traverse distances of up to 250 km.

fiber optic

A **physical medium** for computer networking and telephony that employs pulses of light to transmit data. The cable is a thin fiber of glass or silica. At one end is a light source, such as a light-emitting diode (LED) or a laser, that emits light when an electrical impulse is applied to it. At the other end is a detector that produces an electrical impulse when it *receives* light.

What keeps the light from escaping the cable, despite its twists and turns? When a beam of light travels from one medium to another, such as from the glass fiber to air, it is bent (refracted). At a certain critical angle of refraction, all the light is bent back into the fiber, where it remains trapped. There is virtually no loss for several kilometers.

A fiber optic system for local area networks called Fiber Distributed Data Interface (FDDI) can carry 100 Mbps of computer data over a distance of 2.5 kilometers. Currently under development are two fiber optic standards for **wide area networking (WAN)** called **Synchronous Optical Network (SONET)** and **Synchronous Digital Hierarchy (SDH)**. Both are capable of **data transfer rates** ranging from 54.84 Mbps to 2.5 Gbps, significantly greater than **twisted pair** or **coaxial cable.** The coming **gigabit networks** of the **National Information Infrastructure (NII)** will be constructed from fiber optical physical media.

Fiber optic cables have another advantage besides speed: They emit no electromagnetic radiation, which could allow eavesdroppers equipped with special remote sensing equipment to tap the network's signals.

Driven by powerful lasers, high-bandwidth fiber optic cables can be dangerous: If a curious user detaches the cable and looks directly into it to "see how it works," severe eye damage could result. For use in **local area networks (LANs),** designers prefer to sacrifice **bandwidth** for the sake of safety by using LEDs instead of lasers.

FidoNet

A **store-and-forward** network that links more than 20,000 **bulletin board systems (BBS)** using inexpensive, late-night telephone connections. FidoNet applications include **electronic mail**, echoes (the FidoNet equivalent of Usenet **newsgroups)**, and file transfer. Internet users can exchange mail with FidoNet sites by means of a **gateway**.

The basic unit of data storage on the computers linked to the Internet. A file is a named unit of information that is stored on the computer's disk. It may contain a program or text.

In a personal computer **communications program**, a program feature that allows you to "capture" incoming data (via a **modem**) to a disk file.

The existence of a file capture feature in popular communications programs attests to the inherent drawbacks of **dialup access**: Your access to the Internet is based on the **host** on which you have an account, so that the mail and files you retrieve and view are stored on the host computer rather than your PC. You cannot print these files (or, if they're program files, execute them on your PC) without first **downloading** them in a time-consuming **file transfer**. Capturing the file bypasses downloading by enabling you to save to your PC's hard disk a copy of the characters displayed on-screen. However, this is not suitable for executable files (programs) because the text (ASCII) display you are viewing probably lacks error correction. It is not a particularly good solution for printing your electronic mail messages, either, since you must open the captured file with a word processing program and perform substantial editing to print the message you want. These and other difficulties supply the motivation for **direct connections** to the Internet. In a direct connection, the Internet's basic units of data exchange—the **packets** defined by the **TCP/IP protocols**—come directly to your computer.

| file compression |

The reduction of a file's size by means of a compression program. A compressed file takes up less disk space. In addition, it takes less time to transfer it via a network from one host to another. *See* **file compression program**.

Through various clever techniques, it is possible to reduce a file's size by as much as two-thirds, while still ensuring that the file can be decompressed without losing any data (*see* **lossless compression**). A popular approach is to code each letter, giving commonly-used letters such as *a* or *e* a short code, while infrequently-used ones (such as *q* or *z*) get long codes. When the file is decompressed, the compression program translates these codes back into letters, and the file is usable again. Graphic and video images are compressed using a different technique called **lossy compression**, which sacrifices some of the image's quality in a way that is not perceptible by the human eye. Compressing files helps to conserve network **bandwidth** (not to mention disk space on **hosts**) because the smaller, compressed file takes less time to transfer from one Internet host to another.

Tip: Many of the files you'll access by means of FTP have been compressed using a specific compression program. If you want to obtain the file and use it, you'll have to decompress the file using the same program that compressed it. You can tell which program compressed a given file by looking at the file name's **extension** (a set of characters added after a trailing dot that clarifies the type of data that the file contains). If the extension is .Z (uppercase), the file was compressed by the UNIX **compress** program. If the extension is .gz, the file was compressed using gzip. If the extension is .zip, the file was compressed using PKZIP.

| file compression program |

A program that is designed to reduce the size of a file so that it does not occupy so much disk space or consume so much network **bandwidth** during transmission.

There are two kinds of compression programs. File compression programs such as the compress utility **(UNIX)** use **lossless compression**, in which a decompression step can restore the file to a bit-by-bit duplicate of the original. These programs are used to compress **text files** and **binary files**, and can often obtain a compression ratio of 2:1 (a 50% reduction in the file's size). To use compressed files, you must first decompress them using the same technique that was used to compress them. Used by graphics and multimedia programs is **lossy compression**, in which some of the original information is permanently lost without any perceptible degradation in the quality of the sound or image; see **Joint Photographics Experts Group (JPEG)** and **Motion Picture Experts Group (MPEG)**. Lossy compression techniques can reduce a graphics or sound file's size by as much as 12:1. Decompression is generally handled by the same multimedia utility that compressed the file, called a **codec** (compression/decompression program).

Some lossless compression programs can compress more than one file at a time, producing a compressed **archive** that contains several files. Other programs, such as the UNIX shar utility, create archives without compression.

While browsing for text or binary files with **FTP** or **Gopher**, you'll often *see* file name **extensions** (one to three letters or numbers after the period in the file name). The extension indicates two important facts: first, the file is compressed, and second, it tells you which program was used to compress the file. You need this information so you can choose the correct program to decompress the file. *See* archive, file compression.

file extraction

The decoding (using a program such as **uudecode**) of a **binary file** that was previously translated into ASCII by an encoding program such as uudecode.

Tip: If you run into a uuencoded binary file while browsing through **postings** on **Usenet**, chances are that your **newsreader** includes a file extraction command that automatically calls uudecode and extracts the file to your **home directory**. File extraction commands work with binary files that have been uuencoded into multi-part postings. Check your newsreader's documentation to find out whether the newsreader you're using has this capability.

file ownership

In **UNIX** and other multiuser operating systems, a set of access restrictions that is stored with a file and that governs what file owners and other people can do with the file. With read-only access, the file can be viewed or copied, but not altered in any way or deleted. With write/delete access, the file can be altered or even deleted. With execute access, a program file can be run as an application. *Compare* **read only access, delete/write access**.

Tip: If you are viewing UNIX directories with the DIR command, you will notice codes that indicate the access restrictions assigned to the files displayed in the directory list, as in the following example:

```
-rwxr—r— electronic-freedom-today
```

The codes preceding the file name, *electronic-freedom-today*, indicate the access restrictions assigned to the file: read-only (r), write/delete access (w), and execute access (x). The first character, a dash, indicates that the item is a file rather than a directory. The following three codes (rwx) indicates the priveleges open to the owner of the file—here, this person can read the file, change it or delete it, or execute (if it's a program). The next three codes (r--) describe the privileges granted to the group to which the file's owner belongs, such as a department within a university. Members of the group can read the file, but they can't change it, delete it, or execute it (the dashes indicate that an option is denied. Of interest to you, a public user of the file, are the last three codes; if full access were available to the public, you would see *rwx*. Instead, you see *r--*, indicating that read-only access is enabled (r), but write/delete and execute access are not (this is indicated by the dashes).

file server

In a **local area network (LAN)**, a computer—generally, a fast one with an especially large hard disk—that has been set aside to store frequently-accessed files, such as a large database that is useful for everyone on the network.

file server site

An Internet-accessible **host** in which part of the computer's hard disk has been set aside to make files of a certain type available by means of **anonymous FTP**.

file system

A means of organizing files on the computer's disk so that you do not see an endless series of file names when you try to view the disk's contents. This is done by organizing the files by means of **directories** and **subdirectories**.

The file system used on most of the **UNIX** computers connected to the Internet is hierarchical: At the top of the directory hierarchy is the **root directory**. This directory contains several subdirectories, the names of which are preceded by a slash (/). These subdirectories in turn may contain their own subdirectories, as in the following example:

```
root
    /pub
        /rfc
        /fyi
        /ien
    /cgrn
        /docs
        /bib
```

In UNIX systems, the root directory stores the UNIX **kernel** and other essential system programs, such as **daemons**, startup programs, and programs that support peripheral devices such as disk drives. In the /usr directory, you find most of the programs that are available for use. In addition, every person who has an **account** on the computer has a **home directory**.

In many **Unix** commands, you can directly access a subdirectory by typing a **pathname**. For example, the command

```
cd /cgrn/docs
```

opens the /cgrn directory.

file transfer

One of the basic operations made possible by internetworking, the transmission of one or more files from one computer to another by means of network links. For file transfer to work, both machines—the sending machine and the receiving one—must be running file transfer software that conforms to the same **file transfer protocol** (standard). *See* **file transfer protocol, File Transfer Protocol (FTP)**.

file transfer protocol

A protocol (standard) that governs the transmission of data from one computer to another. The protocol is necessary to ensure that the data arrives without errors introduced during the course of transmission. For **modems**, common protocols include **Kermit, Xmodem, Ymodem,** and **Zmodem**. File transfer protocols for use over the Internet's high-speed connections include **File Transfer Protocol (FTP)** and **Trivial File Transfer Protocol (TFTP)**.

File Transfer Protocol (FTP)

An Internet protocol for exchanging files with remote **hosts**. FTP employs the **client-server model**: You (or an application such as **Gopher** or **WWW**) use a local **client** program, which accesses the corresponding **server** on the remote host. FTP can copy a single file or multiple files between hosts. In addition, it provides the tools needed to identify the current **directory** on the remote host, list the files in this directory, change to other directories, and rename or delete files. Using FTP, you can remotely access files on a host for which you have a valid account and password, or you can use **anonymous FTP** to access files in public directories.

FTP directly addresses the problem of how files can be transferred on an Internet composed of computers made by several manufacturers. These computers have differing ways of organizing and naming files for storage and even differing character sets for representing the stored information (*compare* **ASCII** and **EBCDIC**).

You can transfer three kinds of files with FTP: **ASCII** text files, **EBCDIC** text files, and **binary** files. By default, FTP assumes you are transferring ASCII text files.

> **Tip**: If you want to transfer a binary file, such as a computer program, don't forget to use the SET BINARY

command to switch FTP to the binary file transfer mode. Otherwise FTP will not transfer the file correctly.

filter

Any automatic utility that screens incoming data and disposes of unwanted portions; in **electronic mail**, a program (or a command in an electronic mail **client** program) that automatically deletes unwanted email messages.

Do check with your system administrator to find out how to set up an email filter if you persistently receive unwanted email.

finger

An Internet **client** program that permits you to obtain a list of the users currently logged on to your Internet **host** system. You can also use finger to obtain informmation about users on remote systems.

To use finger to obtain information about a user on another Internet system, you need that person's electronic mail address. You type *finger* followed by the person's electronic mail address, as in this example:

```
finger rudolph@north.pole.com
```

You receive a response such as this one:

```
Login name: rd      In real life: Rudy Reindeer
Directory: /home/rd         Shell: /bin/ksh
On since Apr 23 16:07:32
20 seconds Idle Time
No Plan.
```

"No plan" doesn't mean the individual is disorganized. It means that he or she hasn't created a .plan file, which would have been automatically retrieved by this command had such a file existed.

Tip: If you would like to supply more information to those who finger you, you can do so by creating and saving a file called .plan to your **home directory**. Consult your system's help desk for more information.

The .plan file (and another that works the same way, called .project) were originally created to allow scientists to exchange information about their current research work. Today, some people use .plan files to tell something about themselves. Their files amount to an extended poem, phrased in ASCII art, quotations, reflections, and poetry.

Do remember that you can't hide behind an obscure **login name** (*lv213@bigbucks.com*) to hide your **identity**; you can be fingered to find out your name in real life.

Don't disclose too much personal information in your .plan file, if you decide to create one; remember that *anyone* can retrieve it.

| firewall |

A **host** that has been designed to serve as the first line of defense against **crackers** and other malicious users who are trying to access a network. The firewall is placed between the Internet connection and the network that the firewall protects. *Compare* **access control**.

A firewall is designed to provide services to those who access the network remotely, whether by means of the Internet or **dialup access**, and to make available whatever resources the network wishes to make public (for example, **anonymous FTP**), while at the same time blocking access to malicious uses.

Firewalls work by blocking IP packets. Unlike a **router**, a firewall doesn't forward packets to destination hosts on the network; instead, it accepts packets that are addressed to the network, and stores them. Users on the network who wish to receive electronic mail or transferred files must log on to the firewall to obtain them.

Because firewalls block IP packets, they inconvenience network users. Rather than insulating all of the network users from the Internet, it frequently makes more sense to divide the network into two parts, a sensitive part where security is of utmost importance, and a non-sensitive part where security doesn't matter as much. The sensitive part can be blocked by a firewall, giving the rest of the network full Internet access.

The inconvenience imposed by firewalls may be lessening, thanks to the development of **proxy servers**. A proxy server is a program that runs on the firewall machine. It acts as a trusted agent to handle the risk-free exchange of data between machines located behind the firewall and other computers located elsewhere on the Internet. Proxy servers have been developed for **Mosaic**, **Gopher**, and other popular **resource discovery tools**.

The use of firewalls is spreading due to growing concern, even alarm, concerning the vulnerability of the Internet to computer criminals. Compaq Computer Corp., of Houston, Texas, maintains a 1.544 Mbps direct Internet connection, but this is not fully used owing to fears concerning Internet security. Users accustomed to full Internet access, however, may not take kindly to the inconveniences introduced by a firewall. Recently, a U.S. Department of Defense (DoD) agency announced plans to install a firewall owing to fears concerning Internet security, but the planners faced an open rebellion from agency Internet users.

---

flame

In **Usenet** and **electronic mail**, an ill-considered, highly emotional message that, in the extreme, may be filled with foul language and personal attacks.

Communicating via the computer is convenient, but it's all too easy to send a blistering email message before you've cooled off. Perhaps the only advantage of **snail mail** is that, after you write a flame on paper, you'll have some time to think about the wisdom of sending it—and, if you're smart, you'll throw it in the trash can. With email, you finish writing, choose the send command, and presto! It's out of your hands. And with most systems, you can't get it back.

Do take some time to consider whether you should send a message. Take a walk, have a cup of coffee, go to the bathroom—just don't choose the send command until you've had some time to think about it. Many electronic mail **clients** have a command option that lets you postpone writing and sending a message until later. Learn how to use it.

Don't make unsupportable or untrue accusations against a person or company in a **Usenet** posting; you could find yourself on the wrong end of a defamation lawsuit.

| flame bait |

In **Usenet**, a **posting** that is virtually guaranteed to produce a harvest of **flames** in your mailbox.

Do read the newsgroup for a while before posting. Make sure you clearly understand the group's purpose and range of topics. Before you post, make sure you've found the right newsgroup. And be sure to read the group's **Frequently-Asked Questions (FAQ)** document before posting a question to the group. The group's old-timers sometimes resent (and flame) **newbies** who ask a question that's answered in the FAQ. (Instead of flames, you might wake up the next morning to find several dozen copies of the FAQ in your **mailbox**.)

Don't advocate censorship if you see something that offends you, unless you're prepared to find yourself on the wrong end of some very vitriolic messages. The Usenet community, in general, strongly favors free and open communication—typically, Usenet people believe that if there's some type of material that offends you, don't read it.

flame war

In **Usenet**, a protracted, vitriolic exchange of opinion concerning an unresolvable issue, typically degrading into name-calling. The war begins with a dispute between two individuals who are bent on undermining each other by means of public postings, and widens when others get involved. If the flame war seems likely to produce more heat than light, the proper remedy is a new entry to your **kill** file. *Compare* **holy war**.

flame warrior

A **Usenet** participant who cruises **newsgroups** randomly, looking for **postings** that contain flawed logic, naivete, sentimentality, or factual errors, and replies with a withering, vitriolic **follow-on posting** with *ad hominem* attacks and biting sarcasm. *Compare* **net.police**.

Do ignore flame warriors. What they want more than anything else is attention; if you reply to their posts, even to flame them in return, you validate their actions.

flow control

In **point-to-point data transmission**, a method that is used to ensure that the transmitting system doesn't dish out data faster than the receiving station can handle it.

In **Usenet newsgroups**, a reply to an existing message that is added to the newsgroup so that anyone who wishes to do so may read it. If you wish to reply to a Usenet **posting**, you may do so in two ways: by sending **email** directly to the poster, or by sending a follow-up message.

Follow-up postings often quote part of the original message, which is useful for readers who may have forgotten (or never read) the original posting. With most systems, the quoted text is shown by a "greater than" symbol (>), as in the following example:

```
Benny Bungle (bungle@foo.com) wrote:
> The following spring to mind...
Does this mean that we have to wait until next
spring before any more come to mind?
-- Captain Ironic
```

When a posting leads to a **thread** (a series of postings on the same subject), some articles may contain quotations of quotations. In such cases the number of "greater-than" symbols increases to show the logical relations among the quoted postings, as in this example:

```
Captain Ironic opened his posting with this
salvo:
>Benny Bungle wrote:
>> The following spring to mind...
>Does this mean that we have to wait until next
>spring before any more come to mind?
Spring so close to the Arctic Circle doesn't
come until about July, near as I can tell, so
he's still got a chance *this* year.
```

Don't quote the whole article—take some time to edit it down to just the sentences to which you want to reply. If you don't know how to do this, get the documention for your system's **text editor** and find out.

Above all, don't quote the original message's **signature**—this is considered a waste of network **bandwidth**.

Do reply with a follow-on posting if many would find it of interest. Suppose someone posts a query in rec.aquaria about the health hazards of aquarium water. You know of a child who became seriously ill with salmonella poisoning after drinking water from a fish tank. Your reply will surely prove of interest to many readers of this newsgroup. Be sure to reply to the smallest geographic **distribution** that will accomplish your purpose.

foo

A word commonly used by hackers to stand for anything else; a textual wild card. This often appears in domain name examples, such as *fred@foo.bar.com*. The frequent pairing of *foo* with *bar* connotes the acronym FUBAR ("Fucked Up Beyond All Recognition"), commonly used in the U.S. military.

For Your Information (FYI)

A series of Internet publications that are distributed in the same manner as **Requests for Comments (RFC)** but with content that is considerably less technical. FYIs do not propose new protocols.

Tip: FYI 1206, available through **FTP** from any **Network Information Center (NIC)**, is titled "Answers to Commonly-Asked 'New Internet User' Questions." This is well worth reading if you're just getting started with the Internet.

fragmentation

In a **packet switching network**, the division that occurs en route, during the transmission of a message, into **packets** (called **datagrams** in the Internet context) of sufficiently small size that they can meet the packet size restrictions of the next network on the message's route.

Fragmentation is necessary because there are no widely-shared standards for the size of the **maximum transmission unit (MTU)** of a packet; Ethernet allows packets 1500 **octets** in length, while **ARPANET**-derived networks limit the length to 1000 octets. As a message travels to its destination, it may encounter a network that can't handle the size of its current packets, so further reduction in the size of the packets is required. Fragmentation produces new **datagrams,** each with the necessary **header** that contains routing and destination information. These are **reassembled** when the packet reaches its destination.

frame

At the **data link** layer in a point-to-point transmission line, the technique used to demarcate the data so that it can be received in an orderly and meaningful way. *Compare* **packet, tunneling**.

frame relay

At the **data link layer** in a **wide area network (WAN)**, a protocol for transferring **packets** at speeds of up to 1.544 Mbps, depending on the physical medium employed. Frame relay, standardized as part of the developing **Broadband ISDN** specifications developed by **CCITT**, is very similar to **X.25**, a protocol that governs point-to-point computer communications over noisy **analog** telephone lines, but at the cost of high **overhead** for error correction. Frame relay is designed for noise-free **digital** lines and, in consequence, omits the unneeded error correction facilities. The result is a big payoff in **bandwidth**: Frame relay can use a variety of physical media, including telephone lines. *Compare* **cell relay**.

Defined in 1991, frame relay has become the most quickly adopted data link protocol in WAN history, thanks to the fact that frame relay software can be installed on existing X.25 equipment, such as **routers**. Many firms are using frame relay to create their own private networks.

Free Software Foundation

A Massachusetts-based, not-for-profit organization that is dedicated to eliminating restrictions on the copying, redistribution, and modification of computer programs. To promote this goal, the organization is currently developing an integrated software system called GNU (short for "GNU's Not UNIX"). The software is made available under the organization's General Public License, a **copyleft** that specifies that the software is freely redistributable provided no commercial use is made of the underlying program instructions (the source code).

Freedom of Information Act (FOIA)

A U.S. federal law that provides the principle means researchers can use to force government agencies to divulge information, with the exception of information deemed sensitive for reasons of national security. However, FOIA expressly refers to documents on paper. Several U.S. agencies have resisted attempts to secure computer-stored information on the grounds that the legislation applies only to printed documents. Now that most government information is stored on computers rather than in paper files, the ability of researchers to access government information is once again in doubt.

Electronically-available information that people can freely retrieve, use, and distribute for others, as long as no commercial gain is involved. An example is an **electronic text** (such as an electronic version of Plato's *Symposium*), a graphic image, or a sound recording that has been made available for access via such means as **anonymous FTP, Gopher**, or **World Wide Web**.

A freelore document is not entirely "free"; it is not in the **public domain**. Its author makes it **freely redistributable** under the terms of **copyleft** (a copyright statement which specifies that unlimited copies of the document can be made for any non-commercial purpose). Underlying the freelore concept is a democratic philosophy of information availability, namely, that computer users the world over should have free access to informative materials in every field of human knowledge. A freelore author sacrifices the opportunity to profit from the document, and does so for the public good. The purpose of copyleft is not to restrict the free flow of information, but rather to safeguard its integrity: The copyleft statement specifies that no changes should be made to the original information unless the exact nature of the changes is specified and the original author is notified.

A freelore document should contain *lore*—information that is useful and valuable in its own right. Just what constitutes lore is, naturally, a subjective matter, but surely the *Federalist Papers* count for more than a college student's disjointed ramblings about the strong and weak points of various hamburger chains.

Tip: If you've just obtained an electronic text that's loaded with weird characters, chances are that it has been encoded with a **markup language** such as **SGML** or TeX. This language is used to describe how the document should look when displayed or printed. You may need special software, called a **parser**, to display and print these documents properly.

Do contact the author of a freelore work if you have any questions about legitimate use; many authors will grant permission for limited commercial uses.

Don't modify freelore without explicitly listing your modifications and sending a copy to the author. The point of copyleft is to make works freely available without risking violations of their integrity.

freely redistributable

In **copyleft**, an assignment of rights to duplicate and disseminate a document or program, but without making any changes to the original or charging a fee for the duplication. The work's author retains the copyright but wishes to make the work widely available without charge—on the condition that no one alters it.

freenet

A grassroots, community-based Internet **host** that is designed to bring free networking access to a community. Access is provided through public libraries or **dialup access**. Typically, freenets are designed as model "towns" that you can "walk through," stopping wherever you please—at the mayor's office, for example, to read announcements and leave suggestions. Also offered are **bulletin boards**, **electronic mail**, and **Internet access**.

freeware

Software that may be subject to copyright protection, even though it is freely available without any apparent protection or conditions on its distribution or use (*compare* **copyleft,**

shareware). An intellectual work is not in the **public domain** unless it has been expressly defined as such by the work's author, or the period of copyright protection has expired without renewal.

Frequency Division Multiplexing (FDM)

A approach to **multiplexing** (combining several data sources for transmission on one line) in which each signal is given its own frequency, like a radio station.

Although this technique is used to provide **leased lines** with data transfer rates of up to 56 Kbps, it is not the best solution for computer data communications. Unlike voice transmissions, computer communications are inherently "bursty": They're characterized by periods of heavy transmission (for example, when you're sending a file) followed by long periods of silence (you're reading it on your screen). For this reason, **time-division multiplexing (TDM)** makes somewhat effective use of a given line's **bandwidth** for data communications purposes. However, the best practical solution is found in **packet switching networks**, in which the bursty data streams from many computers are broken down into **packets** (segments), each of which contains **header** information that tells the receiving station how to deliver the packet to its destination.

Frequently-Asked Questions (FAQ)

Pronounced "fack." In **Usenet newsgroups**, a posted document that contains lists of questions typically asked by new users (**newbies**), with informative answers that should be read by anyone who wishes to participate by **posting** messages to the group. The FAQ contains answers to questions that regular group members grow weary of answering—and it also contains answers to questions that aren't asked very often, out of fear that asking such a question would make one look stupid!

TIP If the newsgroup you're reading has a FAQ, by all means read it—in fact, save it and print it. Chances are good that it contains a great deal of valuable information, and not just about the mechanics of using the newsgroup. The multi-section FAQ for rec.pets.cats, for instance, is a treasure-trove of knowledge about the care, feeding, and enjoyment of our feline companions.

Not all newsgroups have FAQs; in fact, the existence of a FAQ is taken as evidence of a newsgroup's high quality. If the newsgroup has a FAQ, it is usually automatically posted to the newsgroup at a periodic interval (such as once a month or every two weeks). Some FAQs are so lengthy that they are divided into two or more sections, numbered in a way that shows how many total sections there are (for example, "2/4" means "this is the second part of four total").

At the beginning of a FAQ, you usually see a list of the questions that the FAQ answers. Here's an example:

```
PC GAMES FAQ Guide To The Gaming World (Part 1)
1.1: What are the comp.sys.ibm.pc.games groups
     for?
1.2: How did the comp.sys.ibm.pc.games groups
     come to exist?
1.3: What topics are commonly discussed?
1.4: What groups are in the
     comp.sys.ibm.pc.games hierarchy?
1.5: What are the differences between
     subgroups?
1.6: Are there other newsgroups related to PC
     games?
1.7: What guidelines should I follow when
     posting?
1.8: What do I have to avoid when posting?
```

```
1.9: How do I post a spoiler?
1.10:How do I post to csipg.announce?
```

Tip: To skip to the question you want answered, type a slash mark (/) followed by the number of the question you want answered. For instance, to skip to question 1.9, type */1.9* and press *Enter*.

DO look for your newsgroup's FAQ in one of the several Usenet FAQ archives, accessible via Gopher servers. You can also look for FAQs in the various **.answers** newsgroups (alt.answers, misc.answers, news.answers, rec.answers, sci.answers, and soc.answers).

DON'T post a message to a newsgroup asking whether there's a FAQ for the group—at least, not until you've made a good-faith effort to find the FAQ yourself. Such messages are considered a waste of network **bandwidth**, and you may find yourself the recipient of a number of **flames** from self-styled **net.police**.

| front end |

In a computerized information retrieval system, a program that provides the user with a "friendly" means of operating the retrieval system's commands and procedures. A well-designed front end program can make an otherwise difficult and forbidding system approachable for people who are not full-time computer specialists. The front end program is installed on the user's personal computer or workstation, so that its substantial library of help screens, menus, databases, and other resources are readily available to the user without taxing network links. Today's front end programs employ **graphical user interface (GUI)** principles, including the use of a mouse, windows, pull-down menus, and icons. Increasingly popular on the Internet are the GUI front ends **Eudora** (for **electronic mail**) and **Mosaic** (a resource discovery tool that emphasizes the **World Wide Web**).

FTP

See **File Transfer Protocol (FTP).**

full duplex

In computer networking, a connection between two computers such that both can send and receive at the same time. The Internet's **Transmission Control Protocol (TCP)** enables full duplex communication between two **hosts** on the Internet. *Compare* **half duplex.**

full screen editor

In an **application** designed to run on a computer network, a text editing utility that allows the user to move the cursor at will through an entire screen of text. A full-screen editor permits the user to go back into previously written text and make additions, corrections, or deletions. This is what people familiar with word processing programs expect from a text editor. *Compare* **line editor.**

full-motion video

The display on a computer screen of a moving image that appears to the viewer to be a smooth, continuous TV picture.

Why can't your expensive computer display full motion video as easily as your $300 TV set? The reason is simply that your computer is a **digital** device, and your TV is an **analog** device. Analog devices require much less **bandwidth** to display full-motion video. A digital device can't display analog video directly; it must instead simulate the analog video by precisely controlling every one of the hundreds of thousands of individual dots (pixels) on your computer screen. And then it must display a series of what are essentially still graphics images, and do so fast enough to trick the eye into thinking that the motion is smooth and continuous. And that adds up to a tremendous amount of digital information. To display a digital video image on a 640- by 480-pixel screen with the same quality that your VCR displays, your computer would have to process 9.2 million pixels and deal with 27 MB of data per second.

If you've *seen* computerized full-motion video, you've probably had a good laugh—the video runs for a few seconds in a postage-stamp-sized area of the screen (and it's jerky, as well). Thanks to sophisticated compression/decompression utilities called **codecs**, however, those days are about to end. A standard recently adopted by **CCITT**, called **Motion Picture Joint Experts Group (MPEG)**, employs a combination of **lossy compression** and **lossless compression** to achieve compression ratios of up to 200:1. Thanks to MPEG, it's possible to display full-motion videos that can run for several minutes, occupying a window of about half the size of an ordinary PC's display. Accompanying the video, which approaches VCR quality, is CD-quality stereo sound.

full-text database

A **database** (a collection of information about a specific subject) that does not merely contain references to published works, but instead contains the full, original text of these works.

From the user's point of view, full-text databases represent a major improvement over previous bibliographic databases, which contained citations and abstracts of published works; if the retrieved citations proved of interest, the researcher had to obtain the full text of the works by means of document delivery, fax, or a visit to the library. A full-text database is more convenient because the database contains the original source texts, making it unnecessary to obtain these texts through the previous, time-consuming means.

Fully Qualified Domain Name (FQDN)

A **host name** that includes all the information necessary to locate the host on the Internet. For example, *foo.virginia.edu* is the fully-qualified domain name for the host named *foo*.

FYI

See **For Your Information (FYI).**

gateway

A networking hardware device that handles communication between two completely different types of networks, and allows limited data exchange (for example, electronic mail). There are gateways between the Internet and popular commercial on-line services, such as **CompuServe**.

In the early days of the Internet, the term *gateway* was used to refer to a **router**, that is, a device that directs messages *within* the Internet. To ensure conformity with prevailing terminology in the data communications industry, Internet people now prefer to use the term *gateway* as it's used outside the Internet context—that is, to refer to a gateway between two dissimilar systems. But note that older Internet documents, and some textbooks, use the term *gateway* to mean *router*.

gatewayed newsgroup

In **Usenet**, a newsgroup that reflects a public **mailing list.**

In a one-directional group, postings can be made only to the mailing list; the Usenet newsgroup is only a reflection of the action that's taking place elsewhere. A bi-directional group allows postings to be made to the Usenet newsgroup as well as to the mailing lists.

Gbps

Abbreviation for gigabits per second; approximately one billion **bits per second.** *See* **data transfer rate**.

General Public Virus

An ironic name for the **copyleft** agreement, called the General Public License (GPL), included with the **Free Software Foundation**'s products. This license specifically states that the organization's software products may be freely redistributed and altered, so long as the altered versions are themselves freely redistributed. In other words, the license is said to carry with it a "virus" of free redistribution that "infects" everything made with the organization's software tools. For this reason, software developers who hope to create commercial products avoid using these products. The Free Software Foundation's position has been that the GPL applies only to modifications that would incorporate significant amounts of its code, and not to new programs created by using that code.

GIF

See **Graphics Interchange Format (GIF).**

gigabit network

A computer network capable of transferring data at speeds of more than one billion bits per second (1 Gbps or more).

global kill file

In a **newsreader** program for **Usenet**, a **kill file** that contains **kill** (delete) specifications for all the newsgroups to which you subscribe. A kill file lets you exclude unwanted postings so that they do not appear in the newsgroups you read. *Compare* **newsgroup kill file.**

gnu hierarchy

In Usenet, one of several **alternative Usenet hierarchies** that are carried and propagated only by those Usenet sites that elect to do so (in contrast to **world newsgroups**, which are automatically fed to every Usenet subscriber). The Gnu **newsgroups** offer discussions of the products and services of the **Free Software Foundation**.

god

In a **MUD** (a multi-user, computerized role-playing game), the game administrators who possess the irrevocable right to determine who may play and how they may play.

A **resource discovery tool** that permits you to **browse** in search of diverse Internet **resources,** such as files, graphics, **WAIS** databases, or **phone books**, by using on-screen menus (lists of items). Gopher enables you to retrieve these items without having to know the technical details of where these resources are located and how to operate the programs that retrieve them. Gopher employs the **client-server model**: You use the Gopher **client** that is available on your host system, and this client helps you contact **servers** on the same or other hosts. You can also access Gopher servers by means of a **World Wide Web (WWW)** client, such as Mosaic.

Unlike **FTP**, Gopher hides the details of accessing resources on a **remote system**, such as **domain names** and directories. When you choose a Gopher item from the menu, the Gopher client makes the connection, contacts the Gopher **server** on the remote system, and displays that server's Gopher menu. When you choose a resource such as a file name, Gopher automatically starts the appropriate utility to retrieve the resource. There is no need for you to memorize and use complicated commands and syntax.

There are several Gopher clients available for several brands of host computers, including IBM PCs, NeXT workstations, and Macintoshes. In widespread use on UNIX systems is the **curses client**, which gets its name from a standard UNIX terminal interface software utility called curses. The examples that follow illustrate the on-screen appearance of the curses client. Clients that employ **graphical user interfaces (GUIs)** employ **icons** to indicate the type of resource an item retrieves. Some clients have advanced features, such as the ability to create **bookmarks** and play sounds.

When you start Gopher on your **host**, the client contacts its **home server**—the Gopher server that's installed on your host system. If you're accessing Gopher from a university, chances are good that the home server will display a **Campus-Wide Information System (CWIS),** listing items of information about the university, as in this example:

```
Root gopher server: gwis.virginia.edu

     1. About this Service/
     2. News and Announcements/
     3. Library Services/
     4. Arts and Sciences/
     5. Schools of the University/
     6. Health Sciences/
     7. Academic Information/
     8. Administrative Information/
     9. Search for UVa Faculty, Staff, or
        Students <?>
     10. Organizations and Publications/
     11. Computing and Communications/
 ->  12. Worldwide Internet Services
         (i.e.,non-UVa services)/
```

Gopher got its start as a CWIS, and is widely used for this purpose at campuses throughout the world. The first Gopher was developed at the University of Minnesota—the home of the Golden Gophers—to serve as a "go fer" for information about the university. This program was developed to provide an easy-to-use interface to a variety of campus information resources, including class lists and databases of telephone numbers. It enabled the user to access these diverse resources using the same simple commands and menus. It was soon realized that Gopher's **client-server model** for accessing diverse information resources could be extended throughout the Internet: a local Gopher client could contact remote Gopher servers by means of **Telnet.** Gopher was subsequently made available to the Internet community by means of **copyleft,** and there are now hundreds of Gopher servers worldwide.

Gopher menus list two basic items, **directory titles** and **resources**. A directory title is indicated by a slash mark at the end of the item, as in this example:

    3. File compression information/

If you choose a directory title, Gopher makes the connection to the server that makes this directory available, and you see another Gopher menu.

You can tell whether an item is a file because its menu name is followed by a period:

    5. Compression FAQ.

If you choose a file name, Gopher starts **FTP** and retrieves the file for you. Subsequently, you can read it on-screen or save it to a disk file, if you wish.

Other types of resources are indicated by special symbols. A question mark indicates a database:

    9. Search for UVa Faculty, Staff, or
       Students <?>

If you choose a database, Gopher starts the correct search utility (such as **Archie** or **WAIS**). Users of UNIX systems should note that your Gopher client gives you the best means of accessing **WAIS** databases; look for a Gopher menu item called

    WAIS based information/

You may see an item that ends with <CSO>:

    8. Green Valley College Faculty and
       Students <CSO>

This indicates that the item is a **CSO name server**, a program that allows you to search a database **white pages** phone book.

Another item you may see in a Gopher menu is <TEL>, indicating that the item makes a **Telnet** connection to a remote host:

    11. University Library Catalog <TEL>

If you choose a <TEL> item, Gopher starts Telnet and makes the connection with the remote host.

As a tool for information browsing, Gopher is easy to use but sometimes frustrating. It is very easy to get lost in Gopher menus without finding the information you're looking for. For this reason, two search utilities, called **Jughead** and **Veronica**, were introduced to allow you to search **Gopherspace** for just the items you want. Jughead searches for directory titles only, while Veronica searches for directory titles and resources.

Tip: If you want to access a Gopher server on a remote host, you can find it by displaying an item called "All the Gopher Servers in the World." If you know the remote host's **domain name**, there's a faster way. At your host's command prompt, type *gopher* followed by the name of the server you want to access, as in this example:

```
gopher fpio.uu.no
```

This command will connect you to the remote system and start the Gopher server there.

gopherspace

The searchable and browsable computer space made possible by **Gopher** servers worldwide

gov

In the **domain name system**, a **top-level domain** name that is assigned to a federal, state, or local government organization. The top-level domain name follows the last period in the site's domain name (such as nsf.gov).

Grand Challenge

An unsolved problem in science or engineering whose complexity exceeds the capability of human researchers, even with the aid of today's fastest **supercomputers**. For example, a program that tries to match a gene pattern to the three billion base pairs of the human genome (inventory of genetic patterns) would require several hundred years of supercomputer time. To meet these challenges, researchers will need not only faster supercomputers, but **gigabit networks** as well, so workers at geographically separate sites will be able to parcel out parts of the program for concurrent work, as well as to exchange massive amounts of data (including high-resolution **graphic** and video images) without delay.

If science can be conceptualized as a quest to find the underlying laws of nature, which can be expressed in equations as simple as Newton's $f=ma$, it's run into a disturbing roadblock. Many of the phenomena of nature are now known to be complex dynamic systems, whose behavior is not predictable by any known simple equation. A few examples: the Earth's weather, ozone depletion, the behavior of turbulent fluids, the functioning of the human immune system. Disturbingly, these problems—such as predicting weather more accurately, understanding the consequences of pollution, and grasping the biology of cancer growth—include many that are vital to the improvement of human life.

If complex dynamic systems behave unpredictably, what's the point of studying them? Mysteriously, they tend to show some regularity—despite year-to-year variations in temperature and precipitation, for example, the seasons come and go. And in the fall, hurricanes make their way eastward across the Atlantic. Just which way they'll go, though, is very difficult to predict. One way to study complex dynamic systems is through **interactive visualization**, a technique that models the system on a reduced scale within a computer, so that its dynamics can be observed. By changing the underlying variables (for example, the temperature of the ocean in a hurricane simulation), the researcher can view an animation that shows how the real system might behave.

A simulation is only as good as the assumptions that underlie it, as anyone who has created a financial model with a spreadsheet program knows very well. But the Grand Challenges present another problem: The higher the model's resolution, the better the results. Here, resolution refers to the ability of the computer program to mimic fine-grained details of the system under study; the best simulation of the world's atmosphere, for instance, would require a computer capable of representing every atom in the atmosphere by a unique data point. That's impossible, and likely to remain so. But the higher the resolution, the better. But here's where an inconvenient fact comes in. To double the resolution of a simulation model, you need roughly 100 times more computing horsepower (measured in teraflops, or billions of operations per second).

Scientists believe that a supercomputer capable of resolving weather conditions to a level of 5 square kilometers—about the size of a small town—would be sufficient to incorporate conditions known to affect the course of tornados and severe thunderstorms. A weather-prediction system capable of 5km resolution could produce highly accurate forecasts every 6 hours, but would require a nationwide system of supercomputers operating at 20 teraflops and a **gigabit network** to connect them.

graphical user interface (GUI)

A design for handling the interaction between the user and the computer that presents options using on-screen pictures (called icons), which the user may choose by clicking the icon with a mouse. GUI's typically include the following, additional features: windows (each application runs its own rectangular window screen), pull-down menus (command options are found in hidden menus, which appear when you click the menu name), and on-screen fonts. The on-screen display of icons, fonts and other graphic elements makes heavy demands on computers

Graphical user interfaces are supposedly easier to use than **menu-driven interfaces** and **command line interfaces**, but some users aren't so sure. An unfortunate trend in recent software design is iconitis, the (unfortunate) tendency to create little, incomprehensible icons for every conceivable computer operation. Frequently, it's difficult—or impossible—to tell what the icons stands for. One program, for instance, displays a button with a little picture of a flashlight; this turns out to be the the "Search" command.

Graphics Interchange Format (GIF)

A graphics file format originally developed by **CompuServe** and widely used to facilitate the exchange of graphics files throughout the computer community, including **bulletin board systems (BBS)** and the Internet. GIF files, stored with the .GIF **extension**, are compressed to shorten transmission times.

The GIF standard employs a **lossless compression** technique to reduce the size of graphics files for economical transmission; the image is decompressed by a graphics program that can read GIF files. Although GIF files are common and well supported by communications and graphics programs, the GIF file format is giving way to **lossy compression** standards such as **JPEG.** With a lossy compression technique, the file size is reduced even further than GIF can manage, albeit at the cost of losing some visual information. However, the human eye cannot perceive this loss.

Great Renaming

In Usenet, a 1986 administrative action that reorganized Usenet newsgroups into the world, alternative, and local newsgroup hierarchies. Previously, newsgroups were organized into just two categories, net (newsgroups to which anyone could post), and mod (**moderated newsgroups**). The renaming was expressly intended to permit **system administrators** to exclude delivery of certain newsgroups that were not felt to be desireable additions to a system's resources (such as alt.sex, owing to its erotic content, or the comp.binaries groups, which consume huge amounts of disk space).

grep

In **UNIX**, a utility that scans a file in an attempt to match a **pattern** you have supplied (such as a **key word**). The utility then displays the lines that contain the string. Here's an example of grep in action. Suppose you're looking for all the lines in a file called modems.txt that include the text "V.42bis." You type the following:

```
grep "V.42bis" modems.txt
```

and grep displays the lines that contain this text, if any.

Group 3

The reigning international standard for fax machines and **fax modems** that can transfer a single page of information in a minute or less. A fax modem that is compatible with the Group 3 standard should be able to communicate with most of the fax machines in common use today. The Group 3 standard is maintained by the ITU-TSS.

The Group 3 fax standard does not specify the speed at which fax transmission occurs; this is handled by additional standards. The **V.27ter** standard specifies fax transmissions at rates of 4800 bits per second (bps). The **V.29** standard regulates fax transmissions at rates of 9600 bps, while the **V.17** standard regulates speeds of 14,400 bps.

GUI

See **graphical user interface (GUI).**

gzip

A popular **UNIX** file compression program. When you use **resource discovery tools** such as **Gopher**, you will frequently encounter files that have the extension .gz, which means they have been compressed with gzip. *See* **compression**.

hacker

A computer enthusiast who possesses considerable knowledge and expertise regarding computers and computer networking, and who applies this knowledge in creative ways to solve computer problems and challenges. Hacking has a long and distinguished history in computing and is responsible for a large share of the significant technical innovations that have occured both in the software and networking industries. In the computing community, this term has positive connotations and should not be confused with **cracker**, a computer criminal who may possess hacking skills but who employs them for malicious purposes. To the deep chagrin of many in the computing community, the popular press uses the term hacker as if it were synonymous with cracker, in effect negating the positive meaning of hacking.

Don't confuse the terms hacker and cracker in a **Usenet** posting unless you love to have dozens of **flames** in your mailbox.

hacker ethic

A set of beliefs developed by youthful computer hackers, originally at the Massachusetts Institute of Technology (MIT) in the late 1960s and early 1970s. These beliefs hold that computer systems and networks represent a societal resource of immense value, and that there is therefore no principled justification to deny access to this resource to individuals and groups who could make good use of them.

The Hacker Ethic is sometimes seen as a veiled rationale for **crackers** who seek to gain unauthorized access to computer systems for malicious or criminal reasons, but this is a serious mistake. The Hacker Ethic indeed holds that all computer resources should in principle be accessible, and hackers have long attempted to gain unauthorized access to computer systems. But the Hacker Ethic also holds that it is immoral to destroy computer resources or prevent others from enjoying them.

The Hacker Ethic has contributed positively to the computer industry in general and the Internet in particular. It provided not only the rationale for the development of personal computing, but also the sense of social purpose that led early PC innovators to accomplish almost heroic feats of sustained intellectual achievement. In computer networking, it has played a positive role as well. Much of the Internet's value stems from the actions of individuals who, with no expectation of private gain, make valuable resources available to all Internet users. Organizations such as the **Electronic Frontier Foundation (EFF)**, the **League for Programming**

Freedom (LPF), and the Open Software Foundation (OSF) embody the best principles of the Hacker Ethic.

half duplex

The transmission of data in one direction at a time. A half duplex **modem** can send or receive information, but it cannot do both at the same time. All of the popular modems for PCs today are duplex modems, but can shift to half duplex if you're trying to connect to a really ancient mainframe computer. *Compare* **full duplex**.

handshake

In computer networking, the exchange of information between a transmitting and receiving computer that indicates that the receiving computer is ready to receive data. Handshakes are required to communicate by means of **connection-oriented protocols** such as the **Transmission Control Protocol (TCP)**; they are not required for **connectionless protocols** such as the **Internet Protocol (IP)**.

hardware independence

The ability of a computer program to function effectively on a variety of computers, even if they are made by different manufacturers. Much of the success of the **TCP/IP** protocols stems from the fact that they can operate on a wide variety of computers and computer networks, providing the means by which very different **physical networks** can be linked to form what appears to the user to be a single **logical network**. In brief, this is what makes the Internet possible.

header

In an **electronic mail** message or **Usenet** posting, the portion of the message that contains the sender's and recipient's addresses; it may contain additional lines of information about the message, such as the subject. In an Internet **datagram**, the initial portion of the data segment that contains information about where and how to deliver it.

HEPnet

In **Usenet**, one of several **alternative newsgroup hierarchies** that are carried and propagated only by those Usenet sites that elect to do so (in contrast to **world newsgroups**, which are automatically fed to every Usenet subscriber). HEPnet, short for the High Energy Physics Network, is a computer network that links physics and nuclear physics research institutes; the HEPnet hierarchy carries **newsgroups** pertaining to physics-related conferences and workshops, job opportunities, computer resources, and announcements of general interest.

Heterogeneous Distributed Computing (HDC)

In scientific computing, the direct use by scientists of a panoply of diverse and geographically distributed computer resources, including **supercomputers**, graphical resources for scientific visualization, and **multimedia databases**. These resources are made conveniently accessible for **real-time** computation by means of forthcoming **gigabit networks** such as the **National Research and Educational Network (NREN)**.

hierarchy

In **Usenet**, a collection of **newsgroups** that have been grouped together under a common name. The **world news-**

groups are organized into seven hierarchies (**comp, misc, news, rec, sci, soc,** and **talk**). The **alternative hierarchies** contain additional newsgroup categories (such as **alt, biz,** and **clari**), but not all **Usenet sites** carry these newsgroups.

High Performance Computing Act of 1991

A U.S. legislative act intended to support the development of high-performance computing—specifically, **supercomputers** and **gigabit networks**—through the allocation of funds to several government agencies, including newly-created High Performance Computing and Communications (HPCC), a multi-agency program. A key component of the bill was increased funding for the development of the **National Research and Education Network (NREN)**.

High Performance Computing and Communications Program (HPCC)

A multi-agency U.S. federal program, founded in 1992, that is devoted to fostering the commercial availability and use of high-performance **supercomputers** and **gigabit networks**. HPCC draws on existing resources in several government agencies, including NASA, the Defense Advanced Research Projects Agency (DARPA), and the National Science Foundation (NSF). One of HPCC's projects is the **National Research and Education Network (NREN)**.

High-speed Digital Subscriber Loop (HDSL)

A proposed solution to the **last mile problem** that involves adding an additional **twisted pair** wire to the single wire that serves most homes. This would allow digital services at **data transfer rates** approaching those of **T1** lines (684 Kbps). One drawback to HDSL is that it would require expensive termination equipment so that the home user could attach devices such as computers, televisions, and phones. *See* **local loop**.

holy war

In the computer community, an unresolvable argument concerning issues in computing. A holy war takes on the attributes of a religious controversy in that the various positions boil down to very deeply held, irreducible propositions about the correct way to design and implement computing technology. Classic holy wars: the debates concerning whether the most significant bit in a unit of data should come first or last (*see* **big endian** and **little endian**), as well as the user-friendliness of the Macintosh vs. the speed and technical accessibility of MS-DOS. On the Internet, holy wars may manifest themselves as **flame wars**.

The latest holy war—and it's a fire fight—pits the advocates of the **Internet protocols** against the proponents of the OSI protocol suite (*see* **Open Systems Interconnection [OSI] protocol suite**). The war concerns not only the respective merits of the two protocol suites; each side accuses the other of being undemocratic in the methods used to develop protocols.

home directory

In **UNIX** systems that are accessed by more than one person, the **directory** (a named file storage area) that was assigned to you when the system administrator set up your account. The home directory includes several important configuration files, such as .newsrc (the file that specifies the **Usenet** newsgroups to which you've subscribed), .plan (a file containing information about you that people can obtain using the **finger** utility), and .signature (a file that many electronic mail clients and newsreaders will automatically append to messages you send). You can also use your home directory to store files.

> **Don't** keep your home directory loaded with files you're not using—you're gobbling up precious disk space. Delete the files or download them to floppy disks for archiving.

home page

In **World Wide Web (WWW)**, the **hypertext** page that appears by default when you access a WWW **client.** Typically, a home page lists general information about the Internet and WWW, and provides access to navigation tools such as **virtual libraries**. With most clients, you can create your own home page that includes frequently-accessed, useful items.

home server

In **Gopher**, the server that appears by default when you access a Gopher client. If you're using a **host** at a college or university, this is likely to be a **Campus-Wide Information System (CWIS)**. *Compare* **remote server**.

hop

In a **packet-switching network** such as the Internet, a single **point-to-point data transmission.**

An Internet **datagram** may make several hops along the way to its destination. It may also traverse many different **physical media** (such as **coaxial cable, T1** telephone lines, **fiber optic**, or even **communications satellites**) along the way. In addition, each hop is governed by its own protocols for encapsulating the data in **frames** (*see* **data link layer**). The **Internet protocols** are not concerned with these low-level matters. By separating these protocols from the low-level physical facts of physical media and data transmission, the Internet's architects ensured that Internet communications could traverse virtually any existing or future data communications medium.

host

A computer that can function as the endpoint of a data transfer on the Internet. The computer could be a single-user personal computer or **workstation** that is part of a **local area network (LAN),** a minicomputer, or a huge mainframe computer (**big iron**). All of these computers can run the **Internet protocols**.

This term is confusing because it implies that you are using the computer as a guest. That is true for the many users who use **dialup access,** but it is also true that a single-user workstation or PC can be a host if it is **directly connected** to the Internet. In other networking contexts, the term *node* is used to describe a single, addressable computer on the network. The term *host* is synonymous with *node* and carries no "social" implications about hosting anything other than the Internet protocols.

A host is one of only two basic devices that can be connected to the Internet. The other is the **IP router,** which handles the task of sending messages (broken up into **packets** called **datagrams**) from one network to the next.

host address

The **IP address** of an Internet **host** (a computer that's directly connected to the Internet).

host name

A unique, **fully-qualified domain name** (FQDN) that identifies the location of an Internet **host**. The name is expressed using the **domain name system,** in a form such as *watt.seas.-virginia.edu* (the computer named Watt, in the School of Engineering and Applied Science, at the University of Virginia). The host name provides a convenient handle for users, who would otherwise have to type the host's numerical **IP address**.

HTML

See **HyperText Markup Language (HTML).**

HTTP

See **HyperText Transport Protocol (HTTP).**

HTTP server

In the **World Wide Web (WWW),** a **server** that can communicate using the **HyperText Transfer Protocol (HTTP)** and provide **hypertext** documents to WWW **clients**.

hypermedia

A **hypertext** system that is capable of displaying **multimedia**—including graphics, sounds, video, or animations—in addition to text.

hypertext

A non-sequential method for reading a document displayed on a computer screen. Instead of reading the document in sequence from beginning to end, the reader can jump to topics by selecting a highlighted word or phrase (called an **anchor**). This activates a **link** to another place in the same document, or to another document altogether. The resulting matrix of links within and among documents is termed a **web**.

Hypertext suits some documents better than others—it's not very useful for fiction, for example, because sequential reading is necessary to keep track of the story! But it's perfect for dictionaries, reference manuals, and textbooks, in which the links enrich and enhance the presentation of information.

Writing a document in hypertext encourages conciseness; if you think some readers might need more information about a subject, you can include an anchor and link to a document that explains the subject in more detail.

Hypertext was first conceptualized by computer visionary Ted Nelson in 1965, who later conceived of Xanadu, a world-wide hypertext system to which people would contribute resources. In 1992, Autodesk Systems abandoned a project to implement Xanadu, but the same year saw the distribution throughout the Internet of CERN's software for the **World Wide Web (WWW).** The Web employs hypertext to provide Internet users with a powerful **resource discovery tool**: When you select an anchor in the Web, the Web software jumps to the linked document—which might be on another computer system, halfway across the world.

HyperText Markup Language (HTML)

The standard **markup language** for documents made available to the **World Wide Web (WWW).** When accessed by a WWW **browser** such as **Mosaic**, a document prepared with HTML will display formatting, graphics, and **links** to other documents.

HTML is a variant of the **Standard Generalized Markup Language (SGML)**, which is frequently used to mark up **electronic texts** for display and analysis purposes. However, it is much easier to learn and use. There are far fewer commands. You need learn only a few to prepare a document for display on WWW.

HyperText Transport Protocol (HTTP)

The **protocol**, as well as the **server** software that implements it, for **hypertext browsing** on the **World Wide Web (WWW)**. The protocol allows a user, who is browsing a hypertext document that contains **links**, to **jump** to another document that may be located on another **host** thousands of miles away, and to retrieve the information in that document (even if this information is in the form of a graphic, a sound, or a short video). In particular, HTTP delineates the form of **Universal Resource Locater (URL)** statements, which allow the authors of hypertext documents to include commands that **jump** to resources available on **remote systems**.

Hytelnet

A **resource discovery tool** that allows a user to **browse** though **hypertext** documents listing more than 1,400 **Telnet**-accessible sites on the Internet, and the resources they contain (with an emphasis on the electronic card catalogues of more than 400 college and university libraries). Hytelnet was developed by Peter Scott of the University of Saskatchewan Library.

icon

In a **graphical user interface (GUI)**, an on-screen picture that represents a computer resource or operation, such as a file or a printing function.

Icons are supposed to make computers easier to use—to do something, you just click the picture of what you want to do. The idea sounds great, but too many icons can prove very confusing. Many of the icons found in today's Microsoft Windows applications, for instance, aren't readily recognizable—what's there to make of an icon showing a computer rocketing off the surface of a desk? (It's an icon for sending a fax.) It's easy enough to represent an operation such as printing (you just use a picture of a printer), but many resources and operations aren't easily paired with a universally-recognized symbol.

identity

In Internet **electronic mail** and related forms of communication such as **Usenet**, the human being who is presumed to be the originator of a message marked with his or her unique **login name** (such as *maryb@wallie.uu.se*).

The operative word in this definition is "presumed," since most of the systems connected to the Internet do not provide secure **authentication** of user identity. To be sure, you are prompted to type a **password** when you log on to an **Internet host**. However, this could be observed over your shoulder as you work in a crowded office or student computer facility.

The fact that login names disclose so little information about the person who originates the message has a positive side: It breaks down social barriers. An undergraduate college student, for example, may have a better chance of communicating with a professor through email than in person. In **Multi-User Dungeon (MUDs)** games (computerized multi-player role-playing games), you can redefine your identity as you please, even to the extent of changing gender or, in the FurryMucker game, becoming an intelligent animal.

> **Tip:** If you would like to learn more about a Usenet poster or someone who has sent you an electronic mail message, you can use the **finger** utility. At the minimum, this will disclose the person's electronic mail address (which you already know), but some Internet users like to use this facility to disclose more information about themselves. At the extreme this may involve a file containing quotations, poems, and reflections that can tell you a great deal about the person.

> **Don't** go away from your computer while it's still connected to the Internet. This is an open invitation for pranksters to appropriate your identity and post outrageous or obscene messages to Usenet. The consequences of such In one such case, a college student who had left a computer running in this way had a visit from the Secret Service; someone had used his account to threaten President Clinton's life.

> **Do** change your password frequently, and follow standard procedures for choosing a secure password. *See* **password**.

A UNIX program that provides a means for other programs to determine a remote user's login name after an Internet connection is established. (A **daemon** is a program that operates in the background, ready to spring into action if needed.) Obviously detrimental to **anonymity**, the use of identity daemons attests to the security concerns of UNIX **system administrators**. Such software could be used, for example, to determine the login name of problem users.

IEEE

In **Usenet**, one of several **alternative newsgroup hierarchies** that are carried and propagated only by those Usenet sites that elect to do so (in contrast to **world newsgroups**, which are automatically fed to every Usenet subscriber). The IEEE **newsgroups** offer discussions of interest to members of the Institute of Electrical and Electronics Engineers (IEEE). Topics include announcements of general interest to members and descriptions of forthcoming conferences.

IEEE 802 Network

A set of **protocols** (standards) for **local area networks (LANS)** that has gained widespread acceptance. Many of the LANs connected to the Internet are IEEE 802 networks.

Based on the original **Ethernet** specifications published jointly by Digital Equipment Corporation, Intel Corporation, and Xerox Corporation in 1982 (*see* **DIX Internet**), the IEEE 802 standards call for a family of Ethernets employing a variety of **physical media** (including **twisted pair**) and **data transfer rates**. The original DIX Ethernet standards (recast in IEEE 802.2) called for a network that would employ **Carrier Sense Multiple Access with Collision Detection (CSMA/CD)**, but subsequent additions have added two more workable methods of avoiding **contention** (called **token bus** and **token ring**). Intel standard 802.4 describes the token bus method, while 802.5 describes the token ring method. Confusingly, all three are widely referred to as **Ethernets**, but they are not **compatible**.

Imminent Death of the Net

A non-existent threat to the Internet's survival, which periodically manifests itself in hysterical **Usenet** postings ("They're out to get us!"). *See* **urban folklore**.

incompatible

Not able to work with something. A program that is incompatible with **UNIX**, for example, will not run if you try to install it on a UNIX computer. *Compare* **compatible**.

indirect access

A means of Internet access that makes use of a **gateway** provided by an online information service (such as CompuServe or Delphi) or a computer **bulletin board service (BBS)**. Although indirect access may make limited Internet services available such as **electronic mail, Usenet,** and **anonymous FTP**, it has the same disadvantages of **dialup access** generally: The mail and files you obtain to the information service's or BBS's computer, not to your own. To get the mail or files to your own computer, you must **download** them.

info

In Usenet, one of several **alternative newsgroup hierarchies** that are carried and propagated only by those Usenet sites that elect to do so (in contrast to **world newsgroups**, which are automatically fed to every Usenet subscriber). The info **newsgroups** originate from **mailing lists** at the University of Illinois, but have proven popular elsewhere. Topics tend toward the technical (Convex Corporation computers and the LISP programming language), with the exception of a newsgroup focused on the music of Jethro Tull, a rock group.

Information Superhighway

A term used popularly, and inaccurately, to describe the coming **National Information Infrastructure (NII)**.

What is misleading about this term is the emphasis it places on high-speed **backbones**, such as the proposed **gigabit network** of the **National Research and Educational Network (NREN)**. A high-speed backbone, or data superhighway, is needed only for sophisticated scientific and medical imaging. In fact, an information "highway" (if not "super") already exists, in the form of the reasonably high-bandwidth backbones currently employed by the **Internet's service providers**, such as the national telephone system and **Public Data Networks (PDN)**. The compelling problem lies in how to deliver data communications services to homes, schools, and offices (the **last mile problem**). In addition, current **wide area network (WAN)** technologies do not do an acceptable job of delivering **real-time** data such as voice and video. *See* **integrated services network**.

InfoSource

A repository of helpful information and tutorials concerning the Internet that is maintained by General Atomics, Inc., as part of the **InterNIC** project, administered by the **National Science Foundation (NSF).**

integrated router

In a **packet switching network** such as the Internet, a **router** that dynamically exchanges information with other routers about the network's **topology.** The result of this exchange, called **convergence**, is a table that shows the best paths for sending packets to their destinations. Internet routers, called **IP routers**, perform this task.

Integrated Services Digital Network (ISDN)

Acronym for Integrated Services Digital Network. ISDN is a set of standards for high-speed **digital** communications that can make use of existing telephone lines. Widely implemented in Europe, ISDN is capable of delivering graphics, sound, low-resolution video, and text data as well as noise-free voice transmission to home users without requiring a massive capital investment.

The existing telephone system was designed to handle the human voice. It does so using **analog** technology: A microphone converts the human voice into an undulating current, whose variations match the changing frequencies of human vocal output. At the other end, a speaker reproduces the voice—but, as generations of phone users can attest, with low fidelity to the original and the addition of a substantial amount of **line noise**. During a conversation, the line noise is irritating, but during computer data transmission it's often fatal: error-free data transmission via the telephone system requires **modems** and **file transfer protocols** (such as **Zmodem** or **Kermit**) that retransmit units of data if line noise disturbs the transmission. This substantially lowers the speed of data transmission.

As millions of audio compact disc enthusiasts have discovered, **digital** techniques provide accurate reproduction of the original sound while virtually eliminating noise. This is done by converting the audio signal into **bits** (1s and 0s), the basic units of digital information. A digital telephone system could bring the same benefits to telephone users: accurate rendition of the human voice against a silent, noise-free background. But it would bring benefits to computer users as well. By eliminating line noise (and consequently the need for retransmission), digital telephone lines bring significant gains in data transmission speeds. Existing ISDN systems can handle 64,000 bits per second of data, a figure that can be increased to 200,000 bits per second with data compression. Compared to the 14,400 bits per second achieved with today's standard **modems** and analog phone lines, the benefits in increased throughput are obvious. A high-resolution graphic that today takes ten minutes to **download** could be received in a minute or less. But ISDN lacks sufficient **bandwidth** to realize the goal of **distributed computing**, in which—from the user's perspective—all network resources are accessible at speeds at least approaching those of directly-connected peripherals such as disk drives.

ISDN is a proven digital telephone standard that is already widely implemented in Europe and Japan. The standard was originally proposed by the Comité Consultif International de Télégraphique et Téléphonique (**CCITT**), a United Nations organization that coordinates international telecommunications, in 1984. In the United States, the regional Bell companies have been slow to offer ISDN in the United States. The delay is partly attributable to incompatible standards. This problem has been resolved by the 1991 publication of the ISDN-1 standard, which makes the regional Bell offerings compatible not only with each other but also with foreign ISDN systems. More than 50% of regional Bell system lines were expected to have ISDN capability by the end of 1994.

Because ISDN can make use of existing **twisted-pair** telephone lines, implementing ISDN does not require an enormous capital investment, as would many of the technologies currently under consideration for the proposed **National Information Infrastructure (NII)**. For this reason, public advocacy groups such as the **Electronic Frontier Foundation (EFF)** believe that ISDN holds the key to equitable public access to the NII. In addition, ISDN may provide many small organizations with an excellent alternative to expensive **leased lines** (high-bandwidth, permanently-connected transmission lines set aside for computer data). ISDN lines have sufficient bandwidth to connect a small **local area network (LAN)**—ten users or less—to the Internet.

Integrated Services Digital Network (ISDN)

If your telephone company extends an ISDN line to your home, you can kiss your old **analog** modem good-bye. An ISDN line removes the last vestige of **analog** transmission—and with it, the rationale for modems, which transform the computer's digital impulses into the warbling, analog sounds required by standard analog telephone lines. But you'll still need some equipment, including a $200 device that handles the decoding of the **multiplexed** signal, as well as a **terminal adapter (TA)** that links your computer directly to the ISDN line, such as the Hayes ISDN PC Adapter, an internal expansion board for IBM PCs and compatibles. This equipment could cost as much as $750 at current price levels (which are expected to decline).

In the United States, ISDN services fall into three categories: Basic Rate ISDN (BRI), Primary Rate ISDN (PRI), and Broadband ISDN (B-ISDN). Designed as the basic option for consumers, Basic Rate ISDN offers two 64,000 bit per second channels for voice, graphics, and data, plus one 16,000 bit per second channel for signalling purposes. Primary Rate ISDN provides 23 channels with 64,000 bits per second capacity. Broadband ISDN, still under development, would supply up to 150 million bits per second of data transmission capacity, which is sufficient for high-definition television (HDTV); however, this would require the replacement of **twisted-pair** telephone lines with **fiber optic** cables.

> **Tip:** If you're like many home computer users these days, you're probably thinking about getting an extra POTS ("plain old telephone service") line for your home so that you and others can place and receive voice calls while your modem's in action. But before doing so, call your local telephone company to find out if ISDN service is available for your residence. A single ISDN line can carry two "B" (64,000 bps) channels, and might be cheaper—or the same price—as two POTS lines. But bear in mind that you'll run into addi-

tional costs for the equipment needed to connect your computer system to the ISDN line. Also, expect to pay a stiff fee—$200 is the going rate—for ISDN installation, which requires extensive line testing to make sure that the circuits can handle the increased data flow.

integrated services network

A **wide area network (WAN)** that will be able to handle all kinds of data efficiently, including voice and video as well as computer data and text. Such a network, still in the planning stage, will probably employ **fast packet switching network** technology, and will form the basis of the future **National Information Infrastructure** of the next century.

Integrated services networks, still on the drawing board, address the inability of today's network technologies (**circuit switching networks** and **packet switching networks**) to handle all kinds of communications, including voice, video, computer data, graphics, and text.

A **circuit switching network**, such as the telephone system, creates a direct connection between the sender and the receiver, and excels at transmitting voice and video without interruption. With both voice and video, users can tolerate some loss in what they receive (such as minor line noise or a slightly degraded image), but they do not want delay. Circuit switching networks allow minor losses but eliminate delay.

Packet switching switching networks, such as the Internet, handle data and text communication more efficiently by breaking data down into individually-addressed **packets** of a small size (several thousand bits), and then reassembling the message at the destination. A variety of mechanisms are used to guarantee that the received message is an exact duplicate of the one that was sent. Some of the packets may be delayed, but this is not serious: Computer users can tolerate some delay but they cannot tolerate loss (an error in just one line of a computer program could prevent the program from functioning properly).

Fast packet networks such as **Asynchronous Transfer Mode (ATM)** seem to offer the pathway to an integrated services network.

| Interactive TV (ITV) |

A **cable television (CATV)** technology, already in use in some test areas, that allows the TV viewer to interact with the content provider, choosing from program options such as movies and limited on-screen information (news, sports, and weather).

Interactive TV typifies the **broadcast model** of the emerging **National Information Infrastructure (NII)**—the delivery of for-profit information and entertainment resources to the home, without giving the home viewers the means or the **bandwidth** to originate content themselves (*compare* **community model**).

| interactive visualization |

A method of scientific analysis that employs high-performance computers and **multimedia** to assist scientists in seeing the patterns in numerical data. A major rationale for the **National Research and Education Network (NREN)** is the promise of rapid scientific progress that could stem from making visualization resources widely available.

Most of the significant problems facing science today (the **Grand Challenges**) are highly complex problems—so complex, in fact, that they could not have been addressed were it not for the development of **supercomputers**. But supercomputers alone can't help scientists solve problems. Supercomputers spew out billions of numbers, far more than humans can interpret. In scientific visualization, these numbers form the basis of detailed graphical simulations, which portray the data in a way that scientists can immediately understand and interpret. It's one thing to see a 300-page description of a new drug; it's quite another to see its molecular shape on-screen, and be able to rotate the image so you can see exactly how the receptors can link with the virus you're targeting. That's the path to discovery. Why? According to a National Science Foundation estimate, more than 50% of the human brain is concerned with vision.

Supercomputers have enabled visualization for more than a decade, but they've had one huge drawback: You had to go to the supercomputer facility if you wanted to make use of its number-crunching capabilities. That's not good enough for physicians and researchers hot on the trail of a disease or a new discovery. **Gigabit networks** holds out the potential of accessing supercomputers remotely, and, more broadly, of distributing visualization capabilities throughout the scientific and professional communities.

interagency network

In the U.S. federal government, an **internet** that links the various regional and national offices of an agency such as the Department of Defense. These networks are part of the Internet, and include the Nasa Science Internet (NSI) and the Department of Energy's Energy Sciences Network (ESnet).

Interface Message Processor (IMP)

The term for **router** that was employed during the design and construction of the **ARPANET**. This term is no longer in common use.

Interior Gateway Protocol (IGP)

A **routing protocol** that governs the routing of **packets** of data within the confines of an **Autonomous System (AS)**, a collection of networks under the control of a single administrative agency, such as a university or corporation. The most popular IGP protocol is **Routing Information Protocol (RIP)**, but the **Open Shortest Path First (OSPF)** protocol is gaining ground because it is more efficient for large networks. *Compare* **Exterior Gateway Protocol (EGP)**.

International Standards Organization (ISO)

An international, non-profit organization that is devoted to enhancing technological and scientific progress by establishing open standards. The organization was founded in 1946. Its membership includes the national standards organizations of its nearly 90 member nations. The United States is represented by the **American National Standards Institute (ANSI)**. With respect to telecommunications, ISO tries to work in concert with the **CCITT** to avoid the creation of incompatible international standards. The ISO developed the **Open System Interconnection (OSI) Reference Model**, which provides a useful framework of concepts for describing and developing computer networks, as well as the **Open Systems Interconnection (OSI) protocol suite**, which currently competes with the **Internet protocols**.

internet

Any collection of computer networks that is connected by means of a common communications **protocol**. *Compare* **Internet**.

There are internets other than the subject of this glossary, *the* Internet (with an uppercase I); that's why Internet users and experts tend to include the definite article *the* when referring to the internet integrated by **TCP/IP**.

The Internet (uppercase I), as opposed to *an* internet (lowercase i). The emerging world network of thousands of physical networks that can exchange data by means of the **TCP/IP** protocols. The result is a **cyberspace** of prodigious dimensions, an enormously valuable global resource of information and collaboration.

The Internet isn't the physical networks that make it up, but that doesn't mean it's an ethereal, nebulous entity that lacks precise definition. The Internet is the computer space created by the Internet's technical means of *connecting* dissimilar networks so that they can exchange mail and data quickly and transparently. In fact, the **TCP/IP** protocols can and are used on very different kinds of networks, spanning the gamut from **local area networks (LANs)** such as **Ethernet**, **metropolitan area networks (MANs)** and **regional networks** that link the LANs in a city or region, to one of several high-speed **backbones** that carry Internet data over transcontinental and transoceanic hauls. Along the way, Internet data may traverse a variety of **physical media**, telephone wires, **fiber optic** cables, **communications satellites,** and **microwave relay** systems. In the future, Internet data will traverse the experimental **gigabit networks** of the coming **National Information Infrastructure (NII)**. In short, the Internet isn't a physical network. It's a way of getting dissimilar physical networks to work together so that users of these networks can exchange data.

Networks and even **backbones** come and go, but the Internet remains—and grows. The Internet is growing so quickly—an estimated 10 to 15 percent per month—that any mention of specific numbers of networks and hosts quickly becomes inaccurate. At this writing, well over 2 million

hosts (Internet-addressable computers) were directly addressable through the Internet, which links an estimated 20 million people in 69 countries, with strong penetration in the U.S., Canada, Mexico, most of Europe, Russia, China, Singapore, Australia, and New Zealand. Internet users can exchange **electronic mail** by means of **gateways** to additional networks in a total of 137 countries. According to **National Science Foundation (NSF)** statistics, the rate at which new networks are added to the Internet in foreign countries (183%) exceeds domestic U.S. network growth (160%). A recent estimate: By 1998, the Internet may have 100 million users worldwide.

Why is the Internet growing so rapidly? There are many reasons.

- The Internet's ability to link physically dissimilar networks frees users to choose the equipment they need. A graphics workshop can run high-end Macintoshes, while engineers can use Sun workstations; in still another office, accountants can use a minicomputer to crank out payroll checks. Yet the Internet can link them all, providing them the means to exchange files and data.

- The Internet is fast becoming the world's de facto **electronic mail** system. By means of **gateways**, Internet users can exchange electronic mail with users of many additional networks that don't use TCP/IP, widening even further the Internet's impressive reach. An estimated 25 million people are now thought to have the ability to exchange electronic mail by means of the Internet and Internet gateways.

- The Internet's **protocols** (standards) are in the public domain and are supported by virtually every manufacturer of network equipment. These manufacturers are also experiencing phenomenal growth—manufacturers of Internet **routers** have recently experienced some of the fastest business growth rates ever observed in the U.S.—

and with this growth comes the economies of scale that send prices of Internet equipment are plummeting. The Internet is a textbook example of the economic and technological benefits of effective **standardization**.

- Once confined to universities, research centers, and government agencies, the Internet is quickly moving out into the mainstream of society. **Freenets** and **online information services** make Internet access available to individuals, while commercially-oriented network **service providers** are hooking up corporations and small businesses at rapidly accelerating rates. In 1993, the amount of commercial traffic on the Internet exceeded other uses for the first time. Firms everywhere are concluding that the Internet is an indispensable resource for business. The **commercialization** of the Internet, as well as the concomitant process of **privatization**, will change the network's character—but in just which ways, no one is certain.

- Yet another reason for the Internet's rapid growth: Viewed as a public communication medium, it's a revolution. As opposed to **broadcast** media that send you only what the broadcaster wants you to see, read, or hear, the Internet is a two-way communication that lets every participant become an originator as well as a consumer of information and resources. This is exactly what makes the Internet so interesting and valuable. The quality of the resources contributed by individuals varies, of course, but it's quite possible to discover on the Internet some material that will prove of tremendous value to you—a bibliography, a utility program, a graphic, or just a few wise words from a very knowledgeable person. These resources don't have much or any commercial value and wouldn't be available in a broadcast medium. And suffusing the Internet is what Mitch Kapor, president of the **Electronic Frontier Foundation (EFF)**, calls a "gift economy": an ethic that stress-

es the common good that arises from everyone contributing to the network in a disinterested spirit.

- For large organizations, it's not very expensive to get a
  dedicated connection to the Internet via a leased line—
  about $1,000 to $5,000 per month. And if this organization
  already has a **local area network (LAN)** to which this
  connection is made, every user on the LAN suddenly has
  a direct link to the Internet. One by one, organizations
  with LANs such as corporations, government agencies, school systems, and non-profit organizations are concluding that the Internet is a very inexpensive way to
  realize dramatic gains in the functionality of computer
  systems they have *already* installed.

Don't go hunting for The Internet Building somewhere in a
big city; there's no central headquarters or central administration. To be sure, the **National Science Foundation
(NSF)** is responsible for the Internet **backbone**, but there are
alternative national backbones now, and NSF's authority does
not extend to them. Each network is an **Autonomous
System (AS)** that is linked to the Internet, which can be
conceptualized as a loose federation of Autonomous Systems
that have found it desirable to link themselves in a cooperative
network. The tasks of coordinating these links, providing the
necessary information, and addressing engineering challenges
falls to the **Internet Society (ISOC)**, a non-profit professional organization in which membership is open to all.

There is no single agency that runs the Internet—and it's
equally vague exactly who pays for it. There is no Internet
Central Billing agency that sends out monthly checks. But
the Internet isn't "free," as some users mistakenly think.
Instead, each participating network pays its share of the operating costs. A university pays a regional **service provider** to
get access to the Internet, and the regional service provider
in turn pays a national **backbone** provider. Individuals
using **dialup access** pay a flat monthly fee to any of a bewil-

dering range of service providers making this kind of Internet access possible—**online information services**, **bulletin board systems (BBS)**, **freenets**, and more.

The Internet is indeed a phenomenon, perhaps one of the most important developments to occur in human communication since the development of the telephone. But it isn't perfect. There are major problems in the areas of **security**, **privacy**, and **authentication**—problems that are keeping many organizations from making a full commitment to Internet connectivity. Moreover, the Internet's underlying **packet-switching network** technology is far from ideal for the transmission of **real-time** services such as voice and video, which can't tolerate delay. It's unlikely, then, that the Internet can provide the foundation for the **integrated services networks** of the future, which will make **multimedia** resources widely and easily available, without fundamental engineering changes. And the Internet's facing some well-organized competition. The **International Standards Organization (ISO)** has developed a competing suite of internetworking protocols, called the **Open Systems Interconnection (ISO) protocol suite**, which has certain advantages for business networking. Moreover, the OSI protocols are solidly backed by European governments and their monopolistic **Postal, Telegraph, and Telephone (PTT)** services, which view the Internet protocols as a form of dangerous anarchy that could only have been devised by cultureless American cowboy types. They look at the Internet with about as much enthusiasm as the French are showing for EuroDisneyland. These attitudes, linked with preferential government contract policies, have slowed the Internet's growth in Europe. An exception: Scandinavia. You won't spend much time on the net before you start to recognize the Scandinavian **domain names,** such as *no* for Norway and *fi* for Finland.

Still, it's arguable that there's no stopping the Internet's growth. It's a proven technology. The alternatives aren't yet ready for prime time. An analogy: For almost fifteen years, experts and prognosticators have been more than ready to attend the funeral of MS-DOS, the operating system of IBM PCs and clones. But it just hasn't happened—in fact, DOS has gone on to become the most widely used operating system in the world. It's simple, inexpensive, widely available, and well supported. DOS computers are cheap, but they're extremely powerful and useful. A winning combination, wouldn't you say? And as Microsoft has eloquently demonstrated with Microsoft Windows, DOS can provide the foundation for a much more sophisticated operating system, Microsoft Windows, which brings to DOS computers all the things that the competition was supposed to offer. Similarly, the Internet of ten to twenty years from now may have a radically different look and feel from the clunky, **command-line** interface of today. But don't be surprised if, beneath the surface glitz, you'll be using the same TCP/IP protocols. And the Internet of tomorrow may be very big indeed: Vincent Cerf, one of the Internet's designers and elder statesmen, sees no reason why the technology couldn't be scaled up to integrate a billion computer networks.

Internet Activities Board (IAB)

An organization created in 1983 to oversee the development of the **Internet protocols** and to coordinate research and engineering work on fundamental Internet problems. There have been several IAB reorganizations, and the organization—currently a unit of the **Internet Society**—is now called the **Internet Architecture Board (IAB)**.

Internet Architecture Board (IAB)

The successor to the **Internet Activities Board (IAB)**, this organization is a unit of the **Internet Society** that is broadly concerned with the technical challenges facing the Internet. The IAB oversees two branches, the **Internet Engineering Task Force (IETF)** and the **Internet Research Task Force (IRTF)**.

Internet Assigned Numbers Authority (IANA)

A unit of the **Internet Architecture Board** that coordinates the assignment of numbers that are employed by various Internet **protocols**. One of the functions of IANA is to keep track of **well-known ports,** which make it possible for your **client** program to access a remote **server** easily and quickly.

Internet Control Message Protocol (ICMP)

A **protocol** (standard) that deals with the problem of what happens when a **router** gets congested or is otherwise unable to send a **datagram** to its destination. ICMP provides **flow control** by sending messages back to the host that tell the host to stop sending datagrams until the problem is resolved. *See* **congestion.**

There are many reasons a router may have difficulty delivering a datagram: It may be temporarily unable to find an open route to a datagram's destination, or the datagram's time to live may have expired. Normally, this isn't a problem, because **TCP** keeps on sending the same datagram over and over until it receives an acknowledgement from the destination computer that the datagram has been received. When a router is congested, however, an unfortunate situation arises: Even though the router is stuffed with as many waiting datagrams as it can accommodate, TCP keeps sending duplicates, making the situation even worse. In such situations, ICMP sends a message that informs TCP that the router is congested and to stop sending datagrams until the backlog clears up.

Internet Draft

The current working documents of the **Internet Engineering Task Force (IETF)**. Although written in the format of **Request for Comments (RFCs)**, they do not propose new protocols (that is the job of the **Internet Architecture Board)** and aren't numbered.

Internet Engineering Steering Group (IESG)

A unit of the **Internet Architecture Board (IAB)** that oversees the activities of the Internet Engineering Task Force (IETF).

Internet Engineering Task Force (IETF)

A branch of the **Internet Architecture Board (IAB)** that addresses the immediate technical problems and challenges of the Internet. The organization is managed by the **Internet Engineering Steering Group (IESG)**. The IETF is a voluntary community of technical people with Internet interests: network designers, network operators, researchers and engineers, and vendors of Internet-compatible equipment.

Internet Experiment Notes (IEN)

A now-abandoned vehicle for the publication of early Internet **protocols**. *See* **Request for Comments (RFC)**.

Internet Hunt

An Internet game, devised and organized by the librarian Rick Gates, that tests the players' ability to find specific information tucked away somewhere on the world Internet system.

Since September, 1992, Gates has offered one hunt per month, with the questions, results, and winners announced in several Internet locations. The purpose of the Hunt is to illustrate the depth and variety of information that is available on the Internet, as well as to encourage Hunters to develop and share clever information retrieval techniques.

A sample question: "What was the total amount of sales in liquor stores in the United States in September of this year? Was this more than last year?"

Internet Monthly Report (IMR)

An on-line report, created for the **Internet Architecture Board (IAB)**, that summarizes the current state of the Internet, including usage levels, technical challenges, and the reports of technical committees.

Tip: Like to see the Monthly Report? It's available by **FTP** from the host *nis.nsf.net*, in the directory /internet-/newsletters/internet.monthly.report. You'll see lots of filenames, which use the form *imr94-07.txt* ("Internet Monthly Report for July, 1994").

Internet Protocol (IP)

At the **network layer** in the Internet's **architecture**, a **connectionless** and **unreliable protocol** (standard) that serves to define the **datagram** (the Internet's basic **packet** structure) and the Internet's method of **addressing** remote computers (**IP addresses**) as well as to handle the task of **routing** datagrams to remote hosts.

As with other protocols in the Internet **protocol suite**, IP refers both to the underlying protocol as well as to specific computer programs that implement it. These programs run on **routers** as well as **hosts**.

Unlike **connection-oriented protocols,** IP is connection-less—that is, it does not seek to establish a connection with the destination computer before sending the datagrams. For this reason, IP cannot verify that the datagrams were received. In addition, IP is unreliable—that is, it does not offer any means for error correction.

From the above, it sounds like it's a very bad idea to send your data through the Internet: IP just spits out packets and doesn't care whether they reach their destination. But there's a reason for denying connection and error handling functions to IP: They're handled at a different **layer**, the **transport layer**, which is one layer up in the Internet's **protocol stack**. At these layers, two transport protocols—the **Transmission Control Protocol (TCP)** and the **User Datagram Protocol (UDP)**—take data from applications, segment it, and pass it down to IP, which takes over from there. At the transport layer, you can choose a connection-oriented and reliable approach—*if you want it*. TCP is a connection-oriented protocol that provides verification and error correction. But it comes with a price: high **overhead** (TCP consumes more **bandwidth** and processing time). UDP, a connectionless protocol, is a low-overhead alternative to TCP that can be used when a "live" connection and reliability are not needed. By separating out the functions of establishing a connection and correcting errors, the Internet's designers give application programmers a choice: When needed, you can send data via TCP and IP, but if connections and error correction are not needed, you can use UDP and IP. For example, **FTP, Simple Mail Transport Protocol (SMTP)**, and **Telnet** send their messages through TCP, while **SNMP** uses UDP.

One of the most important functions of the IP protocol is to define the Internet **datagram**, the data "envelope" that helps Internet routers deliver the packet to the correct address. In a router, IP defines the method used by the router's software to direct the datagram to its destination. This is done by looking up the destination in a **routing table**. Using a table, IP tries to find a route that will get the datagram to its destination. In a small network with few routing options, the routing table might be typed manually by a network administrator, but other Internet protocols can be used to automatically detect the addition of new networks or the temporary failure of some networks.

Internet Relay Chat (IRC)

A **real time**, multi-user **client** program that allows you to "chat" with other Internet users interactively. You can choose from dozens of "channels" on every conceivable subject, ranging from staid (#Over40) to ribald (#HotTub). But don't look for these specific titles; channels come and go; they're organized *ad hoc* by whoever wishes to do so. After joining a channel, you see what others have typed on-screen; when you type a line and press **_Enter_**, your text is seen by everyone else in the channel.

Originally written by Jarkko Oikarinen of Finland in 1988, IRC was conceptualized as a replacement for UNIX's clunky Talk command. IRC has since spread to some 60 countries and attracts hundreds of users every day.

Is IRC another example of how the Internet wastes time and computer resources? Not according to Russians who were trying to figure out what was going on during the abortive coup against Boris Yeltsin in 1993. IRC users from Moscow provided reliable, on-line commentary about the rapidly evolving situation.

Do read the IRC documentation. You'll need to know how to use basic commands such as /list, /join, /nick, /leave, and /quit.

Don't type your password if you see a prompt requesting you to do so. This is a common trick used by **crack-**

ers to hoodwink you into supplying the information they need to access your host system.

Internet Research Steering Group (IRSG)

A unit of the **Internet Society**, this organization coordinates the activities of the **Internet Engineering Task Force (IETF)**.

Internet Research Task Force (IRTF)

A branch of the **Internet Architecture Board (IAB)** that deals with the future of the Internet. In contrast to the **Internet Engineering Task Force (IETF)**, which handles today's problems, IRTF addresses the long-term challenges that the Internet faces, such as the inability of the **Internet Protocols** to deliver **real-time** voice and video.

The IRTF employs a research methodology that protects the Internet from hare-brained schemes that look good on paper but prove disastrous in practice. Before a new protocol is recommended as a standard, it is implemented on a test system and reviewed. A protocol that degrades the Internet's performance doesn't make it past the review process, and never sees light in a **Request for Comments (RFC)**. *Compare* **Open Systems Interconnection (OSI) Protocol Suite**.

Internet Resource Guide

An electronically published directory of Internet **resources**, such as files and databases. The Guide is published by the **NSF Network Service Center (NNSC)** and focuses on the research and educational resources available on the Internet. Catalog chapters include Computational Resources, Library Catalogs, Archives, White Pages (information about users), the networks connected to the Internet, and network information centers.

Tip: You can obtain a copy of the Guide via anonymous FTP from *nnsc.nsf.net*, in the directory "resource-guide".

Internet Shopping Mall

A text list of Internet-accessible businesses that is periodically posted to **Usenet** (news.answers) and is widely available via **FTP**. To be included on the list, a business must make both information and ordering available by means of the Internet. Currently listed are businesses that sell software, books, compact disks, and flower delivery.

Internet Society (ISOC)

An international, non-profit professional organization, founded in January 1992, that is broadly concerned with fostering international cooperation for the promotion of the Internet and its internetworking technology. Membership is open to all. The organization's headquarters are in Reston, Virginia.

The Internet Society seeks to maintain and enhance the Internet's proven system of researching and publishing protocols; to deal with the short-term and mid-range technical challenges facing the Internet as it experiences exponential growth; to address the long-range issues of how the Internet will contribute to the twenty-first century's information infrastructure; to maintain effective administrative organizations required for the effective operation of the Internet on a global scale; and to provide educational materials and activities.

Governed by a Board of Trustees with 18 eminent individuals, most of whom were Internet pioneers, ISOC's many working committees include the **Internet Architecture Board (IAB)**, which approves membership in the **Internet Engineering Steering Group (IESG)**. The IESG in turn supervises the activities of the **Internet Engineering Task**

Force (IETF), which deals with short- and medium-range technical challenges, and the **Internet Research Task Force (IRTF)**, which addresses long-range issues.

Internet Talk Radio

A non-profit Internet service that distributes an Internet "radio show," in the form of a sound file that you can play on a Macintosh, IBM PC, or UNIX computer equipped with a sound board.

Founded by Carl Malamud, Internet Talk Radio addresses the information overload that comes from getting hundreds of electronic mail messages every week—with that kind of reading load, there isn't time to read electronic newsletters. Internet Talk Radio is different. With a computer powerful enough to run more than one program at a time, you can play the radio file in the background while you're doing other work.

And what do you hear? A professional production modeled on National Public Radio's *All Things Considered*. In fact, Internet Talk Radio carries NPR broadcasts that concern technology and computing. A very popular feature: Geek of the Week, an interview with a prominent member of the Internet community. Internet Talk Radio already has an audience of more than 100,000 regular listeners.

Malamud's experiment is the leading edge of an entirely new kind of communications medium, a **multicast** medium instead of a **broadcast** medium: It employs the **Multicast Backbone (MBONE)** protocol to distribute audio and video in **real time**. In the future, thanks to **integrated services networks**, people will be able to choose what they want to hear and when they want to hear it. You'll be able to sit at your computer and design your own afternoon of radio. Let's say you're on your way to Mexico. You can start with the sights of Mexico City, learn more about the Aztecs, and get the low-down on Cozumel. And why not brush up on your Spanish?

Tip: To find out how to retrieve Internet Talk Radio files, send an electronic mail message to *info@radio.com*.

Internet Worm

A well-publicized 1988 incident in which a *worm*, a self-propagating program that tries to spread itself through a network, overloaded the Internet and crashed thousands of Internet **hosts**.

The program was written by Robert Morris, Jr., then a graduate student in computer science at Cornell University and the son of an expert on computer security who works at the National Security Agency. Morris ostensibly wrote the program to test a problem with the protocols used to transport network mail. Morris claimed that the program simply got out of hand and that he had never intended to cause harm.

The program replicated itself so quickly that it brought down the machines it infected, causing damages that were estimated to range from $200 to as much as $50,000. To defend themselves from the worm, sites were forced to disconnect themselves from the Internet, and in consequence did not receive Morris's anonymous letter explaining how to counteract the program. Morris was subsequently convicted under the **Computer Fraud and Abuse Act of 1986**. He was sentenced to 3 years of probation, 400 hours of community service, and a $10,000 fine.

internetworking

The linking of two or more dissimilar networks, consisting of computers made by many different manufacturers, by means of **protocols** (rules) that allow the networks to exchange data. By far the most popular internetworking protocols are **TCP/IP**.

InterNIC

A consortium of three organizations that provide networking information services to the **NSFNET** community, under contract to the **National Science Foundation (NSF)**. These organizations provide the three areas of service: networking information (General Atomics), directory and database services (AT&T), and network registration (Networking Solutions, Inc.).

Interop

An annual trade show, organized by Interop Company of Foster City, California, that has become a showcase for Internet technology.

interoperability

The ability of software or hardware designed for two different computing environments, and probably manufactured by two different vendors, to communicate and perform tasks.

Interpedia

A cooperatively-written, public-domain encyclopedia, still in the planning stages at this writing, that will be accessible via the Internet.

Originally conceived by Rick Gates, the creator of the **Internet Hunt**, the Interpedia concept has taken on a more ambitious goal: It is now conceived as a **hypertext** system that could link the articles with other Internet resources, including on-going discussions. In this way the Interpedia would

grow in complexity, depth, and value as more people coop-
eratively add hypertext-linked information to the existing
text. In keeping with the general push to develop multimedia
resources for the Internet, the encyclopedia is planned to
include sounds, animations, and video as well as hypertext-linked text. This project perfectly captures the spirit of
the Internet—that is, that it can serve as the platform for the
social creation and *exponential growth* of *freely-accessi-
ble* public knowledge.

Current plans call for the project to begin with a published
encyclopedia that is in the public domain, but debate continues regarding the means of access; some argue for
Gopher, others for **World Wide Web**, and still others for
the creation of an Interpedia-specific **browser** with capabilities
suited to the encylopedic nature of the text. In the meantime,
a more traditional approach to the online provision of encyclopedia resources—one that doesn't allow readers to contribute articles—is under developmet by the publishers of
the *Encyclopedia Brittanica*.

Tip: To keep tabs on this worthy project, request a subscription from the Interpedia mailing-list by sending a
message to *interpedia-request@telerama.lm.com*. The
body of the message should contain the the word 'subscribe' and your email address, as in this example:

```
subscribe your_userame@your.host.domain
```

Don't look for the Interpedia any time soon; at this stage, it's
not clear whether, as one critic (Jim Croft) puts it, "it's an idea,
a dream, a vision, a project, an indulgence, an organization,
a movement, an anarchy, a juggernaut, a conspiracy, a
hegemony, a political posture, a social statement, self abuse,
a cause in search of rebels, rebels looking for a cause, or all
of the above."

inverted file

A computer file that contains all the significant words (usually excluding single-letter words and common prepositions) that are found in all the items contained in a **database**. When you perform a **key word search**, the search software consults the inverted file rather than the items themselves, so the search proceeds quickly. **WAIS** servers construct inverted files of the documents contained in a WAIS-accesible database.

IP

See **Internet Protocol (IP).**

IP address

A unique number (such as *128.252.135.4*) that precisely identifies the location of an Internet **host**. This number may include information that specifies the exact location of a host on a **local area network (LAN)** that is connected to the Internet. Synonymous with **dot address**.

You don't normally see this number or use it; instead, you use the **host name** (such as *watt.seas.virginia.edu*), which is easier for people to type and remember. At every host, a database maintained by system utilities keeps a record of the link between host names and IP addresses. The use of the host name allows a system administrator to move the actual physical location of a host without forcing users to learn a new address; all that is required is a simple change to the database that links host names to physical IP addresses.

IP router

One of two basic physical devices that can be connected to the Internet (the other is a **host**). This device, a **router** that is designed to work with the **Internet Protocol (IP)**, sends **datagrams**—the basic units of data transfer—to another host on a network to which the router is physically connected.

IRC

See **Internet Relay Chat (IRC).**

iron box

A customized **host** that is intended to bait, and trap, a **cracker** bent on unauthorized access. *See* **Cuckoo's Egg, firewall.**

ISDN

See **Integrated Services Digital Network (ISDN).**

ITU-TSS

Acronym for International Telecommunications Union-Telecommunications Standardization Section, the successor to the **Comité Consultif International de Télégraphique et Téléphonique (CCITT)**.

joe account

In a multiuser **UNIX** system, an **account** in which the user has, for the sake of convenience, used his or her own first name for a **password**. Joe accounts pose a serious threat to system security because **crackers** can use them to gain **unauthorized access** to a computer system.

John von Neumann Computer Network (JvNCnet)

A regional **T1** network that was one of the original components of the **NSFNET** (prior to its upgrade to **T3** connectivity). Now operated by Global Enterprise Services, Inc., a member of the **Commercial Internet Exchange (CIX)**, JvNCnet provides Internet connectivity in the northeastern U.S. to commercial, educational, research, and government organizations.

Joint Photographic Experts Group (JPEG) graphics format

A **lossy compression** technique for graphics images that is gaining widespread acceptance in the Internet community.

JPEG achieves greater compression than can be obtained with lossless techniques—you can compress a 2 MB file to 100K or less. The technique pulls this trick off by destroying some of the visual information, beyond recovery. But you'll never know it. JPEG exploits the known limitations of the human eye, especially the fact that we don't notice small color changes as much as changes in brightness.

The colors may be slightly altered, but they're far richer than those of the competing graphics standard, Graphics Interchange Format (GIF). JPEG graphics can store 24-bit color information, for a total of more than 16 million colors. GIF, in contrast, can store only 256 colors. GIF graphics may have been acceptable for yesterday's graphics hardware and monitors, but JPEG can take advantage of the high-resolution displays that are increasingly common in middle-of-the-run personal computers.

JPEG

See **Joint Photographics Experts Group (JPEG) graphics format.**

Jughead

In **Gopher**, a search **client** that scans an automatically-compiled index of titles for all the **directory titles** that can be retrieved in **gopherspace**, the world of information accessible to a Gopher **client**. The items include **directory titles** only, and do *not* include the resources (such as files, programs, or graphics) appearing on Gopher submenus. The result of a Jughead search is a Gopher-like menu, which you can use to access the listed directories. *Compare* **Veronica**.

Tip: If you're planning a Veronica search, start with Jughead instead. Because it retrieves directory titles only, you'll see a shorter list of items—and it's very likely that the information you're looking for has been grouped in a Gopher directory somewhere.

jump

In a **hypertext** system such as the **World Wide Web (WWW)**, to move from one document to a related document by selecting an **anchor** (a boldfaced or underlined word or phrase) and choosing the command that makes the jump.

In **Usenet,** to mark an article as read before you actually reach the end of it. Junking the article ensures that the **news-reader** software will remove it from the **subject selector** and **thread selector** lists.

In Usenet, one of several **alternative Usenet hierarchies** that are carried and propagated only by those Usenet sites that elect to do so (in contrast to **world newsgroups**, which are automatically fed to every Usenet subscriber). The K12Net **newsgroups** are **gatewayed** from the K12Net system, a **store-and-forward** system based on late night, long-distance telephone-based propagation via **FidoNet**. The Usenet versions of these newsgroups offer discussions that will prove exceptionally valuable to anyone interested in education from the kindergarten level through the 12th grade. Newsgroups focus on virtually every aspect of schooling, including arts and crafts, business, computers, health and physical education, life skills, language arts, mathematics, music, science, social studies, compensatory education, talented and gifted education, foreign languages, and casual discussion for students and teachers alike.

The K12Net is a loose, decentralized confederation of school-based **bulletin board systems (BBS)** throughout North America, Australia, Europe, and the nations of the former Soviet Union. Using store-and-forward techniques and the long-distance telephone system, messages posted on one BBS's newsgroups eventually propagate throughout the system. They eventually find their way to Usenet, where they become accessible to Internet users. Founded in 1990, K12Net is experiencing the explosive growth that is characteristic of decentralized public access systems; the K12Net has the additional benefit of not requiring expensive hardware (virtually any PC or Macintosh equipped with a modem can become a FidoNet node). Increasingly, K12 BBS systems are becoming **freenets** by forging links with the Internet.

Kbps

Abbreviation for kilobits per second; approximately one thousand **bits per second**. *See* **data transfer rate**.

Kermit

A **file transfer protocol** for use with **modems** that allows two computers to exchange data reliably by means of **dialup access**. Unlike the file transfer protocols commonly used in personal computing (**Xmodem, Ymodem**, and **Zmodem**), Kermit is designed to deal with the problems that arise if one of the linked computers uses the 7-bit ASCII code, commonly used on mainframe computers, while the other one uses the 8-bit **extended character set** used with PCs. The protocol transmits data in variable-length blocks with **error checking** by means of a **checksum**. Enhancements to the original protocol include data **compression** and the ability to send data in long-length packets of 1,024 bytes.

kernel

In **UNIX**, the **operating system** used on many Internet **hosts**, the core portion of the operating system that performs the nitty-gritty tasks of managing system resources such as memory, disk drives, peripherals, and applications, as well as the timing and sharing problems that arise when more than one user is logged on to the system. *Compare* **shell.**

key

In **encryption**, the technique that is used to encipher the **plaintext** message so that it appears to be gibberish. **Decryption** (decoding the **ciphertext**) requires the possession of the key. However, a problem arises here: There must be some secure means for the sending party to give the key to the receiving party. Banks and other institutions that make heavy use of encryption send the key via couriers. Recent developments, however, have made it possible for two parties to exchange encrypted messages without previously exchanging keys. *See* **public key cryptography**.

key word

A word that describes either the special content of a file or document or the topic it shares in common with other, related documents. Key words are used to aid information retrieval in **databases, FTP,** and **WAIS** searches. A good list of key words includes both types of key words. For example, the key words chosen to describe a Microsoft Windows utility program that installs humorous icons should include Windows, utility, icons, and humorous.

key word search

In a computerized information retrieval system, such as **WAIS**, a quest that employs **key words** as a means of matching the searcher's interests to the documents, files, or items stored in the **database**. For example, if you're interested in items related to Arizona, you use the name of this state as a key word in your search. Most Internet search programs, including **Veronica**, permit you to combine key words through the use of **Boolean operators** (AND, OR, and NOT).

kill

In **Usenet**, to exclude certain subjects, words, phrases, or specific individuals from the list of **articles** displayed on your screen.

Usenet is a wide-open public arena for discussion, and as you might expect, it's very difficult to read Usenet without getting shocked, annoyed, and sometimes deeply angry about the things people post. (I don't want to give any examples here—if I do, I'll get so angry I won't be able to write the rest of this entry!) The knee-jerk response is to write a **follow-on posting** that **flames** the original post, but if you do, you're very likely to find yourself on the wrong end of a **mail bombing** that singles you out as an enemy of free expression. Usenet very much embodies the Libertarian ideal that if something shocks you, the proper course of action is simply to stop reading it, rather to call for a massive societal campaign to punish offending writers and to prevent others from judging for themselves.

Happily, there is a simple and very effective solution to the problem of offensive or juvenile postings: the **kill file**. With a kill file, you can exclude certain words, subjects, **threads**, or even specific individual posters, so that you will never again see messages of the type that angered you.

Do learn how to use the kill commands for your specific **newsreader**. You should be able to kill in a number of ways. You can even set up a **global kill file** so that the offending words, phrases, subjects, or posters never appear in any of the **newsgroups** you read.

Don't flame those who post **cascades**, **trolls**, **flames**, and other offensive or juvenile messages; they're trying to get attention so that they can imagine their meaningless lives to have some significance. By ignoring them, you deny the very thing they want.

| kill file |

In **Usenet**, a file that a **newsreader** program uses to exclude unwanted **articles** so that they do not appear in the **newsgroups** you read. When you start the newsreader, the program consults the file, and uses it to mark as read the articles that contain unwanted material. For this reason, these articles do not appear in subject or thread lists.

Usenet is a wide-open forum for public discussion. Unfortunately, Usenet's value is much diminished by the behavior of juvenile, obnoxious, or opportunistic people who exploit the community's openness. The proper weapon against such people is the kill file.

Most newsreaders allow you to kill at two levels: within a particular newsgroup (see **newsgroup kill file**) or all newsgroups (see **global kill file**). Read your newsreader's documentation carefully to learn how to kill messages at both levels.

You can kill unwanted postings in several ways. You can kill a particular subject, an obnoxious individual, all the postings from a particular site, any **crossposted** article, and all **follow-on postings**. In addition, you can kill any article that contains any word or phrase you specify.

Do create a kill file and add to it constantly. Every time you come across an article that contains material you do not wish to see again, add new lines to your kill file.

 Don't get involved in **flame wars** or post replies to juvenile or obnoxious postings. This will only encourage them to continue their behavior.

knowbot

An independent, self-acting computer program that seeks for information on behalf of a user, possibly replicating itself on other **hosts** on the network. As the knowbot performs its task, it sends reports back to the user, and self-destructs when it completes its task.

Knowbot Information Service

A **resource discovery tool** that employs **knowbots** (independent programs that act on the user's behalf) to find information. To hunt for a person's **electronic mail address**, for example, a knowbot will access multiple computer sites and **white pages** databases.

LAN

See **local area network (LAN).**

last mile problem

The sole remaining technical barrier to the development of a **National Information Infrastructure (NII)**, namely, the problem of how to deliver high-**bandwidth** digital networking to homes, schools, and offices. An infrastructure of high-bandwidth **backbone** networks already exists, but the only existing means of connecting these networks to homes, schools, and offices, is the local telephone system, which does not possess sufficient bandwidth to support an **integrated services network** capable of delivering **multimedia**.

About 60% of U.S. homes have two last-mile delivery systems, a **twisted pair** telephone line and an analog **coaxial cable** that provides cable television. Since it is very unlikely that any of the current telecommunications players would contemplate the massive capital investment required to extend **fiber optic** or other high-bandwidth cables to millions of service delivery points, the interim solution to the last mile problem will very likely involve converting local telephones to digital signalling or modifying cable TV systems to permit two-way exchanges of computer data.

With established service to 98% of U.S. households, the telephone system offers excellent penetration. The technical problem lies in the limited bandwidth of the **twisted pair** wires that provide service delivery to the home. The existing **analog** telephone system can carry computer signals by means of a **modem**, but modems in common use today achieve data transmission speeds of only 14.4 Kbps. By the early twenty-first century, the telephone system will convert to **digital** signalling employing the **ISDN** standards, which will permit the simultaneous use of an existing twisted-pair cable for noise-free voice as well as 64Kbps data exchange. This is an improvement over the current system, but the limited bandwidth is insufficient for envisioned applications such as **high definition television (HDTV)** and **distributed computing**. With an estimated capital investment of $130 billion in twisted pair installations, telephone companies are very unlikely to contemplate upgrading their last-mile delivery system, which contains enough wire to run to the moon and back several hundred times. Replacing all of this wire with fiber optic cables would require the largest capital investments in human history. One conclusion: Don't expect a fiber optic cable to show up at your house anytime soon.

In contrast to the telephone system with its huge capital investment in antiquated cabling, cable TV systems currently bring high-bandwidth **coaxial cable** close to 97% of U.S. homes, and provide service to more than 60% of these homes. But these systems were designed with a **broadcast model** of transmission, in which signals emanate from the central office and travel to home TV sets in one direction only. Interim technical solutions allow computer data to traverse cable TV networks to specific TV sets, but are heavily biased toward data delivery. Providing enough upstream bandwidth to realize NII goals and to implement a **communication model** may require the extension of a second coaxial cable to each service recipient.

A likely outcome of the last mile problem is a series of mergers between the **regional bell operating companies (RBOCs)** and cable TV companies; in this way, a telephone company could acquire the last mile delivery system that it needs to implement integrated digital services, while at the same time cable TV companies could acquire the expertise and switching systems that they would need to offer local telephone service.

latency

In a **packet switching network**, the delay that occurs as transmitted data travels through a series of **routers** en route to its destination. Latency is one reason that packet switching networks such as the Internet are poor choices for the real-time delivery of voice and video; latency introduces unde-sirable gaps.

---

layer

In a computer network, a set of **protocols** (standards) that handle a certain class of events, such as handling the details of transferring data reliably through a point-to-point line. *See* **Open Systems Interconnection (OSI) Reference Model.**

Thinking of a computer network as layered allows design-ers to use Caesar's "Divide and Conquer" philosophy— tackle one layer at a time, and design protocols (as well as programs that implement them) that deal with one layer and do it well. Once the layers have been divided concep-tually, designers then create standards so that each layer can hand off data to the next layer in an orderly, predictable way.

From the user's viewpoint, it's helpful to think of each com-puter on the Internet as if it were a layer cake (the fancy term is **protocol stack**). At the top of the stack is the **application layer**. An application creates some data, and passes it down the stack to the **transport layer**, where it's prepared for transmission, and to the **network layer**, where it's shot out of the computer and on to the network. There, the **data link layer** makes sure that the data doesn't get scrambled as it traverses the **physical layer**—the actual wires, fibers, and cables.

When the data arrives at its destination, it goes back up the stack in a reverse of the process that sent the data out. The network layer receives the data, passing it up to the stack to the transport layer and finally to the correct application.

League for Programming Freedom (LPF)

An informal organization, The League for Programming Freedom is a grass-roots organization that seeks to recov-

L

er the freedom of computer programmers to create programs as they wish. They contend this freedom has been lost over the last two decades due to the unwise policy of allowing software patents and the profit-inspired actions of major software publishers to protect the "look and feel" of their user interfaces. The organization's headquarters are in Cambridge, Massachusetts.

leased line

A permanently-connected telephone line that links an Internet **host** to a **service provider**, an organization that provides connections to the Internet. Typically, leased lines can handle between 56,000 and 64,000 bits per second of data, which is enough to handle a minicomputer or a small **local area network (LAN)**. Larger host systems require **T1** lines (1.544 Mbps, sufficient for a larger LAN) or **T3** lines (45 Mbps, used for large corporations or universities).

leeched line

Slang expression for an easy method of Internet access available to users of personal computers linked in a **local area network (LAN)**. If the LAN is directly connected to the Internet, you can equip your computer with the necessary TCP/IP software and **client** programs (such as **Eudora** or **Mosaic**), and your computer quickly and easily becomes a full-fledged Internet **host**.

light emitting diode (LED)

A type of semiconductor (a wafer of silicon that is doped with impurities to give it specific electronic properties) that emits light when current is applied to it. In computer networking, LEDs provide one of the alternative light sources for **fiber optic** cables.

line eater

A bug in an early version of a **Usenet** program designed for reading network news (called a **newsreader**) that caused the last line of a posting to disappear. This is the source of some of the net's **urban folklore**: That the U.S. National Security Agency has a sophisticated program that automatically scans Usenet postings for seditious material and deletes it.

line editor

In a networking **application**, a primitive text editing utility that allows the user to edit only one line of text at a time. This is sufficient for simple **command-line** utilities such as **Archie** or **Telnet**.

line mode terminal

A computer **terminal** that is designed to one line at a time; you type commands on a line (*see* **command-line interface**), and the terminal responds with one-line confirmation and error messages. *See* **Network Virtual Terminal (NVT), page mode terminal, Telnet**.

line noise

In a physical network link such as a telephone line, any extraneous or random signal introduced by interference of many possible kinds, such as telephone company switching operations, lightning storms, crosstalk between adjacent lines, or current fluctuations. Line noise can corrupt transmitted data, forcing retransmissions.

link

In a **hypertext** document, a connection that is established with another document that contains related materials by means of connected **anchors** placed in both documents. When the user selects the anchor, the system displays the corresponding anchor in the linked document.

LISTSERV

In **BITNET**, **EARN**, and other **NJE** systems, a **mailing list** utility program That automatically distributes mailing lists on a wide variety of subjects. Anyone who can send electronic mail to a LISTSERV location—and that includes Internet users—can contribute messages to a LISTSERV mailing list and receive copies of all the messages that are contributed.

Tip: If your Internet **host** receives **Usenet**, you may already have access to as many as several dozen of the most popular LISTSERV mailing lists. *See* **bit hierarchy**.

little endian

A computer system (such as most minicomputers and personal computers) designed to store data with the least significant bit at the beginning of a unit of data, in contrast to **big endian** computers, in which the most significant bit comes first. *See* **holy war**.

local

Peculiar to the physical characteristics and properties of a particular network. As applied to computer networks in general and the Internet in particular, this term is not necessarily synonymous with limited geographic breadth (although most **local area networks [LANS]** rarely extend more than a mile or two). Rather, the term refers to the peculiar characteristics (for example, of **addressing**) within the confines of a particular network. In this sense, a satellite network capable of spanning the globe geographically is "local" in that it has peculiar characteristics that have to be taken into account when linking the system to the Internet. The bridge between the Internet and local networks is provided by the **network access layer**. *See* **Autonomous System (AS)**.

local area network (LAN)

A computer network that links personal computers and workstations within a limited geographic area, such as a building or several contiguous buildings.

Linked by cables such as **coaxial cable** or **twisted pair**, the computers connected to the LAN can access resources on other computers (such as files) and shared peripheral devices (such as fax modems or printers); this is one of the primary reasons for creating a LAN. Unlike a mainframe system linked to terminals that lack their own processing and storage capabilities, a LAN is a peer-to-peer network. Each of the linked computers' users has the right to determine who, and under what circumstances, other users can access files on their own computer. If there is a central network device, it is a **file server** that includes resources (such as applications and a shared database) of use to all.

To keep two workstations from trying to access the LAN at the same time, a problem called **contention,** LANs employ a **Medium Access Control (MAC) protocol.** The first successful MAC protocol for LANs, called **Ethernet**, issued from research undertaken in the 1970s at Xerox Corporation's Palo Alto Research Center (PARC), which was responsible for several key computer innovations (including the mouse, laser printer, and **graphical user interface**). The Ethernet's contention control (MAC) protocol is called **Car-**

rier Sense Multiple Access with Collision Detection (CSMA/CD), and found expression in a standard called IEEE 802.3. More recent MAC protocols include token bus and token ring approaches.

The histories of the Internet and of local area networking are more closely intertwined than most people realize. The ARPANET's pioneering packet switching architecture inspired the PARC scientists, who designed the Ethernet protocols so that PCs and workstations could send their own packets through the network, circulating at speeds of up to 10 Mbps. Each packet contained an address that specified its destination. With this architecture, it became feasible to "translate" Ethernet packets to the Internet protocol (IP) format, so that they could reach Internet destinations beyond the bounds of the LAN. To create the necessary physical and logical bridges to the Internet, ARPANET and industry designers created special routers and translation protocols, called the Address Resolution Protocol (ARP) and Reverse Address Resolution Protocol (RARP).

The Internet's phenomenal growth has been paired with equally impressive growth in local area networking—a fact that isn't surprising, once it's realized that the two are linked developments. With a growing market, the prices of the necessary equipment—network interface cards, routers, file servers, and cable—continue to plummet. Today, an organization contemplating a direct connection to the Internet can do so more cheaply by creating a LAN (see toast-ernet) than by buying a UNIX-based minicomputer.

Within an organization, physically separate LANs can be linked by means of devices called bridges, forming an extended network that can span an entire university or corporation. Bridges linked by wide area network (WAN) connections can effectively break the LAN's geographic restrictions, so that a distant branch office's LAN can appear to users as if it were geographically next door.

local client

An Internet client program, such as **Archie** or **Gopher**, that's available on your **host** system.

Do use a local client, if one is available, before trying to access a **remote client**. The use of a local client lessens the strain on the Internet's **bandwidth** resources because the client can do much of its work by consulting locally-stored databases. For example, every **Gopher** client site maintains an automatically-updated list of the items available in **Gopherspace**.

local loop

The **twisted pair** wire that runs from your telephone to the local telephone company's central office. Employing **analog** transmission technology that was designed to accommodate the human voice (but not computer data), these wires have limited **bandwidth** for computer data communications (56 Kbps is a frequently-cited theoretical maximum with analog technology). A **modem** is required to transmit computer signals via the local loop.

Tip: If you're accessing the Internet via **dialup access** or **dialup IP**, you'll need a fast modem. But before running out and buying a 28.8 Kbps modem, make sure that your **host** is prepared to accept communications at that speed. If not, your modem will **fall back** to a lower speed. Most hosts can accommodate a 9.6 Kbps modem, and growing numbers can deal with a 14.4 Kbps modem.

local newsgroup

In **Usenet**, a **newsgroup** that is maintained only on the local **host** and is not intended for further distribution. At the University of Virginia, for example, the uva hierarchy includes several local newsgroups of interest to Uva faculty, staff, and students.

log off

To end your connection with an Internet **host** computer. If you're using **Telnet**, you log off by typing *exit* and pressing *Enter*.

log on

To make a connection with an Internet **host** computer by typing your **login name** and **password**.

logical network

A physically heterogeneous collection of networks, which nevertheless appears to the user to be a single network because all of its devices seem to operate in the same or much the same way. The Internet, which in fact integrates more than 25,000 distinct networks, appears to its users as if it were a single network in which the same commands and utilities operate throughout.

login name

The name you type as part of the procedure you use to log on to a network. In many (but not all) Internet **host** systems, your login name is the same as the name used for your **mailbox** in electronic mail.

lossless compression

A method of data **compression,** used with program and data files, that seeks to preserve all of the original data without alteration. Lossless compression techniques are used in **file compression programs** such as the UNIX **compress** program.

lossy compression

A method of data **compression**, used with graphics and video files, that sacrifices some loss of the data in ways that are not apparent to a person who is viewing or listening to the file after it has been transmitted.

LPMUD

A combat-oriented **MUD** (a multi-user computerized role-playing game) that includes an object-oriented programming language. This language can be used by **wizards** (game adepts), but not players, to modify and extend the perceived space within the game. LPMUD is named after Lars Penjii, a Scandanavian computer scientist who wrote the game as part of his doctoral issertation. This is the most popular combat-oriented MUD.

ls

One of the essential **UNIX** commands for Internet users, ls displays the contents of a **directory**. Many directories contain dozens or even hundreds of files. To display a directory one screen at a time, you type the following and press **Enter**.

```
ls |more
```

lurk

In **Usenet**, to read a **newsgroup** regularly without posting anything. Such a reader is called a lurker. On occasion, a lurker **delurks** by posting a message containing a public admission of previous lurking.

LYNX

A **client** for the **World Wide Web** that provides **hypertext** capabilities for users of text-based terminals (such as **VT100**). Created by Lou Montoulli of the University of Kansas, LYNX is available for a variety of **UNIX** systems. The program is exceptionally easy to use. To navigate the Web's hypertext links, you use the up or down arrow keys to select a link, and press *Enter* or the right arrow key to jump to the next document. LYNX also incorporates **key word searching** and the ability to display a history list of the jumps you've made.

mail body

The content part of an **electronic mail** message, as opposed to the mail **header**, which lists the source, destination, subject, and additional information.

mail bombing

A form of **email terrorism** in which a person inundates another's electronic mailbox with huge, lengthy files on random subjects. On many systems, this is considered sufficient grounds to **squelch** the offender's account.

mail bridge

A **gateway** that translates **electronic mail** messages from one network's format to another network's format. Mail bridges greatly expand the Internet's reach: Internet users can exchange mail with users of many networks that do not use TCP/IP, such as **BITNET** and **CompuServe**.

mail exploder

A program that makes a **mailing list** possible by forwarding copies of a message to every member of the list. *Synonymous* with **mail reflector.**

mail reflector

A program that makes a **mailing list** possible by forwarding copies of a message to every member of the list. *Synonymous with* **mail exploder.**

mail server

A program that sends you information in response to an electronic mail request.

mailbox

In **electronic mail**, a named storage location on your **host** system that receives your mail. When you log on to this computer, you see a message that tells you whether you've received any new mail. You can then read this mail with an electronic mail client, such as **Pine** or **Elm**.

mailbox name

One of the two basic parts of an Internet electronic mail address, the part to the left of the @ sign that signifies the name of the individual, group, or organization that receives the mail. The other part is called the **host name** (the name of the Internet **host** on which the mailbox has been created). The two parts are separated by an @ sign (pronounced "at sign"), as follows:

mailbox-name@host-name

A (fictitious) example of an electronic mail address is the following:

esmith@eeyore.zeppelin.com

mailing list

A discussion group that has been organized by means of electronic mail. Contributions to the newsgroup are sent via **electronic mail** to the list's manager, who forwards the messages to the **mailboxes** of everyone who has subscribed to the mailing list. To subscribe, you send electronic mail to the list manager, who puts you on the list.

Don't subscribe to too many mailing lists or you'll be sorry—the messages come to your electronic mailbox and tend to hide the important, personal messages you receive.

mainframe computer

A large computer system, dubbed "big iron" in computer slang, that is specifically designed to be able to handle all of the data processing needs of a large corporation, such as calculating and printing payroll checks, tracking clients' accounts and issuing bills, and providing timely reports to management regarding the status of the firm's finances.

Mainframe computer systems permit as many as several hundred people to use them simultaneously. The mainframe computer market has long been dominated by IBM, which employs an **operating system** and a character set (called **EBCDIC**) that is not directly compatible with most of the computers linked on the Internet. *Compare* **BITNET, minicomputer, personal computer, Network Job Entry (NJE), workstation**.

Are mainframes about to go the way of the dinosaur? Mainframes face stiff competition from the model of distributed computing, in which computing power—in the form of minicomputers, workstations, and personal computers—is given directly to the people who need it. Should those people need to share resources and exchange information, computer **networks** can do the job. Even so, many firms find good reason to retain mainframes for the tasks they were designed to perform, such as cranking out payroll checks.

---

malicious use

The use of a computer network with the intention to harass other users, invade their privacy, impede their work, or destroy useful resources.

Malicious use is unfortunately common. In a system that attracts as many as 15 million users, it's not surprising that some individuals just don't seem to grasp the Internet's underlying moral principle: through cooperation and the pooling of shared resources, everyone wins. But perhaps they understand this perfectly well, and something inside them— their own self-hatred, probably—makes them want to reach out and try to smash it. Whatever the cause, malicious use is with us—and it's on the rise.

Do report any signs of suspicious activity. If you find yourself thinking, "Gee, I thought that file was there," or "That's funny, I don't remember putting that program in this directory," *call your network administrator imme-diately.*

man

Abbreviation for manual pages, a **UNIX** resource that displays the pages of software manuals on-screen.

Tip: Having trouble with a UNIX program, such as **EMACS**? Try typing *man* followed by a space and the name of the program you need help with, as in the following example:

```
man emacs
```

After you press **Enter**, you'll see the manual on-screen; it's displayed with the **more** utility, which lets you page through the manual one screenful at a time.

markup language

In an **electronic text** that is made available for computer access, a standard set of marking characters, called **tags**, that describe the various parts of a document and formats such as fonts and paragraph indents or alignments. The purpose of a markup language is to enable the display of complex documents, replete with formatting, fonts, and other typographic features, on virtually any brand of display or printing device. The term is derived from typography, in which a document was "marked up" with typographical instructions before being sent to the printer.

Why is a markup language necessary? The Internet links many incompatible systems; one of the few common denominators linking them is their ability to transfer and display **ASCII** text. A markup language uses ASCII codes to indicate the various parts of a document, as in the following example (note that the tags <Q> and <A> indicate "Question" and "Answer"):

```
<Q>What is a markup language?

<A> A standard set of marking characters,
called tags, that describe the various parts of
a document...
```

One significant drawback to a marked-up document is its cluttered on-screen appearance when viewed as ASCII text. To see what the document *should* look like, you need to view it using a **parser** (a program that interprets the tags, removes them, and displays the document with fonts, formatting, and other typographical features).

Markup languages fall into two categories, **declarative markup languages** (such as **SGML** and **HTML**) and **procedural markup languages** (such as **PostScript**). A declarative markup language merely indicates ("declares") the parts of the document; a procedural language includes instructions that tell the computer how to display or print the document. Declarative markup languages in turn fall into two categories: Some languages (such as Rich Text Format [RTF]) are devoted to the description of specific document formats (such as a specific font and font size), while others are generalized, indicating only the name of the document part and leaving the actual formatting decisions up to the parser. SGML is the standard generalized markup language used for **electronic texts** in the Internet community, while HTML is the standard generalized markup language for **hypertext** documents contributed to the **World Wide Web (WWW)**.

Maximum Transmission Unit (MTU)

In a **packet switching network** such as the Internet, the maximum size of the data **packet** that can be transferred via the network's high-speed communications links. Often, a message exceeds the MTU and must be broken down, in a process called **fragmentation**, into two or more acceptably-sized packets. The packets are reassembled at their destination.

Mbps

Abbreviation for megabits per second; approximately one million **bits per second**. *See* **data transfer rate.**

Medium Access Control (MAC)

In the **Open Systems Interconnection (OSI) Reference Model** of computer networking, a sublayer that was added between the **physical layer** and the **data link layer**. This sublayer describes the protocols for **broadcast networks**, such as **local area networks (LANs)** and **metropolitan area networks (MANs)**.

Most Internet and other **wide area networks (WANs)** are **point-to-point networks**. In contrast, most LANs employ broadcasting: the signals go to all the computers on the network. This doesn't mean that all the data appears on all the workstations; computers other than the one to which the message is addressed just ignore the message. The problem that must be solved by MAC protocols, however, is how to handle a situation in which more than one workstation starts transmitting at the same time (*see* **contention**). A widely-used protocol for this purpose is **Carrier Sense Multiple Access with Collision Detection (CSMA/CD)**.

meme plague

In **Usenet,** an annoying series of postings by people who have been snared by what sociobiologist Richard Dawkins calls a *meme*: An idea that serves few other purposes than to replicate itself. In Dawkins' view, conversion-oriented religious cults provide excellent examples of memes in action.

menu-driven interface

A design for handling the interaction between the user and the computer that presents options in on-screen menus, from which the user may select a desired option by highlighting the option in reverse video and pressing Enter (or by clicking the option with the mouse, if the system supports the use of a mouse). Menu-driven interfaces are considerably easier to use than **command-line interfaces,** which require the user to remember complicated rules and type commands with precision. *Compare* **graphical user interface (GUI).**

Message Transfer Agent (MTA)

In **electronic mail,** a local program that relays electronic mail messages created by electronic mail **clients.** *See* **sendmail.**

Message-Oriented Text Interchange System (MOTIS)

A set of standards for the improvement of **electronic mail** that was adopted by **OSI** in 1988. MOTIS is rapidly gaining acceptance and will influence the future evolution of Internet mail.

The Internet's **Simple Mail Transfer Protocol (SMTP)** does not support a variety of features that would make electronic mail easier to use. For example, if you forward a message, SMTP embeds the forwarding header in the body of the message, producing at least one screen of incomprehensible gibberish (if not more) that your recipient must wade through before getting to the message. MOTIS addresses these and other common deficiencies of electronic mail systems by framing standards for the ideal electronic mail system.

A MOTIS electronic mail system has the capabilities already familiar to Internet electronic mail users, such as the ability to compose, send, receive, forward, delete, and save messages, plus a few new ones: for example, the ability to find out whether a message has been received and read and to include graphics and digitized sound.

As compared to Internet mail, however, the major MOTIS innovation is the concept of enclosing electronic mail in an "envelope" that contains all of the addressing information. This enables the system to separate information regarding delivery from the body of the message.

metropolitan area network (MAN)

A high-speed (at least 100 Mbps) network that is designed to link two or more **local area networks (LANs)** within a limited geographical region, such as a metropolitan area. A MAN can be used to connect the various offices of a government agency, a corporation, or a university.

Michigan Regional Network (MichNet)

A regional Internet **service provider** in Michigan that is operated by Merit Network, Inc., a nonprofit organization. Focusing on education and research, MichNet links universities, colleges, K–12 schools, government agencies, hospitals, and libraries, but connections are also offered to businesses throughout Michigan. Offering dialup connections from 23 Michigan cities, the network also offers direct **TCP/IP** connections at speeds of up to 1.5 Mbps and **gateways** to **public data networks** such as **SprintLink.**

Microcom Networking Protocol (MNP)

A set of **error correction** protocols (standards) for **modems**, originally developed by Microcom, Inc., that has become an important industry standard. See **MNP-5**

MNP protocols are categorized by class (class 1 through class 10), with class 10 representing the most advanced error protection. When two MNP modems communicate, they establish the highest class of error protection that the two can share, and proceed with the transmission. Class 5 through 10 protocols include data **compression** as well as error correction and permit faster data transmission; with class 5 MNP, for example, a 9600 bps modem can transfer data at 19,200 bits per second.

Microsoft Windows

An application environment for IBM and IBM-compatible computers that employs a **graphical user interface (GUI)** and that allows users to run more than one program at a time.

At this writing, it is something of an engineering feat to connect a Windows system to the Internet through anything other than **dialup access.** According to press reports, however, that may change: The new version of Windows (Windows 4) is slated to include **TCP/IP** compatibility. Industry experts estimate that Microsoft will sell 40 million copies of Windows 4.

Midwest Research and Education Network (MIDnet)

A regional Internet network and **service provider**, with headquarters in Lincoln, NE, that offers **dialup access** as well as **direct connections** in the Midwest (Arkansas, Iowa, Kansas, Missouri, Nebraska, Oklahoma, and South Dakota).

mil

In the **domain name system**, a **top-level domain** name that is assigned to a U.S. government military organization. The top-level domain name follows the last period in the site's domain name (such as darpa.mil).

mil domain

One of the **top-level** domain names in the **domain name system**, this domain includes military agencies that are part of the Department of Defense (DoD) internets, including the Defense Data Network (DDN) and the Defense Research Internet (DRI).

Military Standards (MIL STD)

A set of specifications regarding technical standards mandatorily observed by the U.S. military, including many of the core **TCP/IP protocols**. The 1983 Defense Department adoption of the TCP/IP protocols convinced makers of data communication equipment that TCP/IP had a bright future; the consequences, widespread availability of Internet-compatible equipment and falling prices, provided the kick that was necessary to launch the Internet's explosive period of growth. In January of 1988, for example, the NSFNET handled 85 million packets of data; by May of 1993, the figure had reached 6 trillion.

MIME

See **Multi-Purpose Internet Mail Extensions (MIME).**

A computer that is designed to meet the computing needs of a department or a small organization. Smaller and less powerful than **mainframe computers**, minicomputers are nevertheless much more capable than **workstations** or **personal computers**; typically, minicomputers are multi-user systems, permitting as many as several dozen people to use the computer simultaneously. Minicomputers running the **UNIX** operating system are widely used in the academic and research settings that nurtured the growth of the Internet; the proliferation of UNIX-based minicomputers throughout academia can be said to have laid the foundation for the Internet, in that the software most of these machines employed—the Berkeley version of UNIX called **Berkeley Software Distribution (BSD)**—contained the **TCP/IP** connectivity that makes the Internet possible.

Minnesota Regional Network (MRNet)

A state Internet network and **service provider**, MRNet supports education but provides unrestricted commercial access. An independent, non-profit organization with headquarters in Minneapolis, MRNet offers **dialup access,** including **dialup IP**, as well as **direct connections**.

misc

One of the seven **world newsgroup** categories in Usenet, this category includes newsgroups that do not fit into the other six categories (**comp, sci, news, rec, soc,** and **talk**). Examples include misc.consumers (a newsgroup concerning consumer issues), misc.education.adult (adult education issues), the several misc.forsale newsgroups, misc.kids.computers (discussion of computer use by children), and misc.legal.computing (focused on the legal aspects of computer use).

Missouri Research and Education Network (MOREnet)

A state Internet network and **service provider** that links state agencies, K–12 schools, colleges, research institutes, and universities throughout Missouri. Focusing on education, MOREnet also provides Internet access to businesses.

MNP5

A **file compression** protocol that is widely supported by popular modems as an alternative to **V.42bis**. MNP5 compresses outgoing data and sends it to an MNP5-compatible modem, where it is decompressed. By reducing the amount of data that has to be transmitted, MNP5 can double the **data transfer rate** of a modem.

Don't let the promise of a doubled transmission rate get you excited. Much of the information you're **downloading** from **bulletin board systems (BBS)** has already been compressed. Data that has already been compressed cannot be compressed further—and in fact, doing so may actually increase rather than decrease the size of a file.

mobile

In a **MUD** (multi-user Dungeons and Dragons game), a demon or monster that wanders through the game's cyberspace. The cooperative actions of two or more players may be required to defeat it.

A peripheral that permits your computer to communicate with other computers via the telephone system, which can't handle computer signals without modification (called **modulation**). To send signals, a modem modulates (changes) them so that they can be sent over the telephone line; it also demodulates incoming signals. The term "modem" is an abbreviation of MOdulator/DEModulator.

Why can't you just connect your computer to the telephone line directly? The telephone system wasn't designed for computer communications. It's an **analog** communication system that was designed for the human voice. When you speak into your telephone's handset, a microphone transforms your voice into a continuously fluctuating electrical current, which modifies a **carrier**—a continuos tone that you can't hear. The fluctuations mimic those of your voice. On the receiving end, the receiving phone transforms these fluctuations back into sounds.

Computers don't communicate using continuously-varying tones. In contrast, they use on-off pulses, which correspond to the basic units of digital information (**bits**). Since the phone system can't handle a computer's on-off pulses, the modem transforms these pulses into the tones that telephone lines can carry—tones that fall within the normal frequency range of the human voice (from about 100 to 3000 cycles per second). This process is called **modulation**. The modem also transforms incoming sound signals, sent from the computer at the other end of the line, back into the **digital** form your computer can recognize (this is called **demodulation**).

To communicate with each other, the modems at the sending and receiving ends of the line must obey the same **modulation protocol**, a standard that specifies the modulation method. The modulation protocol in turn determines the maximum **data transfer rate** that the modem can achieve, provided it is linked with a modem that conforms to the same protocol.

Modems are inherently slower than direct computer connections, such as those available by means of a **local area network (LAN)**. Within your computer, digital signals (broken into yes-no, off-on units of information called bits) travel side-by-side, like cars on a freeway; to get through the phone line, all those bits have to be put in a row, like cars on a one-lane road. That is why **dialup access** rules out the practical use of **front end** programs such as **Eudora** or **Mosaic**; it would take far too long to convey all that graphical information through the slow, bit-by-bit dialup link. Still, dialup users can make use of **electronic mail, Telnet, FTP, Archie, Gopher**, and other text-oriented Internet services, although to do so you must be content with using the **shell** (user interface) offered by the dialup service.

Modems will be rendered obsolete by innovations such as **ISDN** (a high-speed digital telephone system that can use existing telephone lines), cable TV systems carrying Internet as well as all those junky TV channels, and the **National Information Infrastructure (NII)**, which will extend high-speed digital communications links to homes, offices, and schools. But you'll still need devices such as a **terminal adapter (TA)** to connect your computer to these high-speed lines.

Tip: Going with the herd is always a good idea when you're considering computer communication choices—you want to be able to communicate with as many computers as possible. By this reasoning, you won't go wrong with a modem confirming to the **V.32bis** protocol, which enables communication at speeds up to 14,400 **bits per second (bps)**. On the horizon are modems conforming to the new **V.34** protocol, which will enable communication at speeds up to 28,800 bps.

In **Usenet**, a **newsgroup** in which all the **postings** are sent to a human coordinator, who screens them for conformity to the group's stated aims. As a result, moderated newsgroups show a much higher **signal-to-noise ratio** than unmoderated newsgroups—many or most of the postings are of considerable value and interest. In addition, moderated newsgroups do not share many of the shortcomings of their unmoderated counterparts, such as **carpet bombing, cascading, flame wars, meme plagues,**and **trolling**.

Some **Usenet** users mistakenly equate newsgroup moderation with censorship. But that's not the motivation. Moderated newsgroups sacrifice spontaneity for a specific and rational purpose, such as protecting the group from frequent abuse by malicious posters. For example, the newsgroup may offer informative postings that aren't intended for discussion. Some moderated newsgroups, moreover, are derived from unmoderated groups that have such a high volume of postings that it's hard for the average reader to keep up.

To post a message to a moderated newsgroup, you send it via **electronic mail** to the group's moderator. If the moderater feels that the posting isn't appropriate, you'll get it back with an explanation.

> **Tip:** Looking for the moderator's address? Sometimes you'll find the address in the moderator's **signature** that's automatically added to the bottom of each posting. If you can't find it there, check out the newsgroup net.answers for the List of Moderators for Usenet, which is posted periodically. If you still can't find it, the most recent versions of Usenet software automatically send postings to the newsgroup's moderator, so try posting your message to the group and see what happens.

moderator

In **Usenet** and **mailing lists**, a person who takes on the voluntary task of screening **postings** to make sure they conform to the group's stated aims. Some newsgroups are moderated by a committee of two or more people.

modulation

The process of transforming digital information into a varying audio tone such that the variations convey the same information. This is done by making changes to a continuous tone, called a **carrier**. The technique by which this is achieved is called a **modulation protocol**. Computer modems modulate outgoing computer signals so that they can be conveyed via the telephone system, which is designed for voice communications rather than computer signals. *Compare* **demodulation**.

modulation protocol

The standard that describes the precise technique by which a **modem** modulates (changes) digital signals into varying tones that convey information over telephone lines. The modulation protocol determines the maximum **data transfer rate** that the modem can achieve. Early modulation protocols were developed by AT&T's Bell Laboratories (*see* **Bell 103, Bell 212A**), but these found use only in North America. World-wide standards, preceded by a V as in **V.32bis**, are set by the ITU-TSS, formerly (and still popularly) known as the **Comité Consultif International de Télégraphique et Téléphonique (CCITT)**. Most modems now observe the ITU-TSS standards.

Do buy a modem that conforms to a recent ITU-TSS protocol, such as **V.32bis** (14,400 bps) or **V.34** (28,800 bps). The use of international standards has led to the explosive growth of computer networking. If you stick yourself with a modem conforming to a proprietary standard, you'll be left out.

MOO

The most recent variant of a **MUD** (a computerized, multiuser adventure game modeled on the famous Dungeons and Dragons role-playing games) to be developed, MOOs (such as the original and archetypal LambdaMOO) include a sophisticated, object-oriented programming language. This language, which is built into the game, shares many features in common with C++. For programming adepts, this language can be used to construct additions to the game—at the minimum, a new room with new, active features, and at the maximum, a new mini-environment that other players can experience. In contrast to **LPMUD**, a combat-oriented MUD that also offers an object-oriented programming language, MOOs are positively democratic in making programming tools available: Some MOOs make them available even to new users.

more

One of the essential **UNIX** command for Internet users, more—like **cat**—displays a text file's contents on-screen, but does so one screen at a time. You can press any key to continue reading the document. To display a text file with more, you type *more* followed by the name of the file, as in the following example:

```
more information-superhighway.txt
```

To see the next screen, you just press the space bar. To quit, press *q*.

Mosaic

An easy-to-use **client** program that is designed for **browsing** information available on the **World Wide Web (WWW)** and other Internet information resources. Distributed as **freeware**, Mosaic runs on Macintosh and Microsoft Windows systems, as well as UNIX workstations running **X Windows** software.

Created by the National Center for Supercomputing Applications (NCSA) in Illinois, Mosaic has been described as the Internet's "killer application" (an application so impressive that it helps to usher in widespread public use). Based on **graphical user interface (GUI)** principles, Mosaic allows the user to explore the World Wide Web's **hypertext** links with a click of the button. Suppose, for example, you're interested in whales. After typing in this word, Mosaic connects you to a server in La Jolla, California, that offers an introductory document on this topic. As you pursue more detailed information, you click on a blue-underlined phrase, "migratory patterns," and in an instant you're connected to a server in Vancouver, B.C., that offers information on this subject.

Unlike text-based **browsers** such as **Gopher**, Mosaic is fully capable of **multimedia**; you can view graphics, listen to sounds, and even view **full-motion video**. Although Mosaic is optimized for exploring the World Wide Web, the program can assist the user with other Internet-based information **servers**, such as **Gopher**, **WAIS**, and **FTP**.

Although Mosaic shows the way toward broader, public access to Internet information resources, it requires a direct connection to the Internet (or, at the minimum, a **dialup IP** connection).

Tip: If you're thinking of running Mosaic on a Windows system, note that significant system upgrades may be necessary. Although the Microsoft Windows version of Mosaic will run on a 386, the recommended configuration is a 486DX running at 33MHz with 8MB of memory. In addition, Mosaic requires software that provides Windows with **TCP/IP**-compatibility (but *see* Miscrosoft Windows).

| mount |

To open a **directory** on another computer so that it appears to be part of the directories on the user's own computer.

Motion Picture Experts Group (MPEG)

An organization affiliated with the **International Standards Organization (ISO)**that is attempting to frame standards for the digitization and compression of video images. MPEG has created a standard, colloquially called MPEG, that defines a bit stream of compressed video and audio optimized for transmission at a rate of .5 to 1.5 Mbps. The video standard isn't anything to write home about—it's up to the level of VCR, but decidedly low-resolution—but the audio standard calles for the same, noise-free quality you expect from today's audio CDs. Like JPEG, the compression standard for digitized pictures, MPEG video compression is a lossy compression technique that deletes information in ways that aren't noticed by human viewers.

To view an MPEG-encoded file (usually stored with the .MPG extension), you need an MPEG-compatible viewer, a program that decodes the file, displays the video through your system's monitor, and plays the audio through your system's sound card. Several public domain, shareware, and commercial MPEG viewers are available for a variety of computer systems.

| MPEG |

See **Motion Picture Experts Group (MPEG).**

MUD

See **Multi-User Dungeons (MUD).**

MUD client

A **client** program that runs on your **host** and helps you participate more effectively in a **MUD** (a multi-user Dungeons and Dragons game). Although a MUD client isn't needed to play, it helps you perform tasks that would otherwise be very confusing or tedious, such as formatting input lines, typing a prepared line of text at the touch of a key, and suppressing output from certain obnoxious players that you'd prefer to ignore.

multicast

In a computer network, to transmit a message to a subset of all the possible **hosts** that could receive the message. The message is sent to a **multicast group**. Multicasting is useful for a variety of applications, including **teleconferencing** and **MUDs**, and provides the basis for **Internet Talk Radio**. *Compare* **unicast**, **broadcast**.

Multicast Backbone (MBONE)

An experimental implementation of **real-time** audio and video **multicasting** services via the Internet.

The major weakness of the **TCP/IP protocols**, which form the technical basis of the Internet, is their unsuitability for real-time audio and video. These protocols were designed to assure the error-free delivery of text and program files, at the cost of some delay if necessary. Audio and video, in contrast, can tolerate some loss of data—which might not even be noticed by the user—but delivery delays would introduce intolerable gaps. The MBONE experiment is one of several that are testing ways to upgrade the Internet protocols and physical hardware to accommodate real-time audio and video. Because existing Internet hardware cannot accommodate time-sensitive messaging, MBONE requires the creation of an alternative **backbone** service consisting of workstations equipped with special hardware and software, together with long-distance linkages that have been specially modified to accommodate the audio and video transmissions.

Don't expect broadcast-quality video from MBONE. To create the illusion of smooth action, a **full-motion video** device must be capable of displaying 30 frames per second, but MBONE can handle only 3 to 5 frames per second, generating a noticeably jerky picture. But that's sufficient for a number of useful applications, including interactive audiovisual **teleconferencing**. A unique MBONE teleconferencing feature is a "whiteboard," an area of the screen that can be set aside and viewed by all participants as a collaborative worksheet.

multicast group

In **multicasting**, a list of **IP addresses** to which messages are multicast.

multihomed host

A **host** that is connected to more than one network. For example, a host might be connected to a **leased line** that accesses an **X.25 network** as well as to a **local area network (LAN)**. Each connection requires its own **IP address**, and it is quite possible for the multihomed host to have more than one **host name** (one for each IP address).

multimedia

In a computer system or network, the presentation of information by means of more than one medium at a time (including, for example, graphics, sounds, video clips, and animations in addition to text).

The promise of multimedia is improved understanding. Suppose, for example, I'm trying to explain to you how a jet aircraft engine works. Maybe you could get the idea from a good technical description, but certainly a picture would help. Or, better yet, an animation that shows what happens through the cycles of compression, ignition, and the generation of thrust.

Now that millions of personal computer users have access to systems equipped with high-resolution color monitors and stereo digital sound, the demand for multimedia is rising. One problem: as personal computer users have come to realize, multimedia files require huge amounts of disk space—and they also gobble up equally enormous amounts of network **bandwidth**. Internet technology was originally designed to transmit 7-bit ASCII text. One of the more severe **scale-up** problems faced by the Internet is the growing demand for multimedia service delivery, which will require the emergence of **gigabit networks** in place of the Internet's current **T3** (45 Mbps) backbones.

multimedia database

In scientific and educational computing, a database that contains graphics and visualization resources in addition to text and bibliographic references.

multimedia mail

An **electronic mail** system that allows the user to include graphics, sounds, and video in addition to text. *See* **Multi-Purpose Internet Mail Extensions (MIME)**.

multiplexer

A device used to combine several separate data sources into a composite stream for economical transmission. The two most common multiplexing techniques are **Frequency Division Multiplexing (FDM)** and **Time Division Multiplexing (TDM)**.

Much of the technical research on multiplexing comes from the telephone companies, who have found it much cheaper to combine signals than to dig the trenches for new cables.

multiplexing

The process of combining data from numerous sources into a single continuous stream of data for transmission across the network. The receiving station must be able to **demultiplex** the incoming data so that it is given to the proper **protocol** and **application** (*see* **layer**).

multi-protocol backbone

A high-speed **backbone** network, serving a national or international area, that can transmit data prepared with two or more conflicting protocols (standards).

Multi-Purpose Internet Mail Extensions (MIME)

A **protocol** that enables Internet users to exchange **multimedia email messages** containing enhanced character sets, **PostScript** formatting, recorded sounds, GIF graphics, and digital video.

At present, the Internet's mail protocol, called the **Simple Mail Transfer Protocol (SMTP)**, transfers all mail as plain text. That's true even if you try to include a **binary file** in an electronic mail message: the file becomes **ASCII** text. The recipient is in for a tedious process to decode this text and restore the program. MIME solves this problem by specifying how non-ASCII messages can be included in an electronic mail message. To take advantage of MIME, you—and your recipient—must be using MIME-compatible electronic mail programs, such as **Eudora**.

multivendor interoperability

The ability of a network's **protocol suite** (its standards and their implementations in computer software) to support the exchange of data among computer networks that are radically dissimilar, from a physical and electronic standpoint.

Despite the wishes of computer firms to impose their **proprietary standards** on the networking industry and the work of international standards, vendors keep coming up with computers and networking products that aren't **compatible** with each other. And when organizations start to contemplate networking applications such as **enterprise-wide computing** (linking all the computers and networks in an organization) or **wide area networks** (creating a regional, national, or international data communications network), the value of interoperability—and the **TCP/IP protocols**—come to the fore.

Multi-User Dungeons (MUD)

A fantasy role-playing adventure game, versions of which are available on dozens of Internet-accessible computers, that allows as many as dozens, hundreds, or even thousands of logged-in users to explore a virtual world and interact with one another. Each player takes control of a specific character; most of the other characters with whom you interact are similarly controlled by a human player (but see **bot**). In every MUD, you can build lasting relationships with other participants—relationships that can and do lead to meetings and even marriages in **RL** (real life). You can even construct and define additional game features, such as a private room that only you can enter.

MUDs have their origins in a combat-oriented game written by Richard Bartle and Roy Trubishaw of Aberstywyth University in 1979–1980. Much emulated, the original MUD has spawned a number of direct descendants, called **Aber-MUDs**. Newer variants include additional combat-oriented MUDS (including **DikuMUD** and **LPMUD**), that play down or eliminate the combat orientation in favor of social interaction and character role-playing. The first social MUD was **TinyMUD**, the first version of which appeared in 1989. Newer versions, whose names reflect a play on words on the original TinyMUD, are called TinyMuck and TinyMush.

Don't expect to see graphics, save in a few experimental systems (such as BSX-MUD, which requires a workstation running **X Windows** software). MUDs are text-oriented games. When you enter a room, for example, you see a text description ("It is very bright, open and airy here with large plate glass windows looking southward over the pool to the gardens beyond..."). By typing a WHO command, you can find out whether there are any other characters in the room—characters with whom you can interact. A MUD's text orientation isn't necessarily a bad thing, as MUD players are quick to insist; after all, how many times have you read a good novel, only to find that the movie is a disappointment? MUDs, like novels, open the gateways to the imagination. That they combine this with computer interactivity and the creativity of other participants makes for a heady brew indeed.

What's there to do on a MUD? That depends on the MUD's theme. The original MUDs emulated Dungeons and Dragons games, with their stock of magicians, demons, adventurers, trolls, and elves. To these have been added dozens of new, imaginative settings. Science fiction themes abound; you can become a Jedi knight, a Ferengi spy, a dragonrider of Pern. A recent trend is to transcend the human: In ToonMUSH, you become a cartoon character; in Furry-MUCK, you become a sexy, cute animal. In most MUDs, though, you can explore, solve puzzles, chat with other characters, construct additional spaces such as rooms, embark on quests, visit bars, and—yes—fall in love.

To join a MUD, you first decide whether you want to join a combat-oriented or social MUD. You must then find a MUD location—no easy task, since there's no official list of MUD sites. Once you've discovered the location of a **MUD server**, a program that makes a MUD available to players, you can try accessing it. If you're a new user, you may be asked to register by email; this may involve your being assigned a specific character. Once you gain access to the system, try typing *Help, Info, Commands, or News* to get information about the commands you can use and the adventures you can join. But be prepared for disappointment: Many MUDs aren't accepting new players. Assuming you do succeed in gaining access to a MUD, you may want to find out whether there's a **MUD client** available for this game. This is a program that provides an improved interface and automates commands that become tedious when you have to type them repeatedly.

Tip: When you discover a MUD's location, be sure to write down all the information about the server's location (including its Internet address) and port address. You may need all of this information to access the MUD. To access a MUD server using the Internet Protocol port, you use **Telnet** and specify the port address as well as the server system's name. For example, to access a MUD at port 5670 in the system *barney.uu.no.edu*, you could try typing

```
telnet barney.uu.no.edu 5670
```

If this doesn't work, you may need to specify the exact Internet address:

```
telnet 178.00.0.0 5670
```

If even this doesn't work, don't be surprised—MUDs come and go.

Do obtain and read Jennifer Smith's excellent MUD FAQs, as well as documentation specific to the MUD you want to play, before logging on and attempting to play the game. Armed with this knowledge, you'll be less of a pain to experienced players. Above all else, be a good guest on the system that's running the MUD—follow the rules and be nice to others. Playing a MUD isn't a right, and a system administrator may shut down the MUD if your actions cause repeated complaints.

Don't break the basic rules of MUD etiquette: Respect the other players' rights to enjoy the MUD without undue nagging, whining, or harassment from new players. Stop paging other players if they ask to stop. Don't use the Shout command unless absolutely necessary; this annoys other players. Don't leave junk lying around after you've used it; find out if there's a junk or trash command, and learn how to use it. Remember that if you harrass other players in any way, including sexually, you could have your access privileges revoked. And above all, once *you've* learned how to make your way, help new players.

mv

One of the essential **UNIX** commands, mv renames a file. To rename the file *information-glut* with the new name *glut.txt*, for example, you type the following and press ***Enter***:

```
mv information-glut glut.txt
```

narrowband

At the **data link layer** in a computer network, a transmission technique that does not employ **multiplexing**; the cable carries only one signal. More generally, the term is used to mean low **bandwidth** (*compare* **broadband network, narrowband network**).

narrowband ISDN

The lowest-speed (64 Kbps) version of the **Integrated Services Digital Network (ISDN)** standards for digital network connectivity to homes, schools, and offices. Narrowband ISDN offers subscribers two 64 Kbps data channels, called "B" channels, as well as a third "D" channel, operating at 16 Kbps, for the exchange of control information. A key advantage of narrowband ISDN: existing

twisted pair telephone wiring can handle narrowband ISDN signals. *Compare* **Broadband ISDN**.

---

narrowband network

In **local area networks (LANs)**, a network that does not use **multiplexing** to combine many signals on a single line; the cable carries only one signal at a time, which is delivered to all the workstations on the network. Most narrowband networks are limited to speeds of 10 Mbps. More generally, this term is used to describe any computer network that has low **bandwidth**—roughly, less than 100 Mbps. *Compare* **broadband network**.

National Information Infrastructure (NII)

A future public information system, a seamless web of computer networks, publicly-accessible databases, and consumer electronics reaching millions of homes, schools, and offices.

At the root of the NII concept is the notion of technological convergence—that today's computers, televisions, telephones, video cameras, and fax machines are headed for an electronic group marriage. The result will be a very impressive device indeed, and one that doesn't have a name yet—although I'm partial to *infotheater*.

Let's take a trip to the future, at least as it's envisioned by the U.S. government's Advisory Council on the National Information Infrastructure.

* You'll have access to—and interact with—the finest teachers our educational system can provide, without limitations introduced by geography, distance, resources, or disabilities.

* You can join "birds of a feather" communities—com-

munities that exist in the virtual space created by the network—of people who share your interests and needs.

- You'll be able to view the collections of the world's finest museums, even if you don't live in a big city and can't afford to travel there. You'll see these resources in vibrant, high-definition video with noise-free digital sound.

- You could live virtually anywhere you want to, without forfeiting a chance for a good job.

- If you're running a business, you can take orders from anywhere in the world, including orders that involve detailed graphic specifications.

- You can get in touch with professional specialists, who can bring the latest expertise to you even if you live in a remote area.

Sound good? Don't hold your breath. Experts are divided about whether anything like NII will come into being anytime soon.

First, it's by no means clear that convergence will occur, or even that it's desirable. For the next two decades, it's the home computer, rather than the television set or the telephone, that's likely to provide the kind of information access that NII envisions.

Second, crucial decisions now being made could dramatically affect the outcome of NII development. It's clear that cable television firms, giant communications firms, and other key players envision the NII as a new, profitable **broadcast** medium (*see* **broadcast model**). They envision a system that stresses high-bandwidth downstream delivery (signals that go from central databases to homes), with minimal upstream signaling as required for control purposes. But that's not the way to create an NII as envisioned in the current administration's proposals. What has made the

Internet so popular is the fact that ordinary people can be *originators* as well as *consumers* of information.

Will the NII develop in a way that meets the needs of ordinary people? Don't bet on it. The political action committees (PACs) of telecommunications firms have spent $69 million so far trying to influence the U.S. Congress to adopt their plans for the NII—plans that stress the broadcast model. And as for the potential of NII to make information available to all, note this: A recent study revealed that their plans for high-bandwidth local communications (*see* **last mile problem**) don't include lower class and lower middle class neighborhoods.

There's a very good argument, often advanced by people familiar with the Internet, that a relatively low-tech, "good enough" system—one founded on the **TCP/IP protocols** with extensions for real-time voice and video—is just the ticket for the National Information Infrastructure. In tandem with currently-available digital delivery techniques such as **ISDN**, which can use the current **twisted pair** telephone wires that reach 98 percent of U.S. households, such a system could realize the NII's lofty goals in short order. *See* **Electronic Frontier Foundation (EFF), Computer Professionals for Social Responsibility (CPSR)**.

National Research and Education Network (NREN)

A proposed **broadband network**, still under development, that will serve educational and research institutions while at the same time serving as a catalyst for the emergence of the **National Information Infrastructure (NII)**. NREN will develop from the current Internet, but it is specifically intended to broaden networking access and to permit the development of more advanced networking **applications**.

NREN was initially envisioned in the **High Performance Computing Act of 1991**. It is currently under development by the **High Performance Computing and Communica-**

tions **Program (HPCC)**, a multiagency program of the U.S. federal government that seeks to push the envelopes of supercomputing and networking simultaneously. The 1991 program statement called for NREN to operate at **gigabit** speeds by 1996, but it is more likely that the network will employ the maximum 622 Mbps bandwidth that can be achieved with current **Asynchronous Transfer Mode (ATM)** technology.

One of the primary motivations of NREN is to realize the goal of **Heterogeneous Distributed Computing (HDC)**, in which a researcher's physical location in relation to computing resources becomes irrelevant. HDC applications include **composite imaging**, **interactive visualization**, video **teleconferencing**, **multimedia database** access, and **multimedia mail**.

NREN development is plagued by a number of policy issues, which are directly entailed by its contradictory missions of serving the research community while at the same time serving as the catalyst for the emergence of the NII. The first issue concerns the scope of its mandate to serve research and educational communities. Does this mandate include schools as well as colleges and universities? The second policy issue concerns the use of NREN for non-research or non-educational purposes. Today, the Internet shows a clear trend towards **commercialization**, as non-governmental **service providers** increasingly extend Internet services to businesses, homes, and schools, as well as to governmental agencies not currently served by **interagency networks**. Just how NREN would fit into this picture is far from clear. The third issue, related to the second, concerns funding. NREN policy statements insist that the U.S. government should not bear full responsibility for funding the NREN backbone; instead, NREN development will involve a "shared investment" with the telecommunications industry, as well as some mechanism for passing on costs to users.

These questions will doubtless be resolved in the coming years, but NREN's probable impact seems clear: Like the **Internet**, whose **TCP/IP** protocols are well on their way to becoming a world standard, NREN will surely play a vital role in promoting the development of the advanced **broadband networks** of the 21st century.

National Science Foundation (NSF)

An independent agency of the U.S. government, established in 1950, to promote science and engineering through the sponsorship of scientific and engineering research and education. As part of its mandate, NSF seeks to improve and enhance scientific communication, a known component of rapid scientific progress. To foster scientific communication, NSF administrates **NSFNET**, one of the Internet's **backbones**, and is currently participating in the planning for the forthcoming **National Research and Educational Network (NREN)**.

net

In the **domain name system**, a **top-level domain** name that is assigned to an Internet administrative organization. The top-level domain name follows the last period in the site's domain name (such as info.net).

net lag

The delay introduced by **latency** (the time lag introduced when a router relays **datagrams** on the next **hop** of their journey) and by **congestion**.

The information you're transferring by means of the Internet may traverse as many as 30 point-to-point links, including telephone lines, leased lines, fiber optic cables, and even communications satellites. If one of these lines becomes congested or goes down for some reason, the Internet has to find another way of delivering the information, and that takes time. That's why you sometimes experience net lag—a momentary pause, ranging anywhere from a few seconds to a minute.

Net lag isn't fun, but it provides a clue to one of the Internet's design goals: The Internet places greater value on delivering data intact than it does on preventing delays. That's great for computer text and especially for computer program code, but it's not so great for voice or video.

net surfing

Exploring the Internet in search of amusing or interesting information resources.

You'll find out why this is such an addicting pastime if you give it a try. Some gems: A library of high-resolution graphic images of paintings and drawings at the Smithsonian Institution; a **World Wide Webb (WWW)** archive of recipes that have appeared in the **Usenet** newsgroups rec.food.cooking and rec.food.recipes; an archive of downloadable IBM PC utility programs from Ziff-Davis Publishing's *PC Magazine*; a searchable database of movies that allows you to join other Internet users in rating the indexed films; and an FTP-accessible program that lets you plan every aspect of a wedding.

net.character

In **Usenet**, a person who posts amusing, irritating, facetious, or downright offensive messages, with the principal goal of attracting attention. Net.characters include **cascaders, flame warriors, spewers**, and **trollers**. *Compare* **net.deity.**

net.deity

In **Usenet**, a high-frequency poster with sufficient cleverness and wit to become something of a celebrity. One of the several reigning deities is James "Kibo" Parry (*kibo@world.std.com*), who claims to post as many as ten to fifteen Usenet messages per day; an **alt** newsgroup (*alt.religion.kibology*) has been founded by his fans.

net.police

A **Usenet** participant who conceptualizes himself or herself as a protector of the Internet's core values, such as the avoidance of commercial gain and the conservation of network bandwidth. A net.guardian **flames** posters who violate these norms.

Netfind

A client program, currently available only for Sun workstations, that scans **white pages** in search of a person's telephone number and **electronic mail address**. To use Netfind, you need the person's name and a rough description of where the person works.

netILLINOIS

A state Internet network and **service provider** that provides high-speed Internet connectivity in several Illinois cities. The organization is a membership corporation funded by its member institutions (universities, colleges, community colleges, schools, libraries, non-profit organizations, government agencies, and businesses).

netiquette

An informal, open-ended set of guidelines for fruitful, legitimate, and socially responsible use of Internet applications (especially Usenet).

The basic rules of Usenet netiquette can be summed up in the following simple principles.

Do conserve network **bandwidth**. Before posting a message, read the newsgroup for a while to see what kinds of topics are fruitfully discussed. By all means, obtain and read the group's **FAQ** (Frequently Asked Questions), so you can avoid asking questions with which the group has long been pestered. **Stay** away from **flame wars** and debates that seem to go on indefinitely without resolution. Be wary of **trollers**. Ignore **carpet bombers**. If you feel you can contribute something worthwhile, make your points succinctly. Take the time to check your facts and document your sources. If you're answering a **posting** with a **followup posting**, edit it down to just those sentences to which you want to reply. If you're replying to a question, reply via **electronic mail** rather than posting your reply to the net. Keep your **signature** to a minimum, and **crosspost** to more than one newsgroup only when doing so makes sense.

Do consider the needs and feelings of others. Use a descriptive subject line so people can tell what your message is about. Keep your line lengths to a maximum of 80 characters, so people using 80-column terminals can read them. Avoid overly technical language; write clearly and succinctly. Remember that kids browse the net; use **rot-13** to encrypt messages with questionable content. And above all else, remember that there's a human being at the other end of the computer system; the spelling mistakes you're tempted to criticize may stem from dyslexia or unfamiliarity with the English language. Praise in public; criticize in private.

Don't write anything in an email message or Usenet posting that you wouldn't want to see in your home town newspaper the next day. If you feel you must criticize, attack the idea, not the person, and do so constructively. Don't use sarcasm that might be taken the wrong way.

netletter

A **mailing list** that is distributed in the form of a newsletter, with added editorial commentary and news clippings. An example: EDUPAGE, a thrice-weekly summary of news articles on computers and the information industry.

Tip: Net Letter Guide, a compendium of netletters that includes subscription information, is periodically posted on **Usenet** to the newsgroups alt.internet.services, alt.etext, alt.zine, misc.writing, and rec.mags.

netnews

Synonymous with **Usenet.**

NetNorth

A Canadian branch of the **BITNET** network that links universities, research institutions, government agencies, and businesses. NetNorth can exchange mail with the Internet by means of a **gateway.** Like BITNET, NetNorth uses IBM's **Network Job Entry (NJE)** protocols.

network

A computer system in which computing tasks are tackled by distributing interconnected computers to the people who need it, rather than forcing them to use a single, centralized computer system (called a **mainframe** computer). A computer network consists of **autonomous computers**, which can exchange information as equals (rather than being controlled in a master/slave relation by a centralized computer). *Compare* **internetworking**.

A properly-designed computer network can improve system reliability (the network is not dependent on the reliability of one, central computer) and enable the sharing of valuable computer resources (such as programs and databases). In addition, it can improve communication among people who work together by providing facilities for the exchange of files and **electronic mail**.

Networks are divided into three categories, **local area networks (LANs), metropolitan area networks (MANs), and wide area networks (WANs)**. A LAN connects up to about one hundred computers located in a relatively confined geographical area, such as a single office, a single building, or a group of contiguous buildings. A MAN links LANs that are dispersed over a metropolitan area. A WAN provides long-haul network connections that can span regional, national, and even international distances.

network administrator

A person who manages a **network's** hardware and software, including planning the network, obtaining and configuring network hardware and software, troubleshooting networking problems, and safeguarding network **security**. *Compare* **system administration**.

Network File System (NFS)

A network file utility, originally developed by Sun Microsystems, Inc., that enables a user to access **directories** and files on remote systems as if they were physically present on the user's computer. Among the many advantages of NFS is that it conserves disk space: With NFS, users of many machines may use the same file without requiring a copy of the file on each computer. Sun published the specifications for NFS in an **RFC** (RFC 1094) and it has subsequently been incorporated into most versions of the **UNIX** operating system.

If you have access to NFS, you can **mount** a remote directory on your own computer, and treat it as if the directory and the files it contains were stored on your own computer's disk. After mounting the remote directory, you can forget about NFS: You simply use the same commands you would ordinarily use to access these files.

Don't assume you can easily get access to NFS on a remote system: Most network administrators regard NFS as a security nightmare because it allows direct access to the files on a remote system. **Firewalls**, computers that are set up to shield a network from malicious use of the Internet, are in part intended to discourage destructive NFS forays. *Compare* **Alex, Andrew File System (AFS), Prospero.**

Network Information Center (NIC)

A repository of network information, including documents such as **RFCs, Internet Drafts**, and **FYIs.** "The NIC," the chief and authoritative repository of these documents, is the **Defense Data Network Information Center (DDN NIC).**

Network Information Service (NIS)

An Internet-wide utility program that automatically develops up-to-the-minute maps of Internet data pathways, and distributes these maps to **hosts** and **routers** throughout the network. Thanks to NIS, correct information about **routing** is maintained by all participating networks at all times.

network interface card

In a **local area network (LAN)**, an expansion board that fits into the expansion bus of a **personal computer** and enables the computer to be connected to the network.

Network Job Entry (NJE)

A suite of **proprietary protocols** developed for IBM for its mainframe computers. NJE-based networks can exchange **electronic mail** with the Internet by means of **gateways**, but the two networking protocol suites are otherwise incompatible. **BITNET**, a **wide area network (WAN)** that links many colleges and universities, uses the NJE protocols.

network layer

In the **Open Systems Interconnection (OSI) Reference Model**, the layer concerned with how a message gets from Point A in the Internet to Point B, even though it will probably traverse several **hops** (point-to-point physical links) along the way. The concern here is with **routing** the packets through the several hops so that they reach their destination. This is handled by the **IP protocol**.

network monitor

A device that tracks the traffic in a **local area network (LAN)**. Equipped with settings that send warning messages if errors exceed a certain count, the network monitor can help a network manager detect problems before they become serious.

Network News Transfer Protocol (NNTP)

In **Usenet**, the **protocol** (standard) that governs the dissemination of Usenet **postings** throughout the sites that have agreed to receive network news. Besides providing the technical means for new postings and new newsgroups to propagate throughout the network, NNTP gives network administrators the capacity to control how long articles are left on-line before they expire and which groups newsreaders can access. In addition, NNTP allows a network to set up **local newsgroups**, which don't propagate beyond a defined domain.

Network Operations Center (NOC)

A central administrative and technical office that is responsible for keeping the network running smoothly. *Compare* **Network Information Center (NIC)**.

network service

A running **application program** that is available to perform services for users of the network.

Network Virtual Terminal (NVT)

In a computer network, a generic terminal **protocol** (standard) that allows programmers to create applications without having to worry about the fact that many different terminals, each with unique characteristics, are in use. An application (such as **Pine**) that offers a **full-screen editor**, for example, must allow users to move the cursor about the screen no matter what terminal they're using. Applications written with a generic terminal definition are linked with support programs, one for each brand of terminal in use, that interpret the application's "generic" terminal instructions to suit the particularities of each terminal in use.

The Internet's network virtual terminal protocol defines a simple **scroll mode terminal**.

 Tip: Virtually all **UNIX** systems are equipped to handle **VT100** terminals. If you're accessing the Internet through **dialup access**, set your **communications program** to emulate a VT100 terminal.

NevadaNet

A state Internet network that links universities, research institutions, and community colleges throughout Nevada. The organization is funded by participating institutions as well as subsidies from the **National Science Foundation (NSF)** and the State of Nevada.

New England Academic and Research Network (NEARnet)

A regional Internet network and **service provider** that connects universities, laboratories, and corporations throughout the New England region. The network was founded by Harvard University, Boston University, and Massachusetts Institute of Technology (MIT). Currently operated by **Bolt, Beranak, and Newman (BBN)**, NEARnet is a member of

Commercial Internet Exchange (CIX) and offers unrestricted business connectivity.

New York State Education and Research Network (NYSERNet)

A state Internet network and **service provider** that focuses on the education and research communities. NYSERNet currently serves approximately 200 member institutions, including universities, research centers, K–12 schools, and public libraries. NYSERNet, Inc., is a not-for-profit organization. The organization is working toward making access available for every person in the state.

newbie

A newcomer to the Internet.

Befitting its roots in the predominantly male culture of computer science, the Internet's culture is partly one of technical achievement and prowess; a newcomer prone to making honest mistakes (for example, **posting** a message to the wrong **Usenet** newsgroup) may be on the receiving end of **flames**. On the other hand, there are many experienced Internet users who are willing to help newcomers and to make them feel welcome.

> **Do** your homework before logging on to the Internet: Read a good introductory book on the use of the basic **resource discovery tools** (such as **Archie, FTP,** and the **World Wide Web**). Know your network's **Acceptable Use Policy (AUP)** and adhere to it scrupulously. Before posting messages to a Usenet newsgroup, be sure to read the group for a while to make sure you understand its topic and purpose. Carefully read the documentation for a **MUD** or **Internet Relay Chat (IRC)** before attempting to join in on the **real-time** interaction. Above all, be sure you understand the basic rules of **netiquette**.

Don't be afraid of making an honest mistake while you're learning. You can't do serious harm to the Internet or its culture by making the kinds of errors that newbies typically make.

news hierarchy

One of the seven categories of **world newsgroups** in Usenet, the news newsgroups deal with Usenet itself—its administration, policies, technical aspects, conferences, announcements, information resources, software, and future.

Tip: If you're just getting started with Usenet, check out news.announce.newusers, which contains plenty of useful information designed for beginners.

newsgroup

In **Usenet**, an electronic conference or bulletin board that is devoted to discussion of a specific topic, such as archery or Amiga computers (and thousands more). A newsgroup consists of **postings**, which are messages that have been addressed to the newsgroup rather than a specific individual. Some postings start a new subject; others are sent in reply to existing postings (these replies are called **follow-on postings**).

The term *newsgroup* is somewhat misleading since few newsgroups contain the sort of "news" found in newspapers or TV news programs (but *see* **ClariNet**). Typically, newsgroup postings consist of questions, opinion statements, information resources such as lists and bibliographies, and—above all—discussion and debate. What makes these postings "news" is their freshness; the more active newsgroups receive as many as several hundred postings a day, often in response to current events and concerns. Within hours of the 1994 Los Angeles earthquake, for example, a newsgroup called alt.disasters.la-quake had been created and more than 600 messages had accumulated. On most systems, messages more than a week or 10 days old are deleted, whether or not you have read them.

Because there are so many newsgroups—more than 5,000 currently exist, and new ones are created every day—they are organized into classifications called **hierarchies**. Each hierarchy has a name, such as **alt** or **talk**, that precedes the newsgroup's name (as in alt.fan.madonna). Within each hierarchy there are dozens or hundreds of newsgroups.

The standard Usenet hierarchies, called the **world newsgroups**, comprise the following hierarchies: **comp** (computers and computer applications), **news** (discussions about Usenet), **rec** (sports and hobbies), **sci** (scientific and scholarly research), **soc** (social issues and socializing), **talk** (discussion of controversial topics such as gun control and abortion), and **misc** (anything that doesn't fall into the other hierarchies). By default, the world newsgroups are distributed to all Usenet sites, although some exclude the **talk** newsgroups.

Found on many systems, and increasingly popular, are the **alternative newsgroup hierarchies** that are distributed only to the sites that request them. These include **alt** (a hierarchy that bypasses the normally stringent rules for creating newsgroups), **bionet** (newsgroups focusing on biology and the environment), **biz** (advertisements and business-related discussions), and **k12** (newsgroups of interest to primary and secondary school educators). In addition, there are many **local newsgroups** that are available only within a specific geographic region (such as California) or an institution (such as a university).

To read newsgroup postings and reply to the messages, you need a **newsreader**. The most popular newsreaders organize the messages into **threads** (subjects). With a **threaded newsreader** such as **nn**, **tin**, or **trn**, you will find all the postings relevant to a given subject grouped together, so you can read them together.

newsgroup kill file

A **kill file** (a list of topics, authors, or origin sites) that applies only to the postings in a specific **newsgroup**. *Compare* **global kill file**.

newsgroup selector

In a **newsreader** program for reading **Usenet**, the level at which you choose the newsgroup you want to read. At this level you can also choose whether to subscribe to new newsgroups, add or delete newsgroups from your subscription list, and change the order in which the subscribed newsgroups are presented.

.newsrc

In **UNIX** hosts, a file kept in your **home directory** that lists the names of the **Usenet newsgroups** to which you have subscibed.

newsreader

In **Usenet,** a program that enables you to read the network news. Newsreaders fall into two categories: **threaded newsreaders**, which group articles by subject, and **unthreaded newsreaders**, which force you to read the articles in the chronological order in which they appeared in the newsgroup. Of the two, threaded newsreaders are much more convenient to use. *See* **nn, rn, tin, trn.**

See **Network Information Center (NIC).**

In an **electronic mail** system, a type of **alias** that lets you receive messages addressed to a nickname (such as "Obi-Wan" or "Flamethrower") in addition to your **mailbox name**. This is a useful way of dealing with common misspellings; a user named *Tourraine* could ask that the system administrator establish the nickname *Touraine*.

See **National Information Infrastructure (NII).**

A respected **newsreader** for UNIX-based systems that allows the user to read and respond to messages posted in **Usenet newsgroups**. Written by Kim F. Storm, of Texas Instruments in Denmark, and released for world distribution in 1989, nn is a **threaded newsreader** that automatically groups Usenet **postings** by **threads** (subjects). This makes it much easier to follow an on-going discussion. The program offers many advanced features that contribute to significantly improved performance compared to other popular newsreaders. In addition, it offers features of great convenience to readers, such as a menu-based **uudecode** command that automatically decrypts and assembles graphics files and an easy-to-use word processing module for replying to postings.

Tip: If you're using an outmoded, unthreaded newsreader such as **rn**, find out whether a **threaded newsreader** such as **nn**, **trn**, or **tin** is available on your system, and switch.

no parity

In **dialup access**, an **error checking** option in which **parity checking** is disabled. Most of the services that offer dialup IP request that you set your **communications program** to disable parity checking.

node

In a computer network, a **workstation** or **terminal** that has access to the network. In the Internet, the term **host** is used instead.

NORDUnet

A regional network and high-bandwidth **backbone** linking the Scandinavian countries and their national networks. Participating countries and national networks include Norway (UNINETT), Denmark (DENet), Finland (FUNET), Iceland (SURIS), and Sweden (SUNET). Founded in 1987, NORDUnet has become one of the most active components of the Internet outside of North America. The network emphasizes research and education.

NorthWestNet

A regional Internet network and **service provider** operated by the Northwest Academic Computing Consortium, Inc., a not-for-profit organization. A regional component of the **NSFNET**, NorthWestNet is also a member of the **Commercial Internet Exchange (CIX).** NorthWestNet member institutions include universities, colleges, K–12 schools, research institutes, libraries, hospitals, state government agencies, and businesses. In addition to offering Internet connectivity in Alaska, Idaho, Montana, North Dakota, Oregon, and Washington, NorthWestNet offers a variety of support services such as training and documentation.

NSA bait

Words or phrases that suggest terrorist activity. In Usenet, you may be advised in a **followup posting** that something you typed is "NSA bait." This refers to the myth that the U.S. National Security Agency (NSA) scans all Usenet postings for signs of seditious activity (see **NSA line eater**). In an ironic, humorous reference to the mythology about the NSA, some **signature** files contain words such as "Uzi."

NSA line eater

A program that is said to be maintained by the U.S. National Security Agency (NSA) to detect signs of terrorist activity on **Usenet**. The program allegedly works by scanning Usenet **postings** for words such as "AK-47" or "plastic explosive." The NSA line eater provides an excellent example of the Internet's capacity to disseminate and sustain **urban folklore**. *See* **NSA bait**.

NSF

See **National Science Foundation (NSF)**.

NSFNET

A high-speed **packet-switching network** based on the **TCP/IP** protocols that currently forms the **backbone** of the Internet, handling data generated by **regional networks**.

Designed as a general purpose backbone, NSFNET carries traffic ranging from ordinary **electronic mail** to data exchanged by some of the world's fastest supercomputers. In December, 1993, the NSFNET backbone carried 10 terabytes of data, the equivalent of 5 billion pages of information.

The NSFNET backbone, spanning the continental U.S., currently employs **T3** links capable of transmitting 45 Mbps of data. The physical network is not actually owned by the U.S. government but is leased from a commercial service provider. The actual amount of U.S. subsidies to NSFNET's operation is estimated at roughly 10 percent of total costs, with the remainder borne by regional service providers and subscribing institutions.

The Internet as we know it at this writing—a federally-subsidized network with an **Acceptable Use Policy (AUP)** limiting the use of the network for commercial activity—is about to come to an end. Users have benefitted from U.S. subsidies to **regional networks** and **NSFNET**, but the U.S. federal government plans to decrease or withdraw these subsidies. The next-generation NSFNET will be limited to its original purpose, namely, to provide very high speed network links between the nation's **supercomputer** centers in Ithaca (NY), Pittsburgh (PA), San Diego (CA), and Champaign (IL). Regional networks and commercial service providers who have benefitted from using the NSFNET backbone will have to make their own arrangements if the Internet is to survive.

To address the impending decommissioning of the NSFNET backbone, several regional service providers have formed a corporation—the **Corporation for Regional and Enterprise Networking (CoREN)**—to provide an Internet backbone and related coordinating services. CoREN addresses the problem of NSFNET's impending demise, but it is far from clear how the Internet will evolve in the long run—or whether the U.S. government will completely abandon some form of direct Internet subsidization. At the same time that the U.S.

government is bent on privatizing NSFNET, it is also planning to construct a **National Research and Education Network (NREN)**, whose technology would not discriminate against messages based on their origin or destination (and would, therefore, very likely handle a large amount of commercial and non-educational traffic). NREN is a high-speed backbone network envisioned in the **High Performance Computing Act of 1991**, and is primarily intended to serve the research and educational communities. But it is also envisioned as a **testbed** for the development of the **National Information Infrastructure (NII)**, which would extend **integrated services networks** to homes, schools, and offices throughout the United States. This implies far broader usage than merely linking universities and research institutes.

| octet |

In the Internet context, a unit of data exactly eight bits in length. In personal computing, a data unit of this size is called a byte. However, some of the computers connected to the Internet have basic data units (bytes) greater than eight bits in length, so this term is used to ensure clarity.

| odd parity |

A method of **parity checking** (an **error checking** technique) in which the number of 1s in each **octet** (8-bit

sequence) of transmitted data must add up to an odd number. *Compare* **even parity**, **no parity**.

offline

Not directly connected to the computer ("OK, you can use the phone now, I'm *offline*"), or turned off ("You can't use the network; it's *offline*").

offline reader

A **newsreader** for reading **Usenet** newsgroups that is designed to run on a computer (such as a home PC) that isn't directly connected to the Internet. You use the program and a **modem** to connect with an Internet **host** via **dialup access**; the program then obtains all the postings you haven't yet read, and **downloads** them to your computer. You then read the messages, and if you wish, reply by **creating followup postings** or postings to a new subject. Finally, you log on to the host again, and the program **uploads** the postings you have created (and downloads any new unread postings that may have arrived since you last logged on). The point of the program is to allow you to read and reply to the news without tying up your telephone.

Ohio Regional Network (OARnet)

A state Internet network and **service provider** that links cities in Ohio with a high-speed **backbone.** In addition to offering Internet connectivity to individuals and organizations throughout the state, OARnet also offers Gopher services, mail consultation, and assistance with Internet installations.

online

Directly connected to a computer via telecommunications or network links ("You can't use the phone right now because I'm *online*), or activated and ready for operation ("OK, the printer's *online*). Compare **offline**.

online information service

A for-profit computer service, accessible via **dialup access**, that makes files, news, discussion groups, and product information available to home computer hobbyists. Most services offer additional features of interests to home users, such as airline and hotel reservations, consumer information, up-to-the-minute stock quotes, and dating services. The leading services are CompuServe and Prodigy, followed by smaller competitors such as Delphi and GEnie. Most offer limited **electronic mail** access to the Internet by means of **gateways**; some are planning, or have already implemented, additional Internet features such as **FTP** and **Usenet**.

> **Tip:** Be forewarned that Internet access by means of online information services is in**direct access**, and has the same disadvantages of **dialup access** generally: You're not directly connected to the Internet, so your mail and files go the service's computer, not yours. You'll have to download mail and files if you want to print or use them.

Open Shortest Path First (OSPF)

An **Interior Gateway Protocol (IGP)** that handles the routing of **datagrams** within an **Autonomous System** (a collection of networks under the control of a single administrative agency, such as a university or corporation). Unlike the **RIP** protocol, which builds **routing tables** through

309

advertising and **convergence**, OSPF routers broadcast throughout the network the information they possess about routes open to them. As each router receives information from all the other routers on the network, it uses this information to build an accurate routing table and computes the shortest routes available to send data to its destination. A network constructed with OSPF routers can respond much more quickly than a RIP network to the failure of a router or connection.

Open Software Foundation (OSF)

A consortium of **UNIX** vendors, led by Digital Equipment Corporation (DEC), IBM, and Hewlett-Packard, that was formed to developing and supporting a version of UNIX other than the one promoted by AT&T. OSF's version of UNIX, released in 1990, is called OSF/1.

open standard

A **standard** (set of rules or specifications for the design or operating characteristics of a computer device) that is published and made freely available to a technical community, without a profit motive, in the hope of promoting **standardization**. The **TCP/IP** protocols are open standards. *Compare* **open systems computing, proprietary standard**.

open systems computing

A philosophy of computer and network system design that avoids **proprietary standards** in favor of **open standards** (a published standard that can be used by any manufacturer). Product specifications are freely available and in many cases can be accessed through the Internet. Open systems computing does not burden customers by forcing them to get all their equipment from just one firm. *Compare* **connector conspiracy.**

Open Systems Interconnection (OSI) Protocol Suite

A set of networking and internetworking **protocols** (standards) created by OSI, a unit jointly supported by the **International Standards Organization (ISO)** and the **CCITT.**

At present, the OSI protocol suite can be viewed as competing with the **TCP/IP** protocols—but not very successfully, save in Europe, where OSI is supported by national policies. OSI has certain strengths for business internetworking, such as the ability to handle remote orders and fund transfers, but the protocols are cumbersome and not well supported by network hardware manufacturers. That may change because, in 1980, the U.S. federal government adopted procurement guidelines that will gradually require agencies to buy equipment that is OSI-compatible. This should not be construed to imply the **Imminent Death of the Net,** however, because hardware devices such as **routers** can and often are designed to work with more than one protocol suite. In addition, a 1994 interagency report harshly criticized the government's choice of the OSI protocols, which have proven in some instances to be unworkable, and recommended the Internet protocol suite as an alternative.

Open Systems Interconnection (OSI) Reference Model

A conceptual framework for understanding and designing computer networks that was developed in the early 1980s by the **International Standards Organization (ISO).** The underlying principle of the OSI model is "divide and conquer": It holds that a network is best conceptualized—and engineered—by breaking it down into seven independent **layers,** each of which carries out a separate function that can be independently optimized for smoothness and efficiency.

Each layer, moreover, should have well-defined, clear-cut **protocols** (standards), which enable designers working on other layers to anticipate how the layer will function.

Useful as it is, the OSI model doesn't perfectly match the **architecture** (design) of the Internet; it doesn't do a very good job of conceptualizing the special problems of **internetworking** (connecting physically incompatible networks). Representatives from the **ARPANET** community made this point to the OSI committee, but their objections weren't taken very seriously—at the time, no one had any idea that the ARPANET's architecture would lay the foundation for the emergence of a global computer network! This, coupled with the fact that the OSI model was very close to one advocated by IBM for proprietary reasons, led to bad feelings between the ARPANET and OSI communities, signs of which can be detected even today (for example, many Internet experts prefer their own layer mapping to the 7 OSI layers). Still, the OSI layers can provide a useful way of conceptualizing how any network—including the Internet—operates.

At the core of the OSI model is a conception of a network as a layer cake—or, if you prefer more sophisticated language, a **protocol stack**. The OSI model calls for seven independent layers, each of which has its own characteristic protocols. The first four layers, called the lower layers, deal with the nitty-gritty details of getting messages from Point A to Point B across the network.

- **Physical Layer** This layer, the lowest in the OSI protocol stack, consists of the physical medium—such as wires or cables—through which the network signals travel. Here, the electrical engineer's job is to keep the circuits functioning without interruption and with as little noise as possible. As far as the Internet protocols are concerned, this layer is the business of each of the physical networks to which the Internet is linked. Internet traffic can be carried over any kind of physical layer yet designed, ranging from noisy telephone lines to **gigabit networks** capable of transmitting the entire text of the *Encyclopedia Britannica* in less than a second.

- **Data Link Layer** This layer deals with the problem of how data can be transmitted across a given point-to-point line so that it comes across as data, not gibberish, on the other end. Typically, this is done by breaking the data down into identifiable units, called **packets**. This may be done in different ways by different kinds of physical networks. Suppose, for example, you're using a PC at home, which is linked through **dialup access** to a **UNIX** computer at your office. The data link problem here is how to get digital signals to traverse a noisy telephone line. From your office computer, the signals traverse a **local area network (LAN)**, move to a **T1 leased line**, and eventually get on to **NSFNET's** high-speed **backbone**. For each of these hops, there is a distinct data link problem, which is handled in a unique way for each type of physical network. That's left up to each physical network. For the Internet, the concern here is how individual computers on very different physical networks can be uniquely identified by means of an **IP address**, so that messages can be routed to this machine and no other. This is handled by **Address Resolution Protocols (ARP)** for LANs and **SLIP/PPP** for computers connected by telephone lines.

- **Network Layer** This layer is concerned with how a message gets from Point A in the Internet to Point B, even though it will probably traverse several hops along the way. The concern here is with **routing** the packets through the several hops so that they reach their destination. This is handled by the **IP protocol**. This protocol doesn't care if the packets actually get there; it just pumps them out.

- **Transport Layer** This layer is concerned with *manag-*

ing the transmission of data from Point A to Point B so that the data arrives intact. There are three Internet protocols at this layer, the **Transmission Control Protocol (TCP)**, the **User Datagram Protocol (UDP)**, and the **Internet Control Message Protocol (ICMP)**.

The next three layers, which deliver services to users, are called the upper layers:

- **Session Layer** This layer is more relevant to **local area networks (LANs)** than to a **wide area network (WAN)** such as the Internet; it's concerned with such things as preventing two machines from trying to access the network at the same time.

- **Presentation Layer** In this layer are found protocols that deal with the representation of the data to be transmitted. In the early days of the Internet, this layer had no special protocols; the ARPANET simply used ASCII text to represent data. Today, there is considerable interest in defining Internet protocols for data **compression** and **encryption** (see, for example, **Privacy Enhanced Mail [PEM]**).

- **Application Layer** At this level are found application programs, which can benefit from standards that define **terminals**, handle **file transfer**, and specify the formats for **electronic mail**. In the Internet, these functions are defined by the Internet's **Network Virtual Terminal (NVT)** protocol; the **File Transfer Protocol (FTP)**; the **Simple Mail Transport Protocol (SMTP)**; and the **domain name system**.

With these layers in mind, here's how a network works—specifically, the Internet. In the source computer, the computer originating a message, an **application** passes data "down" the protocol stack. At the presentation layer (if there is one), it's compressed or encrypted. At the transport layer, one of the Internet's two **transport protocols** breaks the data down into **packets** called **datagrams**. Each datagram contains information that tells Internet **routers** how to deliver the packet to the correct destination. At the network layer, it's **multiplexed**—combined with data originating from many other sources—and routed out through the network's data links and physical connections. At the destination computer, the reverse of this process occurs. First, the incoming **byte stream** is **demultiplexed**. This is done by giving the message to the correct **transport protocol**, which then reassembles the data and passes it on to the correct **application**. In sum, originating data goes "down the stack," traverses the network, and then goes "up the stack" at its destination.

---

operating system

The software that controls a computer's operations, including managing memory, running programs, controlling the flow of data from ports and disk drives, and other essential functions. Operating systems are divided into two portions, the **shell** (the portion that interacts with the user) and the **kernel** (the underlying software that actually performs the system control functions). Many operating systems permit the user to use more than one shell; the **UNIX** kernel, for instance, can work with shells ranging from the very simple, command-line shell found on most university UNIX systems to elegant **graphical user interfaces (GUIs).**

One of the reasons that UNIX systems figure so prominently in the Internet is that the **TCP/IP** protocols are part of the UNIX kernel. Press reports at the time this book was written indicate that the coming version of Microsoft Windows (Windows 4.0) will include TCP/IP connectivity.

Operation Sundevil

A 1990 U.S. Secret Service crackdown on computer **crackers** that was intended to curtail their illegal activities, such as gaining unauthorized access to computers and the theft of long-distance calling access codes. (The Secret Service's mandate includes investigating interstate telecommunications fraud.) Precipitating the raids was the massive AT&T long-distance service outage on Martin Luther King Day in January 1990. The timing, coupled with suspicion that the outage had been cause by a software bomb, persuaded investiagators that the outage was due to an incidious leftist plot. (The problem turned out to be caused by a bug in AT&T's software.) Swinging into action throughout the U.S., investigators seized **bulletin board systems (BBS)** in an attempt to prove that illegally-obtained documents and telephone numbers had been made available on these machines. A few convictions resulted from this massive program, but investigators were much embarrassed by a blunder made in seizing materials from a Texas maker of role-playing games: They seized a disk containing a role-playing game called *Cyberpunk* in the mistaken belief that it was a "dangerous manual for computer crimes." A judge subsequently ordered the secret service to compensate the games company for damages related to this incident.

org

In the **domain name system**, a top-level domain name that is assigned to a non-profit organization, such as a scientific or scholarly association. The top-level domain name follows the last period in the site's domain name (such as cpsr.org). Three organizations that use the org domain name are the **Electronic Frontier Foundation (EFF)**, **Computer Professionals for Social Responsibility (CPSR)**, and the Institute of Electrical and Electronic Engineers (IEEE).

OSI

See **Open Systems Interconnection (OSI) Reference Model.**

outsourcing

The management of a firm's computer network by another firm that specializes in such services. A practical solution to the prodigious problems involved in installing and maintaining a smoothly-functioning computer network, as well as dealing with users' problems, this business is expected to generate revenues in the US$3.5 to $7 billion range annually by the mid-1990s.

overhead

In a computer network, the amount of **bandwidth** that is consumed by the protocols needed to move the data from one computer to another.

packet

In a **packet-switching network,** a physical unit of data that has been broken down to a small enough size so that it can be transmitted efficiently and rapidly across the network. The division of a message into packets is required by the network's **maximum transmission unit (MTU)** limitation, which specifies the largest unit of data that can be physically transferred by the network. *Compare* **datagram**.

Packet Internet Groper (PING)

In **UNIX** systems, a diagnostic utility program that indicates whether a remote **host** is actually connected to the Internet. If you're having trouble accessing a remote host using an application such as **FTP** or **Telnet**, use ping to determine whether the host is accessible. To use ping type *ping* followed by the host name, as in the following example:

```
ping walthers.hltco.com
```

If the host is working and connected to the Internet, you'll see statistics on the delivery of test packets, or, with some systems, a message indicating that the host is "alive." If there's trouble, you'll see one of the following messages: "unknown host" (the host name does not appear to be correct), "network unreachable" (your system does not have a route to the host you are trying to contact), or "no answer" (the host appears to exist but does not respond). If you receive any of these messages, contact your system administrator for assistance.

packet radio

A **packet switching network** that employs radio signals at the **physical layer**. Packets originate from a host that is equipped with a radio, and travel to a central station, where they're routed to other computers on the same network (or to other networks via more conventional physical media). Packet radio networks are ideal for rural locations.

packet switching network

A **wide area network**, such as the **Internet**, in which a given message is broken up into **packets** of data—blocks of information that contain the addresses necessary to deliver them. The packets travel through the network independently, taking whatever route is freely available as they seek their destination. The packets are reassembled at their destination.

A packet switching network operates on very different principles than the **circuit switching network** that you're already familiar with—the telephone system. When you make a telephone call, the telephone system uses switches to create a single, electrical circuit between your telephone and the one that you're calling. A packet switching network, in contrast, is called a **connectionless** network because it is not necessary for two linked computers to establish a physical **connection** before the transmission can take place. Instead, the data is broken down into **packets** (units of digital data), each of which contains a destination address (very much like the address on the front of an ordinary first-class letter).

When the packets have been properly addressed, the sending computer sends them out through the network's complex web of **routers**. Each router examines the destination address, and uses a **routing algorithm** (a utility program) that decides how best to get the packet to the next destination. At the end of each **hop** (each leg of the journey, from router to router), a router is waiting to send the packet on its way. At the destination, the packets are reassembled, and if any were damaged or lost en route, the receiving computer automatically requests a retransmission.

Many Internet users find the division of their messages (such as **electronic mail**) into several or even dozens of packets somewhat disconcerting, but there is ample justification for this "chop-'em-up" approach: It's more efficient. Computer communications tend to be "bursty"—a given computer sends a huge amount of data, and then doesn't send any for hours. So it doesn't make much sense to try to set up a single physical circuit for each pair of communicating computers—the line would be disused except for infrequent bursts of activity. In a packet switching network, thousands of linked computers share a single, high-speed line, which is often continuously occupied.

The fact that each computer's data is broken up into hundreds or thousands of small packets makes it all that much easier to send them efficiently. Imagine that there are thousands of people at the top of a mountain, all wanting to get their letters to people in the town below. They dump their letters into a big funnel, which empties into a long tube that runs down the mountain to the post office at the bottom of the tube. There's a continuous flow of letters at very high speed.

Packet switching networks are great for computer data, but they aren't the best choice for voice or video. Voice and video communication require continuous communication, which a circuit switching network can easily provide. In a packet switching network, not all the packets arrive at the same time. If two packets are addressed to the same destination, one may have to wait. With voice and video, this could lead to disconcerting gaps or jerky motion.

With the rapid growth of **multimedia** applications that combine computer data with voice, video, and graphics, it is increasingly clear that neither packet switching nor circuit switching networks will be adequate in the future, which will see the rise of **integrated services networks** that can efficiently handle all kinds of transmitted data.

page description language (PDL)

A programming language that is designed to specify precisely how a compatible display device, such as a monitor or printer, should show or print text and graphics. Printers that work with PDLs are more expensive than ordinary printers because they require their own microprocessor and memory, similar to a personal computer's, to decode and carry out the PDL's instructions. The benefit gained is increased control over minute details of the printing process. *See* **PostScript**.

page mode terminal

A computer **terminal** that is designed to display an entire page of text or graphics at a time, not just one line. *Compare* **line mode terminal**.

parity checking

A simple method of **error correction** that involves a **checksum** performed on each transmitted character. The two most common methods are **even parity** and **odd parity**. Parity checking is infrequently used in **dialup access** to a remote computer using a **modem**. Most of the **hosts** that offer dialup access to the Internet require that you disable parity checking by choosing the **no parity** option with your **communications program**.

parser

A program that enables you to read a text on-screen that has been prepared with a **markup language** such as **Standard Generalized Markup Language (SGML)**. The parser hides the **tags** (the markup language's commands), and in their place formats the document so that it is readable on-screen.

password

A secret code, known only to you, that enables you to **log on** to a multi-user computer system or **local area network (LAN)**. The password is the only means of **authentication** that most of today's Internet hosts can offer. After you type the password, the system checks what you've typed against a list of authorized passwords. If the computer finds a match, you're logged on to the system.

Passwords are a very weak line of defense against the abuse of computer system security: If a **cracker** can guess a password and gain entry to the system, the system may be in for big-time trouble. Many people think these crackers are using sophisticated computer programs to guess passwords, but that's not the case: According to an estimate by the **Computer Emergency Response Team (CERT),** 80 percent of network security problems are caused by people choosing passwords that just about anyone could easily guess, such as using their first names (see **joe account)**.

 Don't make up a password using one of these poor methods:

- Using your first name or part of your last name, even if you add a number

- Changing or reversing part of your name or initials

- Using personal information that's associated with you, such as part of your telephone number or social security number

- Using a password made up only of numbers

- Using someone else's name (such as a girlfriend's name)

- Using a common acronym (USA, PC)

- Using any word that appears in any kind of dictionary

- Using jargon that you think would be known only to a person in your field or profession

- Using something that's easy to type (qwertyuiop)

  Do create a safe password. Here's one technique: Make seven scraps of paper. On the first, write down a number picked randomly from 0 to 9. On the second scrap, pick one of the punctuation marks that appears on the top row of your computer's keyboard. On the third scrap, pick a lower case letter beween a and z. On the fourth scrap, pick an upper case letter from A to Z. For the fifth, sixth, and seventh scraps, choose more letters. Now try to rearrange the scraps into something that you can pronounce and remember (such as 7Brmow!). That's your password, and it will be impossible to guess (or even to read over your shoulder while you're typing)—but hopefully you won't forget it.

| password aging |

A mechanism employed in most multi-user **hosts** that keeps track of the last time you chose a password. When the password reaches the end of its lifetime, such as three months, you're asked to create a new one. This is a security measure that isn't employed by all systems.

| pattern |

A specific sequence of characters, such as "European Unity" or "pmr05.txt," that you ask the computer to match.

Tip: If you're using the **UNIX** utility called **more**, which shows you a page of a text file at a time, you can skip forward to a pattern you specify by typing a forward slash mark (/) followed by the pattern. For example, if you type /1995, more will skip to the next screenful of text in which "1995" appears.

Pennsylvania Research and Economic Partnership Network (PREPnet)

A state Internet network and **service provider** that links Pennsylvania cities with a **T1 backbone.** A not-for-profit consortium with over 120 members from the higher education, government, health care, K–12, library, and not-for-profit sectors, PREPnet also offers commercial service through its connection to **ANS CO+RE**.

Performance Systems International Network (PSINet)

A national **backbone** and **service provider** that focuses on the commercial market as well as providing Internet connectivity for individuals through **dialup access**. Spanning the continental United States with a high-speed (**T3**) backbone network that employs **Asynchronous Transfer Mode (ATM)** fast packet switching, PSINet offers direct Internet connectivity at 45 **Points of Presence (POPs)**. In addition, you can access the firm's PSILink Global Messaging Service in more than 175 cities by means of dialup access using a **modem**. Using PSI's software, you can access Internet electronic mail and **Usenet** newsgroups. In comparison with the software found on **UNIX** hosts, this software is extremely easy to use.

personal computer (PC)

A computer designed to meet the computing needs of an individual, as opposed to minicomputers and mainframes, which are designed to meet the needs of organizations. Free from administrative constraints, PC users can configure their systems as they please, choosing the software and peripherals they want. The acronym PC connotes computers compatible with the IBM Personal Computer (IBM PC) standard, as opposed to the competing (and incompatible) Apple Macintosh standard, but both are personal computers.

Until recently, PCs were substantially less powerful than **workstations**, high-end desktop computers specifically designed for processor-intensive tasks such as high-resolution graphics simulation. With the marketing of systems based on the high-performance Pentium (developed by Intel Corporation) and PowerPC processors (jointly developed by Apple Computer, IBM, and Motorola), this distinction is rapidly eroding. However, some computing experts believe that the internal architecture (design) of Intel microprocessors is inherently flawed due to the need to retain compatibility with previous versions of Intel microprocessors, and that there are insurmountable limits to the further improvement of PCs based on the Intel architecture.

The diffusion of personal computers throughout society provides one of the most important spurs for Internet growth. Although PC users still face formidable installation and system configuration challenges if they attempt **dialup IP** (access using **SLIP** or **PPP**), **dialup access** is widely available and inexpensive (as low as $9 per month for unlimited access). High-speed Internet access by means of **cable television (CATV)** is undergoing field testing in several areas of the U.S. With over 100 million PCs in use in North America alone, the so-called Information Superhighway is most likely to reach homes, schools, and offices through PCs rather than a marriage of the television and telephone.

| physical layer |

In the **Open Systems Interconnection (OSI) Reference Model** of computer networks, the layer that consists of the physical medium—such as wires or cables—through which the network signals travel. Internet messages traverse a huge variety of physical media, including **twisted pair** (ordinary telephone wires), **coaxial cable**, **communication** satellites, fiber optic, microwave relay, packet radio, as well as T1 and T3 trunk lines.

physical medium

The cabling through which network signals travel, including twisted pair telephone wires, coaxial cable, T1 and T3 telephone lines, and fiber optic.

physical network

In the Internet, one of the more than 25,000 distinct computer networks that the Internet links. They are made by many different manufacturers and have very different means of addressing individual computers. What has helped lay the foundation for the emergence of a global computer network is the worldwide acceptance of the TCP/IP protocols, which make it possible for these different networks to exchange data.

Pine

A well-designed electronic mail client program for host systems running UNIX. Unlike earlier email clients that forced you to use a default editor such as vi or the difficult EMACS, Pine includes its own easy-to-use word processing program and spelling checker for writing and editing letters.

pingable

An Internet-connected host that is able to respond to the ping diagnostic utility, and should therefore be able to respond to Telnet and FTP commands.

plain ASCII file

A file that contains nothing but the standard **ASCII** characters and control codes.

Plain Old Telephone Service (POTS)

A **physical medium** consisting of a **twisted pair** cable that's set up for **analog** transmission, which is the service that's delivered to virtually all homes and offices. *Compare* **Integrated Services Digital Network (ISDN)**.

plaintext

The "raw material" of **encryption**, that is, a message that could be easily read by an intruder.

plonk

In Usenet, to establish or amend a **kill file** (a file containing lists of subjects and posters that you do not want to read) so that an annoying individual's posts do not appear on the screen. The term "plonk" suggests the sound of refuse hitting the bottom of a trash can.

Point of Presence (POP)

In a **Public Data Network (PDN)**, an area—generally a metropolitan area consisting of a city and suburbs—where it is possible to connect with the network's high-speed long haul lines by means of **leased lines** or local **dialup access**.

point-to-point data transmission

The physical medium through which a data transmission occurs in one **hop** of its journey through the network. An example of a point-to-point transmission is the transfer of a file from a **UNIX** system to a user's home PC by means of **twisted pair** telephone lines and a **modem**.

point-to-point network

A network in which a message originates from one computer system and travels to one or more destination computer, but not to every computer on the network. **Wide area networks (WANs)** are point-to-point networks, while most **local area networks (LANs)** are **broadcast networks** that send all network data to every computer connected to the LAN.

Point-to-Point Protocol (PPP)

One of the two most prominent protocols for **dialup IP access** (the other is **SLIP**). The PPP protocol establishes a method of Internet access in which a personal computer, linked to an Internet **host** via the telephone system and a high-speed modem, appears to the host as if it were an **Ethernet** port on the host system's **local area network (LAN)**. This establishes a temporary but direct Internet connection in which **packets** of data can travel directly from and to your computer system, eliminating the mediation of the mini- or mainframe host computer (compare **dialup access**). Because a direct Internet connection is established, you can run **clients** such as **Eudora** or **Mosaic** on your computer system. The successor to SLIP, PPP offers superior data compression, data negotiation, and error correction.

port address

A number that identifies the location of an **application program** that is running on an Internet **host**. This number appears in the **header** of a **datagram.** It tells the destination computer to deliver the data to the appropriate application. This number is part of the information needed to **demultiplex** incoming messages—in other words, to break down the incoming byte stream into meaningful data that can be delivered to the correct application. *Compare* **protocol address, socket.**

Some port numbers, called **well-known ports**, are standardized with a fixed number because they provide access to **well-known services** such as **FTP** and **Telnet.** Others are dynamically allocated as needed.

Positive Acknowledgment with Re-Transmission (PAR)

In a computer network, a method of ensuring the reliable delivery of data. A computer using PAR keeps sending the message until it receives a confirmation from the destination computer that the message was received intact. The **Transmission Control Protocol (TCP)**, one of the fundamental **TCP/IP** protocols, uses PAR.

Post Office Protocol (POP)

In **electronic mail,** a **protocol** that functions as a **Message Transfer Agent (MTA)** (a mail handling utility) for users who are accessing the host from single-user machines, such as personal computers. The protocol provides the means to store incoming messages until the remote user logs on. Then, the protocol automatically **downloads** new messages to the user's computer. Subsequently, the user can use a **client** program such as **Eudora** to read and reply to new messages. The replies are then **uploaded.**

For PC users accessing the Internet, the advantage of POP is that you aren't stuck with the mail-reading program that's available on the **host** system you're accessing. Instead, you use user-friendly client programs such as **Eudora** to read your mail. Because this program runs on your system, it can directly access your printer, making it much easier to print your incoming and outgoing messages.

| posting |

In **Usenet**, an **email** message that has been sent to a **newsgroup** rather than to a specific individual.

Like an email message, the posting has a **header** that includes information about the person who sent the message, the subject of the message, a synopsis of the message's contents, and keywords that help to categorize the message's content. The header is followed by the body of the message, as in the following example:

```
alt.usage.english #29010 (15 + 141 more)
From: tuffy@mage.bmc.uu.se (Bernard Kludge)
Newsgroups: alt.anagrams
[1] Three Letter Acronyms (TLA)
Date: Mon Apr 18 10:18:26 EDT 1994
Organization: Uppsala University
Lines: 15
Distribution: world
Is there a list anywhere of self-referential
three-letter acronyms? Here's my start...
TLA     Three letter acronym
TTM     Three too many
ITA     Ignore This Acronym
Send me yours and I'll post 'em en masse..
```

The term "posting" suggests the public nature of sending a message to Usenet; anyone who wishes to do so can **subscribe** to the newsgroup and read any of the postings. Usenet postings fall into two categories.

Do read a newsgroup for a while—at least a couple of weeks—before posting. You'll get a better feel for the nature of the newsgroup's discussions. In addition, carefully observe every detail of Usenet **netiquette**: for example, write a useful and descriptive subject line for your posting, and be polite and show consideration for others. Above all else, remember that many people will read your posts (and draw conclusions about you).

Don't post a question to a newsgroup without first obtaining and reading the newsgroup's **FAQ** (Frequently Asked Questions). And don't post a "test message" to see if it gets through—this is highly irritating to regular Usenet readers, and you may get **flamed**. If you feel you must perform a test, post your message to alt.test or misc.test, which were provided for this purpose.

postmaster

Within an **Autonomous System (AS)**, the person who has the responsibility for handling **electronic mail** and dealing with the many problems that arise, such as misdirected messages.

PostScript (PS)

A **Page Description Language (PDL)**, a programming language that can be used to specify precisely how text should appear on the printed page, that is widely used to encode text files. A file that has been encoded with PostScript has the extension ps. To read or print this file, you need a **text editor** that is capable of displaying PostScript on-screen, or a word processing program (such as Microsoft Word) and a printer (such as a PostScript-compatible laser printer) that is capable of interpreting the PostScript commands. PostScript files cannot be read on-screen without a PostScript-compatible **parser**.

POTS

See **Plain Old Telephone Service (POTS).**

PPP

See **Point-to-Point Protocol (PPP)** and **Point of Presence (PPP).**

presentation layer

In the **Open Systems Interconnection (OSI) Reference Model** of computer networks, the layer that governs the representation of the data to be transmitted, including **encryption** and **compression.** This layer has not been considered to have a direct analogue in the Internet's **architecture.** However, there is increasing interest in the Internet community to safeguard user **privacy** by means of encryption protocols—for example, see **Privacy Enhanced Mail (PEM)**—and to cut down the costs of data transmission by means of compression techniques such as **JPEG.**

privacy

In the Internet, a presumed right to have exclusive access to your account and the files stored in your **home directory** (the portion of your **host** system's disk storage that is set aside for your use), such that you are not subject to searches of this area without your permission.

Many Internet users are shocked to learn that privacy, as defined above, is almost completely illusory on the Internet. Put simply, Internet usage is not secure under default conditions (but *see* **cryptography**). Devices and programs exist that are capable of detecting and logging virtually every keystroke you type. Unscrupulous system administrators may read your messages and browse through your directory without your knowing. A misdirected email message is "bounced" back to your system **postmaster**, where it can easily be read by computer staff people. Even if you erase information you do not want someone to find, it can be recovered through "undelete" programs or recovered from extensive tape backups.

A celebrated example of the lack of privacy on the Internet: As one of the puzzles posed as part of the **Internet Hunt**, a monthly information retrieval game, librarian Rick Gates supplied nothing more than the **electronic mail address** of a volunteer and challenged players to find out as much as possible about this volunteer. The winning team discovered no fewer than 148 separate facts about the volunteer, including his employer (the CIA!) and the name of his fiancee. Much of this information was gleaned by searching **archives** of **Usenet** postings.

As the Internet comes to the fore as the medium of choice for interpersonal communication, and eventually grows into a **National Information Infrastructure (NII)** in which voices and images will flow as easily as text and data, the issue of Internet privacy will take on additional importance. When a new communication system emerges, deliberate action may be required to extend previous legal protections to the new medium. Technological innovations, notably in **cryptography** and the emerging **Privacy Enhanced Mail (PEM)** standards, may work to increase the privacy of Internet communication, but many agencies of the U.S. federal government oppose these measures out of the fear that organized crime will be able to exchange messages without fear of detection (*see* **Clipper Chip** and **Electronic Frontier Foundation**).

Privacy Enhanced Mail (PEM)

A proposed addition to the **Simple Mail Transfer Protocol (SMTP)** that would ensure the **privacy** of **electronic mail** communication on the Internet by allowing users to employ **encryption**, so that only the intended recipient of the message would be able to read it. PEM is currently under development.

The existing Internet mail **protocols** provide no means for ensuring the **authentication** or **privacy** of electronic mail communication. For example, if someone should obtain your **login name** and **password**, that person could send threatening or harassing messages in your name. A college student recently learned this to his dismay after failing to log off after using a public terminal in a crowded campus computing center; someone used his account to send President Clinton a death threat. And if an investigative agency wishes to do so, it is not technically difficult to obtain archives of the electronic messages you have sent, even after you have "deleted" them, as the Iran-Contra conspirators learned to their dismay. Fawn may have shredded the paper trail while Ollie deleted the email, but a tape tucked away in the computer center's archives told all.

One doesn't need to be a terrorist or drug dealer to desire more confidentiality and privacy in electronic communication. It is but a small feat for a knowledgeable hacker to assemble a remarkably accurate picture of an Internet user's political opinions, employment situation, and sexual inclinations by ransacking electronic mail and Usenet archives.

Private Branch Exchange (PBX)

A local **digital** telephone exchange that can be installed in an organization, providing noise-free voice and data communications internally. Some organizations use PBXs as the physical basis for **local area networks (LANs)** and for Internet access. Current PBX designs limit data transfer to 64 Kbps, too slow for most LAN uses and only adequate for external Internet access.

privatization

The devolution of publicly-owned resources to the private (business) sector, often with the assumption that a government lacks the experience and competitive drive to manage such resources effectively, or that a government should not compete with private sector firms involved in the same industry.

Current plans call for the privatization of the **NSFNET**, which currently provides the Internet **backbone**, beginning in 1994.

problem user

A user who repeatedly or habitually engages in malicious or destructive acts.

prompt

An on-screen symbol or message indicating that the system is ready to receive command input. In PCs running MS-DOS, for instance, the prompt looks like this: C:>. On **UNIX** systems, the prompt is usually a greater-than sign (>).

proprietary

Designed using secret or only partially documented features by the manufacturer; a *proprietary* communications link, for example, would be defined by undisclosed electronic characteristics that would make it impossible or illegal for another company to imitate it. A proprietary design may be motivated by a genuine desire to retain all the benefits of the innovation and expense that went into product development—or it might be aimed at locking buyers into purchasing more of the same company's products. The networking community has learned to resist proprietary designs because they make it very difficult to achieve **interoperability**, which is the basis of **internetworking**.

proprietary standard

A **standard** (a set of rules or specifications for the design or operating characteristics of a computer device) that is developed and promoted by a single manufacturer.

If the firm can succeed in its goal of establishing its standard as the **de facto standard**, it is likely to profit handsomely: Customers may be forced to buy additional, **compatible** equipment from the firm at high margins of profit (*see* **connector conspiracy**). In computer networking, proprietary standards can cause problems if they prevent the connection of equipment made by different manufacturers. For this reason, the people who buy network equipment and create computer networks prefer **open standards**. A proprietary standard may become an open standard if the firm that created it proposes that it be accepted as an international **de jure standard**. For example, IBM proposed its proprietary protocol for long-distance data linking, the Synchronous Data Link Control (SDLC) protocol, to the ISO for acceptance internationally. The ISO adopted the modified standard as part of its **Open Systems Interconnection (OSI) protocol suite**.

Prospero

A **client** program that enables the user to **mount** a remote directory so that it appears to be part of the **host** system's file system.

Prospero is very much unlike other protocols that provide this service, such as **Andrew File System (AFS), Alex,** and **Network File System (NFS)**. AFS, Alex, and NFS give users access to directories on other systems. The mounted directories appear as though they were part of the file system on the user's machine. In contrast, Prospero provides a way for the user to construct multiple views of what appear to be a single collection of files across the Internet—views that are organized as the user pleases.

protocol

A **standard** that governs the operation of a network communications function by providing a clear-cut set of rules for its operation, as well as the specific computer programs that are designed to implement these rules. A computer network's **architecture** is described by listing the protocols that govern each of its **layers** and describing how they work. *See* **Open Systems Interconnection (OSI) Reference Model**.

protocol address

A number that appears in the **header** of a **datagram** that identifies the **transport protocol** to which it is to be passed. For example, a **datagram** that is sent by **Transmission Control Protocol (TCP)** on the source computer must be delivered to the corresponding TCP on the destination computer, so that (among other things) the data can be reassembled in the correct order. To simplify the delivery process, standard numbers are assigned to frequently-accessed transport protocols such as TCP and **User Datagram Protocol (UDP)**.

protocol converter

In a **gateway** that bridges two networks that operate with dissimilar protocols, the software that converts data formatted with one network's protocols so that it can be transmitted on the other network.

protocol number

A number in the **header** of an IP **datagram** that identifies the **protocol** to which the data should be given after it arrives at its destination. If the number is 17, for example, the data goes to the **Transmission Control Protocol (TCP)** for processing. *Compare* **port address**.

protocol stack

In a **layer** model of a network, a "layer-cake" conception of how a network host originates and receives network communications. Each layer in the stack is governed by a protocol designed to perform a clear-cut task. Applications prepare the data, and pass it "down" the stack to the **transport layer** (where it's broken down into segments), the **network layer** (where it's put into addressed **datagrams** and **routed**), and finally to the **data link layer** and **physical layers**, which handle its transmission across each point-to-point **hop** in the transmission). *See* **Open Systems Interconnection (OSI) Reference Model.**

protocol suite

A collection of related **protocols** (standards) that together comprise the specifications for a computer network. Each of the protocols addresses network functionality at a given **layer**, such as the **data link layer** or the **transmission layer**. The two competing protocols suites for internetworking are the **Internet Protocols** and the **Open Systems Interconnection (OSI) protocol suite.** *See* **Open Systems Interconnection (OSI) reference model.**

pseudo top-level domain

In a **domain name** such as *wrlx.udac.bitnet*, a name that indicates to Internet **routers** that the host with this name resides on a network that lacks full Internet connectivity (in the preceding example, **BITNET**). The name appears to be a **top-level domain** because it appears at the end of the series of host names.

Public Data Network (PDN)

A **wide area network (WAN)** whose services are open via subscription to the general public. Examples include **bulletin board systems (BBS)**, online services such as CompuServe locally accessible through **X.25** access points, and the Internet.

public domain

A work, such as a computer program or short story, that has been expressly made available to the public for reproduction or alteration for any purpose, including commercial gain.

Don't assume that anything you download from the Internet is necessarily in the public domain, just because it lacks a copyright notice. International copyright law specifies that a work's rights remain the author's unless the author has specifically and deliberately given them up.

public domain program

A computer program that has been expressly made freely available to the public, with no restrictions on further use, modification, or incorporation into commercial products. *Compare* **copyleft, shareware**.

Do note the word "expressly" in the above definition. The United States became a signatory to the Berne Convention treaty in 1989, which holds that a work is copyrighted *even if no copyright notice appears*. The Berne convention holds that copyright inheres in the creation of a work.

 Don't use or modify program code you **download** from the Internet for use in a commercial product without getting permission from the author.

public key cryptography

A method of encrypting a message (enchipering it so that it can be read only by its intended recipient) that does not require the sender to convey a **key** (the code used to decode the message) to the recipient. In public key cryptography, the encryption key differs from the decryption key. People can and should make their encryption keys private. This key is needed so that the sender can encrypt the message. When the message is received, the receiver uses a private decryption key too decode the message. This method is secure as long as it is not possible to derive the secret decryption key from the public encryption key. Public key cryptography has been proposed as a means of ensuring electronic mail **privacy** on the Internet. *See* **encryption**.

query

In a computer **database** search system such as the one made available in **WAIS**, a search question that has been formulated in such a way that the system can understand it and use it. *See* **Boolean operator**.

read only

Able to be read but not altered or deleted. A *read-only* file can be opened, but you can't save changes to it or erase it.

read-only access

A mode of remote access in which you are permitted to read and retrieve files, but never to alter or destroy them. **Anonymous FTP** uses read-only access.

real life (RL)

In **MUDs** (multi-user role-playing games), the real world, as opposed to the fantasy world in the game. Two users who develop a friendship in a MUD may decide to meet in RL.

real time

Not delayed; occurring as fast in the computer as the corresponding process would occur if the computer wasn't involved. **Internet Relay Chat (IRC)** provides an example of a real-time Internet application: Your messages are conveyed to other IRC users as quickly, or almost as quickly, as they would be if you were sitting in the same room (or hot tub) with them. You see their replies just as quickly.

reassembly

In a **packet switching network**, the process of reaggregating the data **packets** so that they once again form a coherent message. This is performed by the computer that receives the message.

rec

One of the seven **world newsgroup** categories in **Usenet**, this category includes **newsgroups** relating to recreational interests, such as movies, comics, science fiction and Star Trek, audio systems, sports cars, aviation, backpacking, collecting, brewing, cooking, board games, humor, hunting, kites, music of all kinds, pets, ham radio, skiing, sports, and more.

receipt notification

In **electronic mail**, a feature that lets you know if the recipient of your message indeed received the message and opened it.

recursion

In computer programming, the ability of a part of the program to refer to itself and call itself to perform repeated processing tasks. The prevalence of recursion in programming leads computer people to make puns and jokes with a recursive flavor, such as the name of the popular UNIX-like operating system GNU—short for GNU's Not UNIX.

Regional Bell Operating Company (RBOC)

A regional telephone company that was created as a result of the 1982 divestiture of AT&T, which forced the former telephone monopoly out of the local and regional telephone business.

regional network

A **wide area network (WAN)**, usually constructed of leased 56 Kbps and **t1** lines, that provides Internet access to a defined region, such as a state or several contiguous states. Linked by national and international **backbones**, regional networks have their origins in university consortiums that sought to promote Internet connectivity for educational and research purposes; many are now transforming themselves into for-profit **service providers** that aggressively seek commercial as well as research and educational subscribers.

registered host

A **host** that uses an **IP address** obtained from the **Network Information Center (NIC)**.

Every host that's directly connected to the Internet must have a unique IP address—otherwise, the Internet's **routers** would not be able to deliver information correctly.

Relcom

In Usenet, one of several **alternative newsgroup hierarchies** that are carried and propagated only by those Usenet sites that elect to do so (in contrast to **world newsgroups**, which are automatically fed to every Usenet subscriber). The Russian-language Relcom **newsgroups** are mainly distributed within Russia, but they may appear on some European and North American systems that can handle the display of Cyrillic script.

relevance feedback

In advanced **WAIS clients**, such as xwais (a WAIS client for **X Windows** workstations) an innovative feature that lets you "show" WAIS a document that you've found relevant to your interests, so that it can automatically construct a refined **query** that will enable you to find more documents pertinent to your interests.

reliable

Able to tolerate faults and continue to function. The **TCP/IP** protocols assume that some portions of the network are unreliable, and assure the delivery of data by finding alternate routes or retransmitting the data until it is correctly receieved.

remote host

A **host** that you access via **Telnet, FTP,** or a **resource discovery tool** such as **Gopher** or **WAIS.** *See* **remote login.**

| remote login |

In **Telnet**, the procedure by which you establish a connection with a **remote host**. To **log on**, you must type a **login name** (that name that was provided to you when you established your **account**) and a **password**. If you are connecting to a publicly-accessible application by using a **port address**, you need not type a login name or password.

When you use Telnet to access a remote computer, the program establishes the connection using the **TCP** protocol, which lets you enter into a dialogue with the remote machine. In addition, Telnet handles the job of translating between your computer's screen display and the display technique used by the remote host. For example, you may be using a Macintosh to access a Sun workstation, which is a very different machine. Telnet manages this translation job by creating a **Network Virtual Terminal (NVT)**—a very basic **line mode terminal**.

| Remote Procedure Call (RPC) |

A protocol that allows a **client** to start a program stored on a **remote host**. The output of this program is returned to the client. An example of a client that uses RPC is the **Network File System (NFS)** protocol.

| remote server |

In the **client-server model** of network application organization, a **server** that is located on some computer system other than the user's home system. For example, there are thousands of **Gopher** servers worldwide, any of which can be accessed by any Internet user.

remote system

A computer system located on a network other than the one to which the user's system is connected, so that it must be accessed via Internet links. It's "remoteness" isn't necessarily a matter of geographical distance; the remote system could be next door, or in Sri Lanka.

remote terminal

A keyboard and screen that are linked to another computer located elsewhere. *Compare* **diskless workstation**.

repeat post

In **Usenet**, the reposting of a previous **post** for informational purposes (*see* **FAQ**) or in response to a request.

repeater

In a computer network, a device that extends the practical length of a network cable by receiving, amplifying, and rebroadcasting the network signals.

Request for Comments (RFC)

Acronym for Request for Comments. These documents, more than 1,000 in number, constitute the chief means of on-line, electronic publication for the Internet research and development community. Among them are found the standards for the **TCP/IP** and other **protocols** that form the basis of the Internet. Although not referreed publications in the academic sense, RFCs are subject to technical and editorial review before publication.

The humility of the title "Request for Comments" reflects the democratic, communitarian nature of Internet engineering development: Many of these documents actually contain authoritative statements regarding the Internet standards that have created the fastest-growing communication system in human history. But not all RFCs contain technical standards. Some contain notes on conferences, the minutes of technical committees, or notes for new users.

Request for Discussion (RFD)

In **Usenet**, a **posting** sent to the group news.announce.newgroups that contains a proposal for the creation of a new **newsgroup**. Subsequent postings to this group will contain opinions for and against the creation of the new newsgroup. If the opinion seems positive, the person who proposed the newsgroup may issue a **Call For Votes (CFV)**.

resource

In the Internet, an item available on a **host** that may prove valuable to you. For example, **Gopher** resources include text files, binary files, sound files, image files, phone books, WAIS searches, and Telnet links that connect directly with additional resource locations. *See* **resource discovery tool**.

resource discovery tool

One of several programs that were developed to help Internet users discover and retrieve **resources** (such as files, documents, programs, sounds, and graphics). The most widely-used resource discovery tools are the following: **Archie** (for finding files in directories that are publicly accessible by means of **anonymous FTP**); **WAIS** (for finding documents in more than 1,000 Internet-accessible databases), **Gopher** (a menu-based **browser** that provides user-friendly access to FTP- and WAIS-accessible resources), and **World Wide Web (**a **hypertext** browser).

Tip: Because it seamlessly integrates all of the Internet resource discovery tools, the World Wide Web (WWW) is well on its way to becoming the premier resource discovery tool on the Internet. By means of WWW, you can access FTP, Gopher, and WAIS resources in addition to those available exclusively to WWW browsers.

resource sharing

The basic motivation for **internetworking**. In an **internet**, every **host** on the network is an **autonomous** computer that, ideally, can extend its reach to access **resources** available on other computers. The mere fact that these two computers are separated by several thousand miles should not matter.

Reverse Address Resolution Protocol (RARP)

In the **Internet Protocols,** a **protocol** (standard) that does precisely the opposite of the **Address Resolution Protocol (ARP)**—that is, it converts **Ethernet** addresses to **IP addresses**. The translation is necessary because most of the local area networks connected to the Internet use a different method for **addressing**, that is, directing a message to the correct computer. This protocol operates invisibly, taking care of the details of translating messages between various physical networks so that, from the user's perspective, the Internet is a single **logical network** (a system that appears to be homogeneous because all of its devices seem to operate in the same or much the same way). *Compare* **Address Resolution Protocol (ARP)**

| RFC |

See **Request for Comments (RFC).**

| rm |

One of the essential **UNIX** commands, rm deletes a file. Before you use this command, be sure you really want to delete the file; once you do, you can't recover it. To delete the file called *information-glut*, for example, type the following and press *Enter.*

```
rm information-glut
```

| rn |

A **newsreader** for UNIX-based systems that allows the user to read and respond to messages posted in **Usenet newsgroups**. Written by Larry Wall in the mid-eighties, rn is probably the most widely used news reading program in the world. However, it is outmoded. A serious limitation of rn is its inability to organize Usenet **articles** into **threads** (new subjects and their **follow-on postings**).

> **Tip** If you've been using rn, find out whether your system offers **trn**—a **threaded newsreader** that is an extended version of rn. If not, other threaded newsreaders, such as **nn** or **tin**, may be available.

| robust |

Able to keep functioning in spite of varying network conditions, including failures of some components.

rot-13

In **Usenet**, a simple encryption technique that can be used to make all or part of a **posting** unreadable, save by someone who knows how to decrypt the scrambled text. Rot-13 works by "rotating" or swapping each character with one exactly 13 letters from its position in the alphabet; thus "a" becomes "n."

Rot-13 is not a secure encryption technique, since the commands used to unscramble the text are easily found. It is used to "hide" text that some might find offensive, such as an ethnic joke. The message: If you think you might find the material offensive, don't decrypt it. If you do and you get offended, it's your fault, not the poster's.

Do encrypt anything you post that might prove offensive, and precede the encrypted text with a message explaining what the ciphertext contains and why you've encrypted it.

router

One of two basic **Internet** devices (the other is the **host**), this is an electronic device that connects a **local area network (LAN)** to a **wide area network (WAN)** and handles the task of routing messages between the two networks. A router designed to work with the Internet is called an **IP router**.

A router is essentially a computer that's dedicated to its task (routing messages), so unused computers can be put to work as routers, if need be (*see* **toasternet**). But routers designed especially for this function contain the input and output connections needed to link **local area networks (LANs)** to the Internet.

One measure of the phenomenal growth of computer networking is the equally phenomenal success of companies (such as Cisco Systems) that make networking products, such as routers. Revenues for the networking hardware industry exceeded US$1 billion in 1993.

routing

In a **packet-switching network**, the process of deciding which **router** to use in sending a **packet** of data to its destination. Before it reaches its destination, the packet may travel over several physically distinct networks, each of which has routers that pass it on to the next routing point.

If a **host** has only one gateway to the Internet, there's no decision involved. In a **multihomed host** (a host with more than one routing gateway to the larger Internet world), routing is handled by a dynamic routing program. In multihomed hosts, there is more than one way for the packet to reach its destination, so the routing process involves finding a pathway that's not already overloaded with data (or inoperable for some reason). In the Internet, this decision is made by the **Internet Protocol (IP)** software and is physically accomplished by devices called **IP routers**.

routing algorithm

In **distributed routing**, a routing decision-making technique that is embodied in a computer program, running on a **router.** The router dynamically determines which path on the Internet is best to take a **datagram** to its destination. The most popular routing algorithm is called the **distance-vector routing algorithm**. *Compare* **routing protocol**.

routing domain

An area of administrative control that characterizes an **Autonomous System (AS),** a collection of networks under the control of a single administrative organization. Within this domain, the AS possesses the right to determine subdomain names and **subnets**, as well as to structure the network's **topology** as it pleases.

Routing Information Protocol (RIP)

A popular **Interior Gateway Protocol (IGP)** that is used to route **datagrams** within an **Autonomous System** (a collection of networks under the control of a single administrative agency, such as a university or corporation). Employing a **distance-vector routing algorithm**, RIP builds a table by means of **convergence** and finds the shortest route over which to send the data. Although RIP is widely used and commonly included in **routers**, it has many deficiencies that have led to the development of the **Open Shortest Path First (OSPF)** protocol.

routing protocol

In **routing**, the standard employed to govern the process of deciding how best to send a **packet** of data to its destination. A routing protocol embodies a **routing algorithm** and provides means for building **routing tables**.

In the Internet, routing takes place on two different levels. Within an **Autonomous System** (a collection of networks under the control of a single administrative agency, such as a university or corporation), routing is governed by an **Interior Gateway Protocol (IGP)**. Some of these protocols are proprietary ones that are embedded in particular brands of routers. The most popular **open protocol** is the **Routing Information Protocol (RIP)**. A new IGP protocol that provides a better solution for large networks is the **Open Shortest Path First (OSPF)** protocol. The protocol currently used to route data from the Autonomous System to the wider Internet is called the **Exterior Gateway Protocol (EGP)**, but a newer protocol called **Border Gateway Protocol (BGP)** addresses EGP's deficiencies and is in increasing use.

| routing table |

In an **IP router**, the table used to route a **datagram** to the router on a bordering system that will send it on its next **hop**. For a stub end network that has only one connection to the Internet, this table is very simple and can be written by the **network administrator**: It simply says, "If the datagram is addressed to a network other than this one, send it out through the **router** to the next destination upstream." The table can also be constructed by a **routing algorithm**, a program that decides which of two or more alternative routes is best. Routing algorithms come into play when a network has more than one connection to the Internet.

| scale well |

To continue to operate without degrading network performance despite the exponential growth of the network. A protocol that *scales well* will continue working efficiently while rapid growth occurs.

scale-up problem

The overloading of Internet system capabilities or **resource** accessibility that occurs as the number of new hosts grows at a rapid rate.

The Internet has been faced with a series of scale-up problems, many of which have stimulated creative and even brilliant engineering solutions. A current example: **WAIS**.

The software for this database-accessing program served well when only a few hundred databases were available, but the number is now well over 1,000. WAIS numbers generally— the number of databases, as well as the number of users trying to access them—appear to be doubling roughly every seven months. But the more people who try to access WAIS, the more difficult WAIS is to use. Already, WAIS is one of the least accessible of the several **resource discovery tools** on the Internet; you frequently get the message that the server is busy. In addition, WAIS users feel overwhelmed by the number of databases available and the paucity of on-line information about them. When you access WAIS, you get a list of more that 1,000 databases that you have to page through in search of the information you want.

A project at the University of Lund, Sweden, seeks to remedy the database selection problem by developing software that can automatically detect new WAIS databases, automatically classify them according to a widely-used subject classification scheme, and sort them into a subject-classified Gopher menu, as in the following example:

```
        Subject tree (based on UDC)

  -> 1. General, Bibliography, Library science/
     2. Philosophy, Psychology, Etics/
     3. Religion, Theology/
     4. Social sciences/
     5. Mathematics, Natural sciences/
```

6. Applied sciences, Medicine,Technology/
7. Art, Architecture, Music, Sports/
8. Linguistics, Philology, Literature/
9. Geography, Biography, History/

Internet engineers have had to deal with so many scale-up problems that much effort is expended to make sure that new protocols **scale well**.

sci

One of the seven **world newsgroup** categories in **Usenet**, this category includes **newsgroups** relating to the sciences, including aeronautics, astronomy, biology, economics, engineering, geology, mathematics, medicine, physics, psychology, statistics, and more.

scroll mode terminal

A computer **terminal** that is designed to display one line of text at a time and to scroll up one line to make room for the next. If you've used a PC equipped with MS-DOS, you already know how this works: DOS transforms your expensive personal computer into a very generic scroll mode terminal. The Internet's default terminal definition (its **network virtual terminal**), defined by the **Telnet** protocol, is a simple scroll mode terminal. *Compare* **page mode terminal**.

seal of approval (SOAP)

A SOAP is a message attached to an article in the proposed Internet encyclopedia (called **Interpedia**) that indicates some person's or organization's judgment regarding the quality, veracity, or utility of the document. Seals of disapproval have also been proposed.

The SOAP concept arose in discussion groups about the **Interpedia**, a publicly-created Internet encyclopedia of human knowledge. Since anyone (in principle) can contribute an article to the encyclopedia, the articles will naturally vary in quality. The SOAP concept reconciles the principles of open access to public contribution and academic freedom with the legitimate needs of readers to access reliable information. A SOAP attached to a document by a competent practicing engineer, for instance, would help to attest to its technical accuracy. This interesting concept thus offers a significant democratization of the academic procedure of peer review of scientific journal articles. A negative peer review can keep an article out of print—and often for reasons that are later found to be attributable to professional jealousy, narrow-mindedness, and fear of innovation. In the Interpedia, readers will be able to read the document and its SOAPS, and reach their own conclusions.

security

Collectively, the measures taken by a network administrator to safeguard a **host**, and more broadly the Internet, from unauthorized access and malicious destruction at the hands of computer criminals.

It's a thankless task—and, with current Internet technology, it may very well be impossible. A series of dramatic computer break-ins in February, 1994, that netted thousands of corporate and university passwords illustrated the vulnerability of the Internet's antiquated **authentication** measures. Thanks to the break-ins, the **Computer Emergency Response Team (CERT)** advised every Internet user to change their **passwords**.

In a 1994 interview, Internet pioneer Vincent Cerf singled out security issues as one of the central challenges facing the Internet. A measure of the merit of Cerf's emphasis: Texas computer manufacturer Compaq Corporation has a T1

(1.544 Mbps) link to the Internet, but it's currently utilized far below its bandwidth potential due to fears regarding unauthorized access.

> **Tip:** Change your password frequently—at least every couple of months. And choose a *good* password, one that can't be easily cracked by known methods. *See* **password**.

Security Through Obscurity (STO)

In **cryptology** as well as the field of computer **security**, the philosophy that a message or vital computer system information is secure as long as would-be assailants do not know of its existence.

A major problem for **system administrators** is that, somewhere, your password (and everyone else's) must be kept in a file that the computer can access when you log in. Obviously, that's a prime target for **crackers** who wish to gain **unauthorized access** to computer systems for malicious purposes. In the past, this information was concealed by burying it within innocuous-looking program files, but this is no longer considered to be adequate. Today, password files are not considered secure unless they are resistant to attacks by the programs crackers write in an attempt to decode their contents.

sendmail

A **UNIX** program that serves as **Message Transfer Agent (MTA)** in an **electronic mail** system. Users originate messages using an electronic mail client, such as **Pine** or **Elm**. Sendmail works in the background to receive messages from the user's mail program and route the mail to its proper destination. The program also enables system administrators to create local **mailing lists, aliases,** and **nicknames**.

serial communication

The transmission of data between computers by means of a single circuit, which requires the bits of data to be sent in a stream, one after the other, like cars on a one-lane road. Within the computer, data is transmitted in parallel, like cars on a multi-lane freeway. As the road analogy suggests, serial communication is inherently slower than the parallel communications that take place inside your computer—and with modems, speed is further limited by the inherently low **bandwidth** of the telephone system. Serial communications can employ **asynchronous communication** techniques (in which each byte of data is demarcated by start and stop bits) or **synchronous communication** techniques (in which a block or **frame** of data is transmitted along with control information that synchronizes the arrival of each frame).

Serial Line Interface Protocol (SLIP)

One of the two most prominent **protocols (**standards) for **dialup IP access** (the other is **PPP**). The SLIP protocol establishes a method of Internet access in which a personal computer, linked to an Internet **host** via the telephone system and a high-speed modem, appears to the host as if it were an **Ethernet** port on the host system's **local area network (LAN)**. This establishes a temporary but direct Internet connection in which **packets** of data can travel directly from and to your computer system, eliminating the mediation of the mini- or mainframe host computer (compare **dialup access**). Because a direct Internet connection is established, you can run **clients** such as **Eudora** or **Mosaic** on your computer system.

 Do find out whether you have a choice between SLIP and PPP—and if PPP is available, choose PPP. Although SLIP is still used, it does not provide any compensation for noisy telephone lines; nor does it offer data compression, which could improve effective performance. The more recent **PPP** protocol is considered to offer superior performance and includes data compression, data negotiation, and error correction.

In the **client-server model** of computer applications, a program that receives requests for information from a **client** program, locates this information, and sends the information back to the client (and to the user). The Internet's most popular **resource discovery tools,** such as **Archie, Gopher, WAIS,** and the **World Wide Web,** employ the client-server model: To use these tools, you start a **client** program, which then handles the details of contacting the appropriate server.

Client-server programs provide an efficient means of distributing computer resources across a network. Instead of distributing the resources, such as files or databases, you distribute the means of accessing these resources—the client program. This is efficient because the client program is much smaller than the sum total of the resources it is able to access. An **Archie** client, for example, is able to access files that amount to more than 50 gigabytes (fifty billion characters).

Some of the best minds in the computer industry have been working on client-server computing software, but the technology is still in its infancy. What is the best method for facilitating public access to the diverse information resources of the Internet? **Gopher** employs an easy-to-use system of menus, through which the user can browse by choosing items from hierarchically-organized menus, while **WAIS** employs querying techniques drawn from database technology. Arguably, Internet users are voting with their keyboards: Of all the client-server technologies, **World Wide Web**—organized on **hypertext** principles—is experiencing the most rapid growth.

service provider

An organization that provides Internet access or communications links. A variety of service providers offer Internet access at the international, national, regional, and local levels, and offer a variety of access methods (ranging from high-speed **dedicated access,** for organizations and large local area networks, to **dialup IP** and **dialup access** for personal computer users).

Many of the organizations that currently provide public access to the Internet got their start as part of the **NSFNET,** which restricts commercial use of the NSFNET **backbone** according to its **Acceptable Use Policy (AUP).** Some of these organizations retain NSFNET's commitment to serve the educational and research communities as a public service, usually with state or U.S. subsidies, and maintain similar AUPs. Others, however, have made the transition to entrepreneurial networking, actively seeking business subscribers and working to extend their user bases as rapidly as possible. Several regional service providers have formed an organization called the **Commercial Internet Exchange (CIX),** which expressly aims to bypass the NSFNET backbone and its AUP restrictions.

Most service providers offer far more than mere physical connectivity—and well they might, because linking to the Internet is a complex process. An organization contemplating a **direct connection** to the Internet, for example, will need the proper equipment (including a **router** and **TCP/IP** software), a **leased line** for transport access to the service provider's access point, and assistance with the task of registering **IP addresses** and **domain names.** Some service providers, such as NEARnet, offer assistance with every phase of Internet connectivity.

| session layer |

In the **Open System Interconnection (OSI) Reference Model** of computer networks, the layer that enables a user to establish a **real-time** connection with another computer on the network. This layer isn't relevant to the Internet because its underlying **protocols** introduce delay, if necessary, to preserve the integrity of data. This is one of the reasons that the Internet protocols are not considered adequate for real-time voice and video transmission in the proposed **National Information Infrastructure (NII)**.

| SGML |

See **Standard Generalized Markup Language (SGML)**.

| shareware |

A copyrighted computer program that is made available on a "try before you buy" basis. If you like the program and decide to use it, you are expected to send the user a registration fee, which usually entitles you to receive technical support, upgrade notices, and printed copies of the documentation. *Compare* **copyleft**, **public domain program**.

| shell |

The portion of a computer **operating system (OS)** that interacts with the user. Some operating systems, such as UNIX, are designed so that users can choose the shell they prefer. *Compare* **kernel**.

shell account

A method of Internet access that gives you access to the **shell** (user interface) of a minicomputer or mainframe **host** system. On **UNIX** systems, you can run applications such as **FTP**, **Pine** (electronic mail), and **Gopher**. A type of **dialup access**, shell accounts require you to connect to the host system using a **modem** and telephone line. Owing to several inconveniences (such as the necessity of **downloading** files retrieved by FTP and the difficulty of printing **electronic mail** messages), dialup access is adequate only for occasional use from a home computer.

You'll encounter three different kinds of shell accounts :

- **"Dumped at the UNIX prompt"** In this, the simplest shell account, you're looking at an arcane symbol and a blinking cursor, but there isn't a clue about what to do next.

- **Menu-driven systems** You see an on-screen menu of options from which you can choose. This is an improvement, but the menus may not give you access to all the UNIX options available at the UNIX prompt.

- **Graphical user interface** (GUI) front ends A front end is a program that runs on your PC, providing an easy-to-use interface to the computer service you're contacting. The best of these employ GUI principles, with on-screen mousable windows, pull-down menus, and graphics galore. Several Internet service providers distribute GUI front ends for dialup access.

shouting

Using capital letters in **electronic mail** or a **Usenet** posting.

Do use other means of emphasis besides capital letters, such as **stars** (asterisks): "I'd *really* like to see that proposal by next Monday."

cannot restrain themselves from copying it for their own signature files.

This becomes the object of sarcastic comment, as in the following example:

```
------------------------------------
Steve Smith          lowly student,CMU

ssmith@ivy.edu                sig virus!
------------------------------------
```

signal-to-noise ratio

In electrical engineering, this term refers to the strength of the signal against background noise; in stereo systems, for instance, compact discs have a much better signal-to-noise ratio than cassette tapes. In **Usenet**, it is used ironically to rate the information content of a **newsgroup**. A newsgroup that is said to have a low signal-to-noise ratio may be subject to unproductive **flame wars**, irrelevance, silliness, or frequent flippant postings.

A low signal-to-noise ratio may condemn a newsgroup or mailing list to obscurity. Bruce Lewenstein, an associate professor of science and technology studies at Cornell University, followed a mailing list devoted to discussion of cold fusion research during a three-year period (1989 to 1992). "For the most part," Lewenstein notes, "the people who were active participants in that group were not the people actually doing the work. The signal-to-noise ratio was so bad that people who were seriously interested in cold fusion didn't bother to use that kind of public forum as a place to do their work."

When a newsgroup's signal-to-noise ratio degrades below tolerable levels, there is a solution: creating a **moderated newsgroup**. In a moderated newsgroup, postings are sent to a moderator for review before they are posted to the newsgroup. The result is generally a dramatic improvement in the group's signal-to-noise ratio, at the cost of spontaneity.

signature

A brief closing, appended to an **email** or **Usenet posting**, that provides information about the person who sent the message, such as the person's full name, organizational affiliation, telephone and fax numbers, and email address. Most **newsreaders** will automatically append a signature file, if such a file exists, to every Usenet message the user sends. Often, the signature includes **ASCII art**, such as a little picture of the starship Enterprise.

Do create a signature file if you're using a UNIX system. Create the file with a **text editor** such as **vi** or **EMACS**, name the file .signature, and place the file in your home directory. The system will automatically append the *signature* file to every Usenet message you send. To append the signature file to your email messages, ask for instructions on how to make the necessary modifications to your email software's configuration file.

Don't create a signature file that's inordinately lengthy (roughly 10 lines or more). Lengthy signature files waste network **bandwidth** and reflect a low commitment to Usenet and Internet ideals.

Simple Mail Transport Protocol (SMTP)

In the Internet's **application layer**, the layer in which one finds **protocols** (standards) of use to **application programs**, the protocol that governs the format of **electronic mail** messages. This protocol is also known by the **Request for Comments (RFC)** document that defines it: RFC822.

Simple Mail Transport Protocol　　SLIP

Pioneered by the ARPANET, the first network to witness the development of widespread electronic mail usage, the SMTP protocol has become the world's *de facto* protocol for electronic mail messages. It is understood by non-Internet networks to which the Internet is connected by **gateways**, linking a total (at this writing) of 137 nations in a single global electronic mail network.

SMTP is indeed a simple protocol; it describes an electronic mail message as plain **ASCII** text. It is now recognized that this has significant limitations in a computing environment increasingly capable of **multimedia** and, at the same time, increasingly plagued by **privacy** problems. More recent protocols, including the **Multi-Purpose Internet Mail Extensions (MIME)** and **Privacy Enhanced Mail (PEM)** address these mail-related issues.

Simple Network Management Protocol (SNMP)

A **protocol** (standard) that governs the communication between a management station (a computer running the appropriate software), and a program called an **agent**, which monitors the status of a network hardware device such as a **host** or **router**. For example, a router agent reports the number of **datagrams** that have been rejected due to errors in their headers. The purpose of SNMP is to automate as many network management tasks as possible so that the network administrator can have some semblance of a normal life.

Within the managed device, SNMP maintains a Management Information Base (MIB) that contains information regarding the device's status and configuration settings.

SLIP

See **Serial Line Interface Protocol (SLIP)**.

SLIP/PPP

A term used generically to refer to the two Internet protocols (standards) for **dialup IP**, called **Serial Line Interface
Protocol (SLIP)** and **Point-to-Point Protocol (PPP)**.

smiley

A sideways face, constructed from **ASCII** characters, that
helps to contextualize the meaning of an **electronic mail** message.

It's tough to convey humor, irony, or sarcasm by means of electronic mail. Consider this example:

```
This is another one of your pet ideas, isn't
it?
```

That could come across as a rather cold put-down. Now try
it with a smiley (a little winking smiley, actually):

```
This is another one of your pet ideas, isn't
it? ;-)
```

The smiley says, "I'm just teasing you in a friendly way."

There are two kinds of smileys—the kind that people actually use, and the kind that people create just to be clever. The
latter category properly belongs to **ASCII art**.

Here's a list of the smileys people actually use:

```
:-)     I'm making a joke; don't take this
        seriously.
;-)     I'm winking or flirting with you.
:-(     This makes me sad.
:-0     I'm overjoyed!
```

And here are some samples of the second kind:

```
@:-)    I'm wearing a turban
3:-)    My pet actually wrote this
[:-)    Can't hear you, I'm wearing a
        Walkman
```

Do use smileys sparingly; the overuse of smileys is considered a sign of **newbie**-ness. Some Internet users believe that the use of smileys testifies to an inability to express oneself clearly in language. Your best bet: Try to avoid the use of sarcasm, irony, and teasing entirely in electronic communications. The potential for misunderstandings, with potentially serious consequences, is high.

| snail mail |

Ordinary, first-class mail conveyed by the postal service (as opposed to **electronic mail**, which is considerably faster if not necessarily instantaneous).

| sneakernet |

The ultimate, low-cost computer **network**: You carry a floppy disk from one computer to another. On **Usenet**, bogus messages frequently appear informing a user community that, in the aftermath of an extensive cost-benefit analysis, a **local area network (LAN)** will be dismantled in favor of undergraduate couriers.

| soc |

One of the seven **world newsgroup** categories in **Usenet**, this category includes **newsgroups** relating to social issues or designed to facilitate social interaction. Topics covered include bisexuality, the issues of college life, discussions focused on the society and culture of dozens of ethnic groups, feminism, homosexuality, human rights, religion, and more.

socket

In Internet **addressing**, a combination of an **IP address** (which identifies a **host**) and a **port address** (which identifies an **application** running on this host). The two together can be used to identify a particular service throughout the Internet. This isn't necessary for **well-known services,** such as FTP and Telnet, because they use standard port numbers. If you want to access a unique program such as a MUD that is running on a remote host somewhere, you may have to supply the socket. To access a MUD, for example, you use **Telnet** and type the numerical IP address followed by the port number.

source

Properly, a computer program that contains source code, the uncompiled program instructions. This term is also used in reference to compiled programs that are ready to run. You can obtain both kinds of sources by means of **FTP**.

Do obtain sources from "official" sites, where the organization responsible for distributing the program has made it publicly available. You are less likely to obtain a program that has been tampered with by **crackers**.

Don't run a program obtained through FTP on a heavily-used central computer without first trying it on a workstation that's not connected to the network.

source address

In the **header** part of a **datagram** (a **packet** format defined by the **Internet Protocol [IP]**), the **IP address** of the user who originated the message.

Southeastern Universities Research Association Network (SURAnet)

A regional Internet network and **service provider** that serves 13 southeastern states (West Virginia, Virginia, South Carolina, North Carolina, Tennessee, Kentucky, Louisiana, Mississippi, Alabama, Georgia, Florida, Washington DC, Maryland, Delaware) as well as Puerto Rico and South America. The network is supported by a consortium of universities, research institutes, government research agencies, and commercial organizations that comply with **NSFNET's Acceptable User Policies (AUP)**.

spamming

A form of computer-based aggression that involves bombarding someone with uninvited, copious information that they must page through before proceeding. This is sometimes found in **MUDs** (multi-user computerized role-playing games), and is a cause for suspension of game-playing privileges. In **Usenet**, spamming is synonymous with **carpet bombing**, the pelting of dozens, hundreds, or even thousands of **newsgroups** with unwanted messages.

spewer

In **Usenet**, a species of **net.characters** who insist on **cross-posting** frequent, vitriolic, and generally unsupported statements of their personal opinion, generally without the slightest regard for the topic of **newsgroup** discussion. The proper remedy is a **kill file**.

SprintLink

A national **Public Data Network (PDN)** that has made a major commitment to providing Internet connectivity. The company makes Internet access available from its more than 300 points of presence (POP) in cities throughout the U.S. Lacking an **Acceptable Use Policy (AUP)** that would discourage business use and offering a connection to the **Commercial Internet Exchange (CIX)**, SprintLink is expected to become a major player in the growth of commercial Internet activity.

squelch

An action taken by an Internet host system administrator to suspend or cancel a user's account privileges.

The use of the Internet is not a right, but a privilege that can be revoked if an individual engages in unacceptable behaviors. These include harassing or threatening other computer users (**email terrorism**), engaging in software piracy, posting copyrighted material to Usenet discussion groups, posting defamatory messages that attack the reputation of Usenet posters, employing **mail bombing** (sending huge numbers of lengthy files) as a form of harassment; or using extreme or habitual profanity. Most system administrators give a warning before terminating your account privileges.

standard

A set of rules or specifications for the design or operating characteristics of a computer device.

Standards fall into two basic categories: **proprietary standards** (standards advanced by companies who hope to impose their way of doing things on the industry at large) or **open standards** (non-proprietary standards that are published and available for use by anyone who pleases). Either type of standard may become a **de facto standard** (a standard that comes into widespread use in spite of the lack of any rational effort to achieve this end). National and international standards organizations may attempt to foster

standardization by creating **de jure standards** (open standards that have the backing of these organizations). The **TCP/IP** protocols are open, de facto standards.

Standard Generalized Markup Language (SGML)

A **markup language** for plain **ASCII text** documents, such as **electronic texts**, that allows these documents to be transferred to a computer made by a different manufacturer in such a way that the formatting identifying distinct parts of the document, such as an abstract or title, can be recovered, displayed, and printed. SGML is defined by an international standard (ISO 8879:1986) of the **International Standards Organization (ISO)**. SGML is a widely-used markup language, particularly in academic fields involving the computational analysis of computer-readable texts.

SGML is a *generalized* markup language in that it does not specify just how the marked portions of the text should appear: It simply identifies a portion of a document as, for instance, a footnote. You need a program called a **parser** to display and read an SGML-encoded document. On an ASCII text display, such as a VT100 terminal, you see all the **tags** (the markup language's commands) in addition to the text, and this makes the document difficult to read. The parser lets you decide how you want the various parts of the document to appear when viewed and printed.

standardization

The widespread acceptance of a **de facto standard** or **de jure standard** in a technical community.

In computer networking, standards encourage capital investment and benefit users. As in other technical fields, they create a uniform market and thus encourage companies to manufacture equipment that embodies these standards. And the more equipment they manufacture, the more costs drop, thanks to manufacturing economies of scale. For networks, standards are all but indispensable. Early networking efforts were hampered by the existence of numerous **proprietary standards** that made it difficult to connect computers made by different manufacturers. One of the reasons for the phenomenal success of the Internet is the fact that its standards, the **TCP/IP** protocols, are **open standards** that anyone may freely use. Most of the networking equipment made today is **compatible** with the Internet protocols. *See* **Apocalypse of the Two Elephants, connector conspiracy.**

Tip: For **Usenet** discussions of standardization, check out the newsgroups comp.protocols.iso, comp.std.misc and comp.std.internat. A FAQ called Standards FAQ is posted to these groups at regular intervals.

star

An asterisk, as in the file-handling wild card expression "star-dot-star" (*.*).

steganography

A form of **encryption** (coding a message) that conceals the encrypted information within the least-significant bits making up a graphic image or a Usenet posting. The existence of such a concealed, encrypted message is virtually impossible to detect. Among the various encryption methods known to **cryptography**, the science of encryption and decryption, steganography is not universally admired; some argue that the encryption techniques are too easy to break and could be detected by programs that search messages automatically.

store-and-forward network

A method for creating a **wide area network (WAN)** by taking advantage of inexpensive long-distance telephone connections. In this system, exemplified by **FidoNet** and **UUCP**, a host gathers the day's **electronic mail** messages and **newsgroup** postings and, at a prearranged time, **uploads** these messages by means of a **modem** to a central distribution site, and **downloads** any mail or new postings from other systems. This system is not fast but it is highly effective; in a matter of days a message can propagate throughout a store-and-forward network of several hundred sites.

stub network

In network **topology**, a network that has only a single connection (by means of a **router**) to the network's **backbone**. The router need not be "intelligent"—if it encounters a packet addressed to a **host** outside the stub, the router simply sends it along the one and only path to the backbone.

subdirectory

In a hierarchical file system such as MS-DOS or UNIX, a **directory** (a catalog of related files) that has been nested within another directory. This is a relational concept; a directory is spoken of as a subdirectory to emphasize its inclusion within another directory.

> **Tip** If you're using **anonymous FTP**, you'll find that most **archive sites** place publicly-available files in a subdirectory called /pub. This may be further subdivided into directories for documents, programs, graphics, sounds, etc.

subdomain

Within the **domain name system,** a set of two or more sub-categories of hosts within the domain name that has been established for the organization.

For example, suppose a University of the Outer Banks applies to the NIC for the domain name *uob.edu.* Without any reference to the NIC, this university is now free to classify hosts within this domain by using subdomains, as in the following examples:

hum.uob.edu	Humanities faculty
soc-sci.uob.edu	Social sciences faculty
sci.uob.edu	Science faculty

subject selector

In a **newsreader** for **Usenet,** a program mode that displays the articles in the chronological order in which they were received. This is inconvenient because it's difficult to follow **threads.** *See* **threaded newsreader, thread selector.**

subnet

In Internet **addressing**, a subunit within an organization's network that has been identified as a distinct entity for datagram routing purposes by modifying the structure of **IP addresses**.

Creating a subnet is a different matter than creating a **subdomain** in the **domain name system.** A subdomain provides a way of organizing domain names in a logical way. Creating a subnet, in contrast, is a way of defining a physical network so that datagrams can be routed in a logical and efficient manner. For example, suppose that the design department in a corporation has two geographically separated branches. They have two separate **local area networks**

(LANs). To facilitate their communication with each other, it makes good sense to connect their LANs by means of a **bridge** and a leased line, and to define the two LANs as a single subnet.

---

subscribe

In **Usenet**, to identify a **newsgroup** as one that you would like to read, so that your **newsreader** program will display this newsgroup's name at the **newsgroup selector**. *Compare* **unsubscribe**.

---

supercomputer

An expensive and extremely fast computer, designed primarily for scientific applications, whose processing speed so markedly exceeds the capabilities of other contemporary computer systems that it is set aside for the exploration of problems that could not otherwise be investigated.

It would be absurd to try to define a supercomputer by stating a fixed number, such as 200 megaflops (millions of operations) per second, for any given definition of a supercomputer in fixed terms will quickly become obsolete. One of the faster supercomputers at this writing was capable of executing 5 gigaflops (5 *billion* operations per second). Today's supercomputers employ parallel processing: they work on the divide-and-conquer principle, with dozens or even hundreds of processing units each working on a part of the problem simultaneously. When all the processors have finished their work, they combine the information to get a final answer. The work gets done much faster than it would have if a single processor were put to work on the problem.

Most Internet users won't access supercomputers; they're designed for sophisticated, cutting-edge research in the sciences. But you can thank supercomputers for the **NSFNET backbone**. The **National Science Foundation**'s justification for creating NSFNET was to provide high-speed (45 Mbps) connectivity for the nation's supercomputer metacenters, such as the Air Force Supercomputer Center at Kirtland Air Force Base, the Center for Theory and Simulation in Science and Engineering (Ithaca, NY), and the National Center for Atmospheric Research (Boulder, CO). But NSFNET isn't fast enough to realize the current NSF goal of **Heterogeneous Distributed Computing (HDC)**, in which scientific researchers will be able to access supercomputers remotely and engage in **real-time**, high-**bandwidth** applications such as **interactive visualization**. In the coming years NSFNET will be **privatized** and the task of linking supercomputers will be taken over by the **National Research and Education Network (NREN)**, which will implement **gigabit networks** (with data transfer speeds of over 1 billion bits per second).

Switched Multimegabit Data Service (SMDS)

A **packet-switching network** that is designed to work in a local or regional telephone system that has converted its lines from **analog** to **digital**. SMDS can support data transfer rates of up to 155 Mbps.

This service, first offered in 1991, is part of a strategy by the **regional bell operating companies (RBOCs)** to provide an alternative to **public data networks**, which currently have most of the data communication business. However, SMDS will require a large capital investment, so rates will probably be high at first. The technology may find its initial application where a local or regional high-bandwidth connection is vitally needed—for example, between a medical imaging center and a physician's office. Because SMDS supports **full-motion video** and other **multimedia** applications, though, it may become a major player in computer networking once the capital costs have been amortized and rates drop to more reasonable levels. This may not happen until well into the next century.

synchronous

Timed, regulated by a timer or clock; at the **data link layer** in a computer network, a method of demarcating data by sending it in equally-sized blocks (**frames**) clocked by equal time intervals (*compare* **asynchronous***)*.

synchronous communication

One of two methods of solving the chief problem of **serial** communication: How to demarcate the beginning and the end of a unit of transmitted data (the other method is **asynchronous communication**). In synchronous communication, the two linked computers exchange timing and control messages so that they can exchange blocks of data, called **frames**. Modems that conform to the **V.42** error correction protocol can set up a synchronous link with another V.42-capable modem; this has the benefit of improving the **effective transfer rate** because it is not necessary to include a start and stop bit with each byte of transmitted data.

Synchronous Digital Hierarchy (SDH)

An international standard, defined by **CCITT**, for high-bandwidth **fiber optic** computer networks that mirrors the **SONET** protocol. *See* **Synchronous Optical Network (SONET)**.

Synchronous Optical Network (SONET)

A set of standards adopted by the **American National Standards Institute (ANSI)** for the use of high-bandwidth **optical fiber** to construct high-speed computer networks. The SONET standards pertain to the **physical layer** in the **Open Software Interconnection (OSI) Reference Model's** scheme of 7 stacked layers. SONET is designed to work with a number of **data link layer** technologies, including **Switched Multimegabit Data Service (SMDS)** and the **Fiber Distributed Data Interface (FDDI)**. Data transfer rates will range from 51.48 Mbps to 2.5 Gbps. A corresponding international version of SONET is called **Synchronous Digital Hierarchy (SDH).** Initially, SONET is likely to be used only for **local area networks (LAN)** and **Metropolitan Area Networks (MAN)**. But SONET technology could eventually provide the foundation for **Broadband ISDN** networks utilizing **cell relay** packet switching, which are likely to provide the **backbones** for the next century's **wide area networks (WAN)**.

syntax

The rules that govern the typing of commands or instructions in a **command-line** interface or a computer programming language. For the command to work, you must carefully observe the order in which the various parts of the command must be typed. In addition, you must exercise caution to insert spaces and other punctuation marks where they are required (and to omit them where they're not).

sysop

In a computer **bulletin board system (BBS)**, the person who operates and maintains the system; an abbreviation for system operatator.

system administrator

A computer professional who manages a single computer
or a collection of systems on a network, and takes care of such
tasks as installing hardware and software, upgrading hardware and software, assigning new accounts, designing and
implementing new applications, troubleshooting and solving problems, and performing routine maintenance tasks such
as checking for **viruses**, and performing regular backups.
Compare **network administrator**.

system utility

A computer program that helps the user cope with the
mechanics of using the computer, such as compressing
files, making backup files, or encrypting messages.

T1 carrier

At the **physical layer** of the Internet, a high-**bandwidth**
telephone trunk line that is capable of data transfer rates of
1.544 Mbps. The line is made of two **twisted pair** copper
cables. Much of the Internet's system of **regional backbones** is constructed from T1 **leased lines**.

T3 carrier

At the **physical layer** of the Internet, a very-high-**bandwidth** telephone trunk line that is capable of data transfer rates of 44.21 Mbps. The line is made of 28 T1 cables that are bundled together. The **NSFNET backbone** is constructed from T3 **leased lines**.

tag

In a **markup language** such as **Standard Generalized Markup Language (SGML)**, the commands embedded within plain **ASCII text** that describe the various parts of a document, such as the title or the abstract. When you open a marked document with a **parser** program, this program reads the tags and displays or prints the text with appropriate fonts and other formats.

talk

One of the seven **world newsgroup** categories in **Usenet**, this category includes **newsgroups** that expressly invite controversy and debate, which is often acrimonious. Topics include abortion, evolutionism vs. creationism, the use and abuse of animals, drugs, guns, and rape.

TCP

See **Transmission Control Protocol (TCP).**

TCP/IP

An acronym and abbreviation for the two fundamental **protocols** (standard) that make the Internet possible, the **Transmission Control Protocol** and the **Internet Protocol**. This acronym is used, however, to refer generally to the entire **protocol suite** that details every significant aspect of the Internet's functionality. In this usage, it is virtually synonymous with the **Internet**.

The use of a home computing system and data communications to avoid the commute to an office.

It's clear that telecommuting can reduce traffic and smog by a significant proportion, but it hasn't caught on—and not just because the boss wants you around to keep track of what you're doing. Workers themselves aren't crazy about telecommuting. They miss the social contact and networking opportunities that the office provides.

An emerging internetworking application in which two or more people can collaborate using the Internet and their computers as a medium. Aided by **real-time** audio and video, the participants work together in a collaborative "white space" that serves as a scratchpad for their work.

The use of the Internet to access geographically distant, computerized research tools, such as telescopes.

Many of today's sophisticated scientific research instruments are driven by computer-controlled systems and produce digital data, which is not meaningful until it has been processed by high-performance computers. And the results of scientific experiments carried out by means of these instruments are computerized images, tables, or other data that can be easily transferred via computer links. For these reasons, it is now possible to conceptualize an expensive, one-of-a-kind research installation as a distributed laboratory, which is accessible to researchers world-wide by means of the Internet.

A case in point is a US$1 million electron microscope for neuroscience applications recently developed at the Microscopy and Imaging Resource of the University of California, San Diego. The installation was designed from the beginning to be accessible on-line. Geographically distant researchers, who may not have sufficient research funding to travel to San Diego, can send specimens for analysis and control the microscope remotely. Networking the site has advantages beyond geographic convenience: The complex, three-dimensional images, which can take up to 10 hours to process on a workstation, can be sent to a nearby **supercomputer** that can process these images in less than a half hour.

Telnet

A **protocol**, as well as the software that implements it, that defines a **Network Virtual Terminal (NVT)** and allows users to log on to **remote hosts**. Based on the **client-server model**, Telnet provides a local **client** that contacts a remote **server**. *Compare* **tn3270**.

The Internet is composed of computers made by many different manufacturers, each with its own proprietary method of displaying information on computer screens (**terminals**). The commands for one computer brand's video display will not work on another's. Even the method of representing text on-screen differs: IBM mainframes use **EBCDIC**, while just about everyone else's computers use **ASCII**. The concept of **interoperability** would not mean much, in practice, if screen display incompatibilities prevented you from logging on to a remote host and operating the system as if you were sitting in front of it.

The Telnet protocol solves this problem by creating a simple **Network Virtual Terminal (NVT)**, which makes all Internet **hosts** appear to the user as if they employ exactly the same techniques for presenting information to the screen and exactly the same user commands for performing operations (such as typing and editing commands).

That's the good news. The bad news is that the terminal Telnet defines is primitive, at best-it's a **half-duplex, line mode terminal** that dates from the dark ages of computing, when you looked at your output on a teletype printer rather than a screen. Such a terminal can't send and receive information at the same time—it's one or the other. And you'll work with just one line at a time—lines you type, and lines received in reply. The terminal gets rid of lines you've already seen by scrolling them up, and they eventually disappear off the top of the screen. (If you've used MS-DOS, you're already familiar with the way this works.)

Here's what a Telnet session looks like. After starting Telnet, you see the Telnet prompt. You then type a command, like this one:

```
telnet>open spock.vulcan.gvsc.edu
```

After you press **Enter,** your command scrolls up one line, and Telnet sends *you* a message to tell you what it's doing:

```
telnet>open spock.vulcan.gvsc.edu
Trying 129.36.99.01...
```

If Telnet's efforts meet with success, you see a confirmation and you're asked to log in:

```
telnet>open spock.vulcan.gvsc.edu
Trying 129.36.99.01...
Connected to spock.vulcan.gvsc.edu.
Escape character is '^]'.
login:
```

The **escape character** lets you interrupt communications with the remote server and talk to Telnet directly. In this mode, you can obtain status information, cancel lengthy processes, or find out if the remote server is still alive.

terminal

A computer monitor and keyboard that can be connected via data communications links to a distant computer system. A "dumb" terminal has no processing circuitry of its own; its only function is to serve as a remote communication station for a computer that's installed somewhere else. When you access the Internet by means of **dialup access**, you turn your expensive PC into what is essentially a dumb terminal of the **host** that you're calling. *See* **terminal emulation**.

terminal adapter (TA)

A device that connects a computer (as well as fax machines and phones) to a digital telephone line. A TA is necessary, for example, if you obtain an **ISDN** line. Like a modem, a TA can be installed internally in a computer's expansion slot or you can get an external TA with its own power supply.

terminal emulation

In **dialup access**, the transformation of a personal computer into a device that electronically simulates the functions of a remote **terminal**. This is accomplished by **communication programs**, which let you choose from several different terminal emulations.

Tip: For dialup access to the Internet, the most commonly-used emulation is called VT-100.

testbed

In technology, a prototype system that has been set up so that researchers can investigate its properties and performance. The ARPANET was the testbed that led to the emergence of the Internet. There are currently several testbeds for the **gigabit networks.** For example, AURORA, a project jointly funded by IBM, Bellcore, MCI, and several universities, is using 2.4 Gbps MCI channels to link computer labs using **ATM** and several alternative technologies. The project's goal is to test the suitability of ATM for high-speed computer networking.

| **test posting** |

In Usenet, a **posting** (contributed article) sent by a **newbie** who isn't confident that the message will actually appear.

Do post a test message, if you must see a test posting to be convinced that it's working, to the groups alt.test or misc.test—that's what they're for. If you want to test whether **crossposting** works, you can post to alt.test and misc.test.

Don't send test postings to a Usenet newsgroup— there's already enough junk to read without someone's post that says, "I'm just trying to see if this will appear."

| **text editor** |

A program that is designed to let you enter and edit text on-screen. Text editors closely resemble word processing programs, except that they contain few facilities for formatting and printing documents. Text editors are designed to assist computer users in preparing text for use in computers, such as computer programs, computer-based documents such as help files, and **electronic mail**. Popular text editors commonly found on **UNIX** hosts include **EMACS** and **vi**.

| **text file** |

A file, containing nothing but the standard **ASCII** characters, that was created by a **text editor** and contains readable text.

This term is often used interchangeably with **ASCII file** (a file of any type that contains nothing but the standard ASCII characters). However, it's useful to make a distinction between text files, which are readable by humans, and ASCII files generally, which include several types of files (such as **uuencoded** files) that represent **binary files** using nothing but ASCII characters. If you try to read such a file on-screen, you'll see nothing but gibberish. You must decode the file with the proper utility, such as **uudecode**.

---

thread

In a **Usenet newsgroup**, a topic or subject that has received one or more **followup postings**. Some threads receive only one or two responses; others receive dozens or hundreds, and a few seem to last forever (much to the chagrin, eventually, of newsgroup participants). In most newsgroups, discussion revolves around several on-going threads, which perpetuate themselves as readers post new **followup postings** to the newsgroup. Occasionally, new subjects appear; they may merit no response at all, or become the focus of a new thread.

Tip: By far the best way to read Usenet is to use a **threaded newsreader**, such as **tin** or **trn**, which organizes the postings by thread topic. At the **thread selector** level, you see all the current thread topics. With a simple command, you switch to the **article selector** level, and you can read all the postings relevant to the thread in sequence. With older newsreaders, such as **rn**, you must read the articles in the haphazard order in which they were posted to the newsgroup; it will probably take quite a bit of manual searching and keyboard fussing to read all the articles pertinent to a given thread.

thread selector

In a **threaded newsreader** for reading **Usenet** news, the program mode that displays the posted articles organized by **thread** topics. *Compare* **article selector, newsgroup selector, subject selector.**

threaded newsreader

In **Usenet**, a newsreader that can organize the posted articles so that they are grouped by subject (**threads**). Using such a program is much more convenient than using a newsreader such as **rn**, which displays the article subjects in the order in which they were received by the system. To follow a thread with a non-threaded reader, you must use cumbersome commands to search for the next subject in the thread. With a threaded newsreader, this is not necessary because the articles have been grouped together by the newsreader software. Examples of threaded newsreaders for **UNIX** systems include **nn, tin,** and **trn.**

Time Division Multiplexing (TDM)

An approach to **multiplexing** (combining several data sources for transmission on one line) in which signals take turns, with each one getting the entire **bandwidth** of the line for a brief period of time.

time-based billing

A method of recovering the operating costs of a network by billing users for the time they spend engaged in various operations, such as participating in a computer conference.

Many Internet users mistakenly believe that the Internet is currently available for "free," and that the impending **com-**

mercialization and **privatization** of the network will lead to its downfall—or at least radically change its character—as profit-seeking **service providers** begin charging what the market will bear. According to Internet expert Dave Farber, a professor at the University of Pennsylvania, "Internet people believe in free goods to everybody: Give each user a straw and let him sip on the pool of wisdom."

But this belief rests on a very serious misconception: The Internet is not free. Somewhere, somebody is paying for the very services that Internet users take for granted. Only a very small proportion of the Internet's operating costs are paid for by U.S. or state government subsidies. Most of the costs are recovered from the flat-fee charges levied on subscribing organizations by **service providers**. Internet users currently benefit from this flat-fee structure, which ranges from as little as $9 per month for **dialup access** to as much as $5,000 per month for fiber optic access at speeds of 1.544 Mbps. But this fee structure contains an inherent inequity: Subscribers are, in effect, subsidizing users whose requests for information (such as **FTP** file transfers, for instance) originate from outside the subscriber-funded systems.

It is far from clear just how the Internet billing structure will evolve in the face of commercialization and privatization. Currently, the Internet lacks a technical basis for time-based billing, but this deficiency—if deficiency it can be called—is about to be remedied by researchers at Carnegie Mellon University. They are developing NetBill, a computerized system for tracking and billing Internet users for small transactions, such as a ten-cent charge for each electronic mail message a user receives. The developers are said to hope that NetBill will evolve into a "universal accounting system on the Internet."

The most likely scenario for future user-based Internet cost recovery is a combination of flat-fee billing (a flat monthly charge, probably based on the **bandwidth** of network access) and time-based or transaction-based billing for commercially-provided services. This scenario does not necessarily conflict with the clear intent of U.S. regulatory legislation to ensure equity of network access; more than 98% of U.S. households have telephones which are operated on a time-based billing basis.

---

tin

A **threaded newsreader** for reading **Usenet** newsgroups. Developed by Iain Lea, tin provides powerful features with ease of use. The program runs on UNIX computers. *Compare* **nn, rn, trn.**

TinyMUD

The first major variant on the original, combat-oriented **MUDs** (multi-player, computerized role-playing games), TinyMUD emphasizes social relationships and cooperation in place of the kill-and-loot orientation of earlier games.

The first TinyMUD, written by Rich Skrenta, gave players the tools to modify their environment by means of commands such as @dig, @create, @open, and @link. Because emphasis is placed on user construction and definition of the game's space, in place of a huge fixed database of predefined features, TinyMUD servers (and their derivatives) take up significantly less disk space (hence the name "Tiny"). There are no predefined rooms, characters, or objects; you define them yourself, or use those defined by others. You can also define command "verbs" that apply to the spaces you create.

More recent versions of TinyMUD are virtually identical to the original from the user's point of view, save that they include programming languages that players can use to add functionality and depth to objects and spaces. TinyMUSH offers a simple scripting language, while the more recent versions of TinyMUCK offer a variant of FORTH. The most recent variant on the TinyMUD theme, **MOO**, includes an object-oriented programming language similar to C++. None of these games require that players possess programming skills.

> **Tip**: Need an excuse to explore a MUD and play? Here's one: The most recent TinyMUDs provide beginning programmers with a perfect and fun opportunity to expand their programming skills. The programming languages included in MUDs are simplified versions of mainstream programming languages, and they're fun to work with—you can write short programs that seem to do a great deal, and you see the results immediately.

TinySex

A form of **cybersex** that sometimes occurs in **TinyMUDs**, which are socially-oriented multi-user role-playing games. TinySex begins with consensual agreement between two characters, and proceeds by means of exchanged messages.

> **Don't** try TinySex until you've had lots of experience in the game and know the other character well. A favorite and reprehensible trick: Someone entices you into TinySex under false pretenses, logs your character's remarks, and posts them to Usenet.

tn3270

A variant of **Telnet** that is designed to facilitate access to an IBM 3270 computer, which uses a **page-mode terminal**. With tn3270, you can access this computer as if you were using a 3270 terminal, which has more features than the simple **Network Virtual Terminal (NVT)** that the ordinary version of **Telnet** sets up.

| toasternet |

A **local area network (LAN)** composed of inexpensive, readily-available, and even unused components that is assembled for the express purpose of facilitating access to the Internet. A small organization may find it significantly less expensive to assemble a toasternet than to obtain **dialup IP** for each computer user.

| token bus |

In a **local area network (LAN)**, a method of dealing with **contention** (the problem of more than one workstation trying to access the network at the same time). Unlike **Carrier Sense Multiple Access with Collision Detection (CSMA/CD)**, the contention avoidance **protocol** used in the original **Ethernet** (*see* **DIX Ethernet**), token bus technology imposes more order on the competing workstations. Physically, the network consists of a linear **coaxial cable** to which workstations are attached. Each workstation has a number. When the network is switched on, the workstation with the highest number gets to transmit first. When it's finished, it passes a special control message called a token to the station with the next highest number, and so on. A workstation can't transmit unless it has the token. *Compare* **token ring**.

| token ring |

In a **local area network (LAN)**, a network that is configured as a physical ring—the ends of the network cable are connected. This has numerous advantages from an engineering standpoint, including the achievement of high data transfer rates with inexpensive **twisted pair** cable and the fact that these networks perform well when load demands are high. Token ring networks are considerably faster than standard Ethernet LANS, transmitting data at a rate of 16

Mbps in comparison to Ethernet's 10 Mbps. To deal with the problem of **contention**, token ring networks employ a token (as do token bus networks). The IEEE 802.6 standard defines token ring networks (*see* **IEEE 802 network**).

top-level domain

In the **domain name system**, the names of the six highest-level organizational domain names (such as *edu* and *org*) as well as the country codes for non-U.S. sites (such as *ca* [Canada] or *se* [Sweden]). **Pseudo top-level domains** allow Internet electronic mail messages to reach users of systems (such as BITNET) that do not have full Internet connectivity.

Domain name	Description
com	Company or corporation
edu	Educational institution
gov	Government organization
mil	Military organization
net	Internet service facility
org	Not-for-profit organization or foundation

topology

In a **local area network (LAN)**, the underlying design or architecture of the network that specifies how the individual computers are wired to the network. In a bus network such as an **Ethernet** LAN, the computers are connected to a single cable that isn't joined at the end. In a **token-ring** LAN, the two ends of the cable are joined in a circle.

Transmission Control Protocol (TCP)

In the Internet's **transport layer**, the layer of its **protocol stack** concerned with managing the transport of data, a **reliable** and **connection-oriented protocol** that can verify whether the data is delivered accurately. *Compare* **User Datagram Protocol (UDP)**.

TCP ensures reliable delivery by means of **Positive Acknowledgement with Re-Transmission (PAR)**. A computer using PAR keeps sending the message until it receives a confirmation from the destination computer that the message was received intact. For PAR to work, it's necessary for the two computers to exchange control information by means of a **handshake**.

TCP does another important job: Keeping the various parts of the message in the correct order. Before sending the data, TCP breaks it down into **datagrams**, which are then routed through the network by the **Internet Protocol (IP)**. Some of the datagrams may travel different paths or suffer delays en route. TCP tells the destination computer how to reassemble the datagrams in the correct order. (This job is done by the copy of TCP on the destination computer.)

Transmission Control Protocol/Internet Protocol (TCP/IP)

A set (called a **protocol suite**) of related **protocols** (rules) that allow computers made by varying manufacturers to exchange messages and share resources across a computer network. The two most important protocols in the TCP/IP suite are the **Transmission Control Protocol (TCP)** and the **Internet Protocol (IP)**, but many others (including applications such as the **file transfer protocol**) are included. The TCP/IP protocol suite, as well as specific programs based on these protocols, form the technical basis for the **Internet**.

The TCP/IP protocol suite has its origins in **ARPANET**, an experimental **wide area network** funded by the U.S. **Defense Advanced Research Projects Agency (DARPA)**. TCP/IP provides the necessary rules for creating a **catenet**, a network that physically consists of a large number of distinct **local area networks (LANS)** that are connected by means of **gateways** (communication links). With TCP/IP, the user can access computers on any of these networks, just as if they were connected to the user's own network. The details of just how data flows from one type of network to another are very complex, but these are invisible (**transparent**) to the user. All you need to know to access another system is its **domain name**.

TCP/IP is unquestionably the emerging world standard for internetworking compatibility, as attested by recent press that Microsoft Corporation is planning to include TCP/IP support in the next version (4.0) of its phenomenally successful Windows software. TCP/IP's widespread acceptance is attributable to its openness (the protocols are in the public domain and are freely available), its **hardware independence** (the protocols are not tied to any specific brand or model of computer or networking hardware), and its **transparency** (from the user's perspective, the entire Internet is a single **logical network**, such that the differences among the many different computers and physical networks is hidden from the user's view).

The use of TCP/IP doesn't necessarily imply connection to the Internet; the protocols can be used to link two or more **local area networks (LAN)** even if no Internet **gateway** is planned.

---

transparent

Actually there but apparently not; *compare* **virtual** (apparently there but actually not).

transparent adaptive routing

In a computer network, the ability of the network hardware to respond to changing network conditions, including the temporary unreliability or destruction of part of the network, by automatically seeking alternative routes. This is one of the cornerstones of the Internet's **architecture**, and was strongly shaped by military considerations (*see* **ARPANET**).

transport layer

In the **Open Systems Interconnection (OSI) Reference Model** of computer networking, the layer that manages the transmission of data from Point A to Point B to ensure reliable delivery.

There are two options here. A **connection-oriented protocol** at this level can establish communication with the receiving computer by means of a **handshake**, and keep retransmitting the data until all of it is received intact. In the Internet, this is the job performed by the **Transmission Control Protocol (TCP)**. A **connectionless protocol** just sends out the message and doesn't care to check whether it actually got received. This may sound irresponsible, but it's not such a bad idea for brief messages such as one-line file transfer commands; sending them this way is very efficient, and it will be obvious to the user if the message doesn't get through because nothing will happen! After a set period of time the program gives up waiting and returns control to you. In the Internet, the **User Datagram Protocol (UDP)** handles messages this way.

transport protocol

A standard that governs the transfer of data from one **host** to another at the **data link layer**. The Internet has two transport protocols, the **User Datagram Protocol (UDP)**, which is a **connectionless** protocol, and the **Transmission Control Protocol (TCP)**, a connection-oriented protocol that establishes a link with a **remote system**.

TRICKLE

A file acquisition utility that lets you "subscribe" to an **archive site**, so that you get a periodic summary of the new files this site contains. You can then request some or all of the files to be copied to your host, if you wish.

Trivial File Transfer Protocol (TFTP)

A simple **protocol** for transferring files that employs the **User Datagram Protocol (UDP)** rather than the **File Transport Protocol (FTP)**. The data is broken down into numbered blocks, which are sent one at a time; when the receiving station gets the block, it sends an **acknowledgment (ACK).** Then the sending station transfers the next block, and so on. TFTP requires very little communications software **overhead,** so it is ideal for downloading software to devices such as **routers**, **servers**, and **diskless workstations**.

trn

A respected **newsreader** for UNIX-based systems that allows the user to read and respond to messages posted in **Usenet newsgroups**. trn is a **threaded newsreader** that incorporates many advanced features, including the ability to perform **file extraction** operations automatically on binary **postings** that have been encoded with **uuencode**.

Trojan horse

A rogue computer program that appears to be an ordinary, useful computer program. Concealed within it, however, are computer programming instructions that can cause annoyance or severe damage.

You know the story: The Greeks defeated Troy by wheeling a huge wooden horse into the city, stuffed with concealed soldiers. Curious, the Trojans couldn't resist it—but they paid a huge price. A recent example: Chinon America, Inc., warned Internet users that a program called CD-IT.ZIP concealed a Trojan Horse. According to the program's description, it would enable users of Chinon CD-ROM drives to write to the disks as well as read from them, a technical impossibility. Curious users who downloaded the program to their PCs and gave it a try lived to regret it: The program corrupted vital system files so that only an aggressive reformat of the hard drive, with total loss of all the data stored on the disk, would eradicate it.

trolling

In **Usenet**, a prank that consists of posting a message so idiotic or facetious that only the gullible, irascible, arrogant, or egotistical would respond with **followup postings**, which expose their stupidity (often hilariously). (The "trolling" analogy comes from fishing, in which you troll with bait to see what bites.)

A recent, classic, and rather clever troll was a message posted to several groups that forbade trolling and spelled out various draconian punishments (which could not possibly have been administered within Usenet's almost non-existent governance structure). Facetious and itself a troll, the posting was nonetheless met with dozens of follow-on postings with a decidedly hysterical tone.

Do ignore trolls. By responding to their messages, you're not only falling into the trap trollers have set for you. You're also wasting network **bandwidth**. Hint: Trolls often **carpet bomb**, which is **cross-posting** a message to a large number of unrelated newsgroups. If you run across a provocative message that has nothing to do with the subject of the newsgroup you're reading, ignore it.

tunneling

At the **data link layer** in a point-to-point transmission line, the "wrapping" of a **datagram** within the **frames** employed by an incompatible system so that the system can transfer Internet data. This must be handled by translation devices at the originating ends of the line—and at the receiving end, too, because the "wrapper" (a non-Internet **header**) must be removed. Tunneling is frequently used to package Internet **datagrams** for transmission over **X.25 networks**.

twisted pair

The standard, two-wire telephone line, consisting of two insulated copper cables that are twisted together in a helical form like a braid. This is done to reduce interference from other wires, because two parallel wires form an antenna (consider the dipole antenna supplied with most stereo receivers). Compare **coaxial cable, broadband coaxial cable**, and **fiber optic cable**.

Don't underestimate the capabilities of twisted pairs. On **analog** lines, fast **modems** can transmit data at speeds of up to 28.8 Kbps. If twisted pairs are used for **digital** transmission, speeds of up to 768 Kbps are possible with **High-bit-rate Digital Subscriber Line (HDSL),** and one-way transfers of a full **T1** rate, 1.544 Mbps, are possible with **Asynchronous Digital Subscriber Line (ADSL)** technology.

unauthorized access

The gaining of entry into a secured computer system through such means as using a stolen or guessed password. Unauthorized access is a crime. *See* **Electronic Communications Privacy Act (ECPA)**.

unicast

To transmit a message from one **host** to another specific host on the network. *Compare* **broadcast**, **multicast**.

Universal Resource Locater (URL)

In the HyperText Transfer Protocol (HTTP) that governs the retrieval of remote resources in the **World Wide Web (WWW)**, a standard for expressing **jumps** to remote resources (as well as the method by which the Web **server** retrieves this information).

A statement such as

```
http://pulua.hcc.hawaii.edu/directory/book.html
```

specifies the type of server to contact (here, an **HTTP server** that's part of WWW), as well as the exact location of the resource (the file book.html at the **host** named pulua.hcc.hawaii.edu).

UNIX

An **operating system** designed at AT&T's Bell Laboratories in 1969 that enables more than one person to use a multiuser computer system at the same time.

Because AT&T was prevented by U.S. regulatory policies from engaging in the computer business at the time UNIX was developed, AT&T gave free licenses to universities, thus beginning a long and close relationship between UNIX and university computing centers. The University of California, Berkeley, modified and extended UNIX, incorporating **TCP/IP** in the process; it was the Berkeley version of UNIX that was subsequently adopted by most colleges and universities. This is the reason for the close association between UNIX and the Internet.

UNIX was never designed for public use. The operating system embodies a philosophy that could only appeal to a computer programmer (or a hacker):

- Instead of making lots of big buggy programs that don't work very well, make lots of little ones you can carefully test.

- Make the output of one program serve as the input for another.

- Do things by combining tools.

It's the third part that makes UNIX hard to use—routing one program's output to another program for additional processing requires typing lengthy, difficult commands. Still, there's no reason that UNIX can't be equipped with a user-friendly **graphical user interface (GUI)**, which is exactly what Steve Job's ill-fated NeXT computer did (and very well, too).

Although UNIX and the Internet are closely related, they're not married. The Internet is designed to link physically dissimilar computer networks and to work with many different brands of computer hardware. As the makers of other operating systems include TCP/IP support, UNIX will fall into its proper place as just one of the many operating systems woven into the TCP/IP web. For now, though, you may find yourself learning how to use a bit of UNIX if you want to learn the Internet.

Unix-to-Unix Copy Program (UUCP)

A **store-and-forward network** protocol for UNIX computers that allows UNIX users to exchange files, mail, and **Usenet** news by means of dialup connections. UUCP played an important role in the early development of Usenet, but it has been largely supplanted by the Internet, which offers much faster connections.

unreliable protocol

In computer networking, a standard for transferring data that does not attempt to determine whether the data arrived safely. The **Internet Protocol (IP)** is an unreliable protocol.

Does this mean the Internet isn't safe to use? Not at all—in fact, data transfers via the Internet are reliable (free from errors). It's just that the reliability is assured by protocols operating at other **layers**. IP doesn't bother with reliability so that it can tackle its main job, packaging data into packets called **datagrams** and shooting them across the net, with a minimum of processing **overhead**. *Compare* **Transmission Control Protocol (TCP)**.

unsubscribe

In **Usenet**, to remove a **newsgroup** from the list of newsgroups that you are actively following. After you unsubscribe from a newsgroup, your newsreader will not ask you whether you want to read this newsgroup again. However, you may re-subscribe at a later time, if you wish. *Compare* **subscribe**.

unthreaded newsreader

In **Usenet**, a newsreader (a program for selecting **news-groups** and reading **postings**) that does not group the post-ings into threads organized by the postings' topics. Unthreaded newsreaders are considerably more difficult and less rewarding to use than **threaded newsreaders** (such as **nn** and **trn**) because they present the postings in the order in which they were added to the newsgroup. To follow a thread, you must skip unrelated postings, a tedious process.

Don't use a nonthreaded newsreader if a threaded option is available—you'll be missing out on one of the joys of Usenet, which is the sense of dialogue you get from following the discussion on a particular topic. Although this is possible with a nonthreaded news-reader, the commands are so tedious to use that you may give up.

upload

To transfer a file from your computer to another computer by means a of modem and a telephone line. *Compare* **download**.

Uploading is one of the several inconveniences of **dialup access**: If you want to send a file to a user elsewhere on the Internet, you must first upload the file to the **host** you're using. If the file is large, this can be a very time-consuming process in comparison with the speed of host-to-host links on today's Internet. A file that takes 12 minutes to upload with a 9.6 Kbps modem can be transferred by **FTP** in a matter of seconds.

To upload a file to your host, you must use a **file transfer pro-tocol** which assures that the transmission is free from errors. The file transfer protocol of choice for computer **bulletin board systems (BBS)** is **Zmodem**. If you're accessing a **UNIX** host, you're more likely to use **Kermit**. Most popular **communi-**

cations programs can transfer files with either of these protocols.

---

upstream bandwidth

In a network designed to provide Internet connectivity to homes, schools, and offices, the part of the delivered connectivity that carries information originated by the system's end users. To permit full and meaningful connectivity to the Internet, a network must offer sufficient upstream bandwidth so that users can become the originators as well as the consumers of information. *Compare* **downstream bandwidth**.

---

urban folklore

A genre of folklore that is spread by fax machines, electronic mail, and—most recently—**Usenet** rather than village tattlers.

The rise of a global computer communications system has delicious consequences for students of folklore, for the old human propensities to pass on (and exaggerate) rumors, create legends with little basis in fact, and spread unsubstantiated stories are well in evidence on the Net. In fact, Usenet provides a beautiful mechanism for the perpetuation of urban folklore. By posting a rumor or legend to newsgroups every so often, it's possible to keep a baseless story going even in the face of repeated attempts by system administrators to warn people that it is without foundation in fact.

A recurrent item of Usenet folklore is the "dying child" who has requested postcards so that he can get into the *Guinness Book of World Records*. Like much folklore, this has some basis in fact: 7-year-old Craig Shergold, diagnosed with a brain tumor, did indeed request that people world-wide send him postcards so he could make the record books. And he did; he received millions of postcards. But Craig recovered; an American billionare flew him to Charlottesville, Virginia, where physicians successfully extracted the non-malignant tumor. The only problem is that, thanks to repeated postings of the story, Craig is still getting postcards—hundreds of thousands of them, an expensive nightmare for the British postal service.

Some of these postings may be **trolls**, facetious postings that are intended to dupe. A case in point is the Nieman-Marcus cookie story, which you will eventually encounter in Usenet. According to the nicely-written story, a Nieman-Marcus customer liked the firm's chocolate chip cookies so much that he requested the recipe. He was told this was "250," which he took to mean $2.50. However, when he got his Visa bill, he found the actual charge to be $250. But Nieman-Marcus refused to refund his money. In revenge, he decided to post the recipe to the Net. It's a hoax; the recipe, which calls for huge amounts of ingredients, doesn't produce anything that comes even close to a chocolate chip cookie.

Tip: You'll find interesting and intelligent discussions of computer-transmitted urban folklore in the newsgroup alt.folklore.urban.

Usenet

A network of (mostly UNIX) computer systems that have agreed to share and propagate a huge (and growing) set of electronic discussion groups, called **newsgroups**, each focusing on a specific area of interest. The network is designed so that a message posted to a newsgroup on one system will eventually propagate throughout the network, with each machine eventually having a copy of the original message.

With an estimated 5,000 newsgroups in widespread use by an estimated 5,000,000 people, Usenet has become by far the most popular computer discussion or bulletin board system ever devised.

The Usenet is neither synonymous nor coterminous with the Internet, although Usenet newsgroups are often available on Internet host systems. Usenet actually preceded the Internet, and does not rely exclusively on the Internet's high-speed **TCP/IP** networking standards; messages were originally exchanged and propagated using the slower **store-and-forward network** called **UUCP** (UNIX-to-UNIX Copy Program). Usenet **protocols** (rules) still allow **dialup sites** to participate by means of UUCP.

Usenet has its origins in 1979, when graduate students at Duke University and the University of North Carolina, Chapel Hill, created the Usenet **protocols** (rules) and developed the first software to handle the propagation of newsgroup postings and replies. Based on UUCP, then widely used to link UNIX systems, Usenet spread quickly to many sites on the UUCP network: Within a year, fifty Unix sites were participating. When these sites joined the growing number of systems linked via the **TCP/IP** protocol, Usenet messages found their way to the Internet.

Usenet is best described as an experiment in controlled anarchy; it has no central administration, no governing body, and no formal sanctions to administer in case of abuse. There are conventions requiring a positive **email** vote to establish a new newsgroup, for example, but this can be circumvented by creating a newsgroup in the **alternative newsgroup hierarchy (alt)**, for which no vote is required.

Usenet freely reflects the character of the male-dominated user communities from which it has grown—meaning, in short, that a Usenet user may encounter unfettered controversy, expletive-ridden language, and male-oriented erotica of every possible kind. Women who try to bring a different perspective to Usenet discussions sometimes find themselves hounded off the net by **mail bombing, flames**, and outright sexual harrassment, and prefer to do their networking in closed, all-female systems (such as the Houston-based Starfleet Ladies Auxiliary and Embroidery-/Baking Society).

Attempts to censor the Usenet generally prove futile: An individual site might decide against carrying potentially offensive newsgroups (notably, the alt.sex.* newsgroups), but their decision will not block the distribution of the affected newsgroup to the rest of Usenet (apart from a few **downstream sites** that have no other Internet connections). Postings can propagate throughout the network along many alternative paths, just as email does.

The quality of Usenet **newsgroups** spans the gamut; some would prove of interest only to the maturity-impaired (notably, alt.flames) or fraternity boys with problematic testosterone levels (alt.binaries.pictures.erotica) while others quickly become an indispensable component of one's information-gathering strategy. The best newsgroups are **moderated newsgroups**, meaning that all the messages are screened for relevance, taste, and accuracy by a human moderator before they appear on your screen, but non-moderated newsgroups offer open-ended discussion that may prove of enormous value to you.

Newsgroups are organized into two broad categories: the **world newsgroups**, which are automatically distributed to all Usenet sites, and the **alternative newsgroups**, which are distributed only to sites that request them. Within each category, newsgroups are further subdivided into classes called **hierarchies**, which make up the first part of the newgroups's name (for example, comp.binaries.ibm-pc is one of the many newsgroups within the **comp** hierarchy). Within the world newsgroups, the standard hierarchies are **comp** (computers and computer applications), **news** (newsgroups about Usenet itself), **rec** (hobbies and sports), **sci** (the sciences generally), **soc** (social issues and socializing), **talk** (no-holds-barred controversy), and **misc** (anything that doesn't fit into the other categories). Of the alternative newsgroups, the flagbearer is the **alt** hierarchy, a huge—and fascinating—

collection of newsgroups created by people who wanted to bypass the world newsgroup voting procedures for creating new groups. Also found among the alternative newsgroups are **bionet** (biology and the environment), **biz** (business discussions and advertising), **ClariNet** (a do-it-yourself on-line newspaper consisting of feeds from major wire services, such as UPI), and **K12** (primary and secondary education).

Although most Usenet sites are not part of the government-subsidized **NSFNET**, Usenet customs (as well as specific regulations maintained by host system administrations) militate against the use of Usenet newsgroups for frankly commercial purposes (see **Acceptable Use Policy**). Exceptions: the **biz** newsgroups and the .for-sale groups found in many hierarchies. Usenet participants are additionally expected to abide by the rules of **netiquette**, which boil down fundamentally to treating other users with care and consideration.

> **Tip: Newbies** (newcomers) often make innocent errors that result in **flames** (vitriolic, critical letters) appearing in their mailboxes, so it's an excellent idea to learn the rules of **netiquette** before you log on.

The value of Usenet discussions is sometimes reduced by phenomena that Usenet participants themselves recognize as aberrant and undesireable, such as **cascading,** excessive **crossposting, flame wars,** and **trolling.** The regular user soon learns to take full advantage of the **kill file,** which stores the names of subjects—and obnoxious posters—that you would like removed before they appear on your screen.

To read Usenet newsgroups, you need a **newsreader,** a program that lets you choose which newsgroup you want to read and presents the current messages, called **postings,** in a list on the screen. There are hundreds of newsreaders, but the best known are those that run on the UNIX systems that make up the backbone of the Internet. The best of these newsreaders, called **threaded newsreaders**, organize the messages by subject (see **nn**, **tin** and **trn**). This is convenient because you can read all the postings relevant to a subject without having to hunt for them manually.

If you wish to add your own two cents to a Usenet discussion, you may do so in three ways: by posting a message on a new subject, by writing a **followup posting** to an existing message, or by replying to an existing postage directly to the poster's **electronic mail address**.

Do learn all you can about Usenet **netiquette**, and read a newsgroup carefully for a while, before posting. And before asking a question that's likely to have been asked many times before, determine whether there's a **FAQ** (a document containing answers to frequently-asked questions) available for the newsgroup.

Don't make the mistake of thinking that Usenet is a right. Access to Usenet is a courtesy extended to you by the computer system you are using, often at considerable expense. Repeated abuse of Usenet netiquette or Internet rules of acceptable use can and should lead to denial of log-on privileges.

| Usenet site |

A **host** that has been configured to receive a Usenet **news feed** and run Usenet software so that local users can read the news on this system.

Becoming a Usenet site isn't a trivial matter: It requires several megabytes (MB) of disk space for the necessary software, as much as 1200 Mb per month of additional disk space for the articles, and the cost of a news feed. Fortunately, this isn't necessary if you just want to read the news. To do so, just log on to a host that's already a Usenet site.

USENIX

A professional association of **UNIX** programmers, users, and system administrators. The organization seeks to share ideas and experience concerning UNIX, to foster innovation and communication concerning UNIX-related research and technology, to provide a neutral setting for the rational and productive airing of issues, and to provide educational and tutorial resources in support of UNIX generally. The organization sponsors annual conferences and workshops, and publishes conference proceedings and technical documents concerning UNIX. Its refereed technical quarterly, published by MIT Press, is called *Computing Systems*.

User Agent (UA)

In an electronic mail **application**, as defined by **X.400**, the **client** program that helps the user compose, send, and receive mail. The user agent communicates with a local **Message Transfer Agent,** which is responsible for relaying the mail to remote hosts.

User Datagram Protocol (UDP)

In the Internet's **transport layer**, the layer of its **protocol stack** concerned with managing the transport of data, an **unreliable** and **connectionless** protocol that doesn't make any attempt to verify that a message is received. UDP sacrifices reliability for economy—a UDP **datagram** makes very low demands on the network's processing capabilities. *Compare* **Transmission Control Protocol (TCP)**.

UDP is frequently used for simple queries that should, if properly received, generate a response. So there's some measure of reliability when UDP is used this way—if there's no response, you know that the message wasn't received!

user interface

The part of a computer program that handles interaction with the user.

The simplest **command-line interfaces**, such as the various **UNIX shells**, present you with a **prompt**; you have to know what to type, and you must carefully follow the rules of **syntax** (arranging the parts of the command in the correct order and following all the rules correctly). Among the Internet **resource discovery tools**, the **UNIX** version of **Archie** employs a command-line interface, as do the UNIX utilities **FTP** and **Telnet.**

Easier to use are **menu-driven interfaces**, which present your options in the form of menus. Typically, to choose an option, you simply highlight the choice you want and press *Enter.* **Gopher clients** employ a menu-driven interface.

Judged easiest to use by most users are **graphical user interfaces (GUIs)**, which let you make choices by pointing at a picture of something (called an **icon**) and clicking a button on a mouse. The most recent Internet resource discovery tools, **Eudora** and **Mosaic**, use graphical user interfaces. However, you can use these programs only if your computer is equipped with a **direct connection** to the Internet and a GUI windowing system such as Microsoft Windows or X Windows.

user name

The name by which a user is known to the computer system; *synonymous with* **login name**.

uudecode

In **UNIX**, a program that decodes (extracts) a **binary file** that was encoded with **uuencode** so that it could be transmitted via Internet **electronic mail** or **Usenet**, which can transmit **ASCII** characters only. *See* **file extraction**.

| **uuencode** |

In **UNIX**, a program that encodes a **binary file** so that it can be transmitted via Internet **electronic mail** or **Usenet**, which can transmit **ASCII** characters only. The recipient must run the **uudecode** utility to decode the file.

| **V.17** |

A **modulation protocol** for **fax modems** and **fax machines** that governs fax transmissions at 14,400 bits per second (bps), with the ability to **fall back** to 12,000 bps if line conditions deteriorate. The protocol is regulated by the **Comité Consultif International de Télégraphiqe et Téléphonique (CCITT)**.

| **V.21** |

A **modulation protocol** that governs transmissions at 300 bits per second (bps). The protocol is regulated by the **Comité Consultif International de Télégraphiqe et Téléphonique (CCITT)**. This standard conflicts with the **Bell 103** standard widely used in North America.

V.22

A **modulation protocol** that governs transmissions at 1200 bits per second (bps). The protocol is regulated by the **Comité Consultif International de Télégraphiqe et Téléphonique (CCITT)**. This standard conflicts with the **Bell 212A** standard widely used in North America.

v.22bis

A **modulation protocol** for modems that governs transmissions at 2400 bps, with the ability to **fall back** to 1200 and 600 bps. The protocol is regulated by the **Comité Consultif International de Télégraphiqe et Téléphonique (CCITT)**. The first modulation protocol to gain world-wide acceptance, V.22bis employs **trellis-coded modulation** techniques. V.22bis modems are in widespread use.

 Don't buy a v.22bis modem! For just a few dollars more, you can get a V.32bis modem that's capable of transmitting data at 14,400 bps.

V.27ter

A **modulation protocol** for **fax modems** and **fax machines** that governs fax transmissions at 4800 bits per second (bps), with the ability to **fall back** to 2400 bps if line conditions deteriorate. The protocol is regulated by the **Comité Consultif International de Télégraphiqe et Téléphonique (CCITT)**.

V.29

A **modulation protocol** for **fax modems** and **fax machines** that governs fax transmissions at 9600 bits per second (bps), with the ability to **fall back** to 7200 bps if line conditions deteriorate. The protocol is regulated by the **Comité Consultif International de Télégraphiqe et Téléphonique (CCITT)**.

v.32

A **modulation protocol** that governs transmissions at 9600 bps, with the ability to **fall back** to 4800 bps. The protocol is regulated by the **Comité Consultif International de Télégraphiqe et Téléphonique (CCITT)**. The v.32 protocol employs **trellis-coded modulation** at the 9600 bps speed.

v.32bis

A **modulation protocol** that governs transmissions at speeds of 14,400 bps, with the ability to **fall back** to 12,000 bps, 9600 bps, 7200 bps, and 4800 bps. The protocol is regulated by the **Comité Consultif International de Télégraphiqe et Téléphonique (CCITT)**. Employing **trellis-coded modulation**, V.32bis modems are inexpensive and in widespread use.

V.32terbo

A **modulation protocol** that governs transmissions at speeds of 19.2 K bps, with the ability to **fall back** to all the rates supported by the **V.32bis** standard. Despite the official-sounding name, V.32terbo is not a **Comité Consultif International de Télégraphiqe et Téléphonique (CCITT)** standard; it is a proprietary standard developed in 1993 by AT&T.

The word "terbo" is a rather ugly neologism that plays on the similarities between the **Comité Consultif International de Télégraphiqe et Téléphonique (CCITT)**'s official term, ter ("the third"), and turbo.

Don't bother with a V.32terbo modem; now the V.34 has been published, V.32terbo will quickly fade into oblivion.

V.34

A **modulation protocol** that governs transmissions at speeds of 28,800 bits per second (bps). Only recently made available, the protocol is regulated by the **Comité Consultif International de Télégraphiqe et Téléphonique (CCITT)**. To achieve the high transmission rate, V.34 modems adapt to changing line conditions in an effort to eke out all the possible **bandwidth** in a telephone line.

Tip: Because the ITT-TSS publishes standards only once every four years, the technology to produce 28,800 bps modems preceded the dissemination of the V.34 standard. As a result, several manufacturers have released what they call **V.fast** modems, which anticipate the V.34 protocols. Most of these modems can be upgraded to the V.34 protocol now that it has been published. To avoid the hassle of upgrading, avoid V.fast modems in favor of the newest ones that implement **V.34**.

v.42

An **error correction protocol**, regulated by the **Comité Consultif International de Télégraphiqe et Téléphonique (CCITT)**, for the correction of errors that occur as a result of **line noise**. V.42 is a **hardware error protocol** that is implemented within the modem, rather than in the communications software. When both the sending and receiving modems conform to the v.42 standard, errors are automatically detected and the sending modem is instructed to repeat the transmission until the information is received intact. V.42 incorporates **MNP4** as an alternative protocol, which will be employed automatically if the other modem cannot use the preferred method, **Link Access Protocol for Modems (LAPM)**.

V.42bis

A **compression protocol**, regulated by **Comité Consultif International de Télégraphiqe et Téléphonique (CCITT)**, that produces the effect of speeding transmission because there is less data to transmit. The protocol specifies how data should be compressed on the sending end and decompressed on the other. If the data is not already compressed, gains in effective transmission speeds of up to 400% can be realized. A competing standard is **MNP-10**.

V.Fast Class (V.FC)

A **proprietary standard** that was developed by a consortium of modem manufacturers in anticipation of the long-delayed **V.34 modulation protocol** (28,800 bps). Most V.FC modems can be upgraded to the V.34 standard.

verbose

Talkative, informative. Many programs have a "verbose" option that explains what they're doing while they're doing it.

Veronica

In **Gopher**, a search **client** that scans an automatically-compiled index of titles of all the items that can be retrieved in **gopherspace**, the world of information accessible to a Gopher **client**. The items include Gopher directory titles as well as resources (such as text files, programs, and graphics) appearing on all Gopher submenus, but they do not include words found within the text of these files. The result of a Veronica search is a Gopher-like menu, which you can use to access the listed items. *Compare* **Jughead**.

Veronica is tightly integrated with Gopher: You will probably find it as an option on your local Gopher client. To use Veronica, you type the term or terms for which you want to search. The result is a Gopher menu listing the first 250 items found that match your request. If you wish to view an item, Gopher retrieves the information and displays it on your screen. You can then read it or save it to a disk file on your **host** system.

Tip: If your Gopher search retrieves too many items, explore ways to narrow the search by reading the item "How to compose Veronica queries" that you'll find in the menu that lists Veronica. Try using the restrictive **Boolean operators**—specifically, AND or NOT—to narrow the scope of your search.

Do start your search with **Jughead**, which searches for directory titles only. You'll find that Veronica retrieves a large number of **false drops** (irrelevant items), including Usenet postings that aren't often informative. Because Jughead searches only for directory titles, the result of a Jughead search is a much shorter list, and each item reflects someone's effort to group together information and resources pertinent to your search term.

| vi |

A simple but cumbersome **text editor** found on many **UNIX** systems. vi is a full-screen editor that lets you work with an entire screen of text at a time. Less complicated than **EMACS,** it is nevertheless difficult to learn for users who are accustomed to the high-quality word processing software available on personal computers. It is widely used—still— as the default text editor for UNIX shell accounts.

video-on-demand

An **interactive TV (ITV)** application that will allow home ITV users to choose from the world library of an estimated 65,000 films, plus thousands of additional documentaries and re-run TV programs, for immediate delivery. Such services could be available as early as 1996.

A glimpse of the future of interactive television is available on many of today's cable TV systems, thanks to addressable channel selectors, a box that sits near your TV and lets you choose the channel you want to view. Most users of these selectors do not realize that they have a unique address that allows the cable TV company to route signals to individual homes. Current video-on-demand services (called pay-per-view) permit you to choose from several movies that are simultaneously broadcast, but you cannot choose to see other options and you must view the movie at the time the cable station begins broadcasting it.

There is a very large technical gap between current pay-per-view systems and video-on-demand, which would allow you to choose from thousands of viewing options at the time of your choice. Few question that video on demand is coming, but the technical problems are prodigious. The thousands of program options would be stored in a giant database, which would require an amount of storage 100 times larger than the largest computer database currently in existence. Moreover, the system must be capable of retrieving and broadcasting the film without delay, which would introduce unwanted distortions and gaps that the viewers will not tolerate. Worse: Imagine a situation in which 5,000 subscribers all wanted to view a popular movie, but they all wanted it to start at a slightly different time.

Prodigious the technical problems might be, but a host of the best U.S. research and development teams are hard at work on solving these problems. One thing seems clear: Much of the processing will have to be handled by a new generation of digital set-top boxes, which will have about as much processing power and memory as today's minimum PC (a 486 with 4MB of memory). Initially, these boxes won't come cheap, and if the price doesn't fall fast enough, video-on-demand may be off to a very slow start.

virtual

Apparently there but actually not; *compare* **transparent** (actually there but apparently not).

virtual corporation

A method of organizing a business in which geographically dispersed resources—for example, engineers in a California office and business strategists in Dallas—can be linked and welded into a team by means of computer networking. The result is enhanced collaboration and a quicker response to rapidly-emerging opportunities.

virtual library

In the **World Wide Web (WWW)**, a **resource disovery tool** that organizes W3 resources by subject. There are several virtual libraries in existence, such as O'Reilly & Associates' Global Network Navigator.

virtual private network (VPN)

A **wide area network (WAN)** that appears to its users to have fixed boundaries and no relation to other networks, despite the fact that much of the network is implemented by public carriers, such as **X.25 networks**, that carry other networking traffic. VPNs are often implemented by corporations to carry private traffic such as establishing connections between point-of-sale terminals and centralized accounting computers. *Compare* **Public Data Network (PDN)**.

A rogue computer program that attempts to duplicate itself, and to propagate as widely as possible, by means of shared computer disks and computer networks (and at their expense).

A computer virus sneaks into your computer unseen, having arrived on an infected disk or by means of an infected program you **downloaded** from the Internet. And from then on, you're in for trouble. To be sure, some viruses are just pranks that display a message on-screen at a pre-arranged time, but even these "well-behaved" viruses may eat up memory or consume disk space. And the worst of them are terrors, capable of wiping out all the data on your hard disk.

> **Tip:** Don't worry about downloading text files to your computer: Viruses can propagate only by means of an **executable program** (a program you can run on your computer) that's been infected by the virus. If you never download a program from the Internet, you'll never get a virus—at least, not from the Internet!

> **Do** equip your system with virus protection software, which can scan your system (including active memory) to make sure that it is free from viruses. Note, however, that virus protection programs cannot detect all viruses. They use a pattern-matching approach, which means that they cannot detect new viruses whose patterns aren't in their databases.

> **Don't** download compiled programs from the Internet to a heavily used computer that's loaded with valuable resources. If you must download a program, transfer it

to a little-used machine that doesn't contain much of value. Before you try running the program, scan it with a virus-checking utility.

VMSnet

In Usenet, one of several **alternative Usenet hierarchies** that are carried and propagated only by those Usenet sites that elect to do so (in contrast to **world newsgroups**, which are automatically fed to every Usenet subscriber). The VMSnet **newsgroups** offer discussions of interest to users of VAX computers made by Digital Electronics Corporation (DEC).

W3

See **World Wide Web (WWW).**

Waffle

A **bulletin board system (BBS)** program that permits an IBM PC to become a functioning **Usenet** site. To obtain the latest Usenet **postings**, the BBS **sysop** (system operator) contacts a **UUCP** site via a **modem** in the late evening, when the phone rates are low, and also sends any postings created by the BBS's subscribers. A **shareware** program, Waffle is currently in use by more than 300 bulletin board systems in the U.S.

See **Wide Area Information Server (WAIS)**.

| **well-known port** |

A **port address** that is standardized with a fixed address number because it provides access to **well known services** such as **FTP** or **Telnet**. For this reason, you do not need to specify the port address when you are trying to access a well known service such as FTP on a **remote system**.

| **well-known service** |

A standard Internet tool, such as **FTP** or **Telnet**, that is assigned a fixed **protocol number** (for **transport protocols**) and a **port address** (for **applications**) so that a **client** will have no difficulty locating its corresponding **server** on a **remote system**.

| **whatis** |

In an **Archie server**, a command that provides additional information about files (including public domain programs, datasets, and text documents).

If you're using an Archie server and you've found a file that looks interesting, but you're not sure what it is, try using whatis to see whether a description of a file has been added to the whatis database (which currently contains approximately 3,500 files). You use whatis by typing the command name and the file name at the Archie prompt, as in the following example:

```
archie> whatis xmoon
```

If any information about this file exists, whatis displays it on-screen, as in the following example:

> xmoon   Dynamically display astronomical data
>   concerning the moon and the sun

white pages

A computer version of the white pages section of a phone book, which lists individuals, their telephone numbers, and their **electronic mail addresses** by name.

If you're looking for a single, unified phone book system for the Internet, forget it—there isn't one (yet). To be sure, there are many organizational white pages available (*see* **whois**); they're often available through an organization's **Gopher** server. But there's no single database that collects all this information in a single, standardized server. That would be a monumental job, considering how often people move and the problems of incompatible standards. The OSI standard called **X.500** may remove the latter problem, however (*see* **White Pages Pilot Project**).

Tip: If you're trying to hunt down someone's phone number or electronic mail address, you can try a number of approaches. **Finger** is a good option if you know where someone works. You can also find out if that person's host system maintains a **whois** service. **Netfind** and **Knowbot Information Service** provide additional means to track people down if you're not exactly sure where they work.

White Pages Pilot Project

An experimental implementation of **X.500** white pages technology that may one day create a unified, computer-searchable world database of electronic mail and telephone numbers.

Whois

A program that provides **white pages** directory service for an organization. You can use Whois to find a person's electronic mail address and telephone number.

The main Whois database is kept by the Network Information Center (NIC), and lists information about people who are professionally involved with the Internet. Other organizations use Whois servers to develop their own internal white pages services.

Wide Area Information Server (WAIS)

Acronym for Wide Area Information Server (pronounced *wayz*). A **resource discovery tool** designed for retrieving documents from **full-text databases** (such as collections of articles, newspapers, electronic texts, or Usenet postings). Unlike the search tools included with **Gopher** (**Veronica** and **Jughead**), which search only the names of Gopher directories and resource names, WAIS bases its retrieval on the *content* of documents retrievable from its databases.

To retrieve information with WAIS, this information must be available in a WAIS-readable database somewhere on the Internet. Since the creation and maintenance of these databases is purely a volunteer effort in most cases, don't expect that these databases will cover every last subject, or even cover one subject comprehensively—for example, there's a database about Indian classical music but nothing about other world music traditions. WAIS will be of most value to you if your interests align with the topic coverage of one of the more than 1,000 available databases. Although there are primitive tools available within WAIS for finding databases that match your interests, your best bet is to scan an Internet resource guide.

The term "database" is normally defined too rigidly to capture the diversity of WAIS resources: some WAIS-accessible databases really are databases in that they offer information grouped in tables or records, but most are collections of text files that have been grouped and indexed for WAIS retrieval.

WAIS is based on the **client-server model**: To use WAIS, you access a WAIS **client** (on your own or on a remote host), choose the **server** you want to access, and select the database you want to search. There are WAIS clients available for virtually all host systems, including Macintoshes, X Windows workstations, IBM PCs running Microsoft Windows, and UNIX systems. These clients offer advanced options such as the ability to search more than one database at a time, convenient access to a **directory of servers** that assists you in finding a database appropriate to your search interests, and **relevance feedback**, which lets you "train" the client to retrieve documents relevant to your interests.

Tip: The UNIX client, SWAIS, is buggy and difficult to use. If you're accessing the Internet by means of a UNIX host, the easiest way to search a WAIS database is by means of **Gopher**. Most Gopher **home servers** include an option with a title such as the following one:

```
12. WAIS Based Information/
```

This option displays a menu of databases, from which you choose the database you want to search. Then you type the search terms. The result of the search is a Gopher menu, which contains retrieved items.

Like other full-text retrieval systems, WAIS uses **key-word searching**: You type one or more search words that describe the topic in which you're interested. However, WAIS does not employ **Boolean operators** (AND, OR, and NOT), as do most key-word searching systems. WAIS retrieves documents based on a numerical score, which is computed according to how many times the search word or words appear in the document. The score is weighted, in that words appearing in the document's title count ten times more than words in the document's body (this is logical, considering that words appearing in the title are very likely to describe the document's content).

To use WAIS, you simply type any and all key words that you think describe the topic in which you're interested. The server then consults an **inverted file**, a list of all the significant words (that is, words longer than 2 letters) in every document contained in the database, and computes a score for each document. The document that contains the greatest instances of the search terms is given a score of 1,000, and appears at the top of the list of the retrieved documents.

WAIS has a distinguished ancestry, stemming from a joint development project carried out by Thinking Machines (a Massachusetts supercomputer firm), Apple Computer, Dow Jones, and KPMG Peat Marwick. To promote the WAIS concept, a freely redistributable version of WAIS was made available to the Internet community in 1991. WAIS, Inc., a newly formed corporation founded by an ex-employee of Thinking Machines, is devoted to developing commercial applications of WAIS. In the meantime, the freely redistributable version, called freeWAIS to avoid confusion with WAIS, Inc.'s products, is supported by CNIDR (Clearinghouse for Networked Information Discovery and Retrieval).

| **wide area network (WAN)** |

A data communications network that is capable of spanning a geographic region larger than a metropolitan area. The Internet is an emerging global WAN. *Compare* **local area network (LAN)**, **metropolitan area network (MAN)**.

Winsock

In Microsoft Windows, a dynamic link library (DLL) file that contains the information and procedures Windows needs to interface with **TCP/IP**. Winsock is needed if you wish to run a TCP/IP-compatible **client** program such as **Eudora** or **Mosaic** on your Windows system and communicate with the Internet by means of an **Ethernet** connection or **dialup IP**. A shareware version of Winsock is provided by Trumpet Software International.

wizard

In a **MUD** (a multi-user computerized role-playing game), a player who possesses the right to judge, censure, or veto the actions of other players. This right is granted by **gods** (here, the MUD's administrators) or, in some MUDs, won through game-playing prowess.

 Don't bug, threaten, or annoy a wizard. In most MUDs, wizards are the only players that have access to a command called @TOAD. This command turns you into a slimy green toad, takes away all the objects you've found, and erases all the work you've done to build up your character.

workstation

A desktop computer system designed for computing-intensive applications such as computer-aided design. Generally, workstations process data in 32-bit chunks and are considerably more expensive than personal computers. However, the distinction between workstations and personal computers is well on the way to becoming meaningless; today's best personal computers are already more powerful than the expensive workstations of five years ago.

world newsgroups

The seven major Usenet newsgroup categories that are automatically circulated throughout the Usenet system (although not every site carries all seven). Sometimes called the Big Seven, the world newsgroup categories are **comp, news, rec, sci, soc, talk,** and **misc.**

These categories are often called **hierarchies** because they are organized in a tree structure; within each category, there are dozens or hundreds of individual **newsgroups** devoted to a single topic. For example, among the hundreds of **comp** newsgroups is found comp.etext, which offers discussion of issues related to **electronic text**. Apart from the **world newsgroups**, there are several **alternative newsgroup hierarchies** (such as **alt, biz,** and **gnu**), which are not carried by all Usenet sites, and **local newsgroup hierarchies** that are regionally distributed (for example, the **uva** hierarchy appears only within the University of Virginia). The organization of newsgroups into the world, alternative, and local newsgroup hierarchies stems from a rather traumatic 1986 administrative reorganization, dubbed the **Great Renaming.**

World Wide Web (WWW)

An Internet **resource discovery tool** that permits you to **browse** for information using the principle of **hypertext** (retrieved documents contain **links** to other documents). Currently, WWW traffic accounts for 3% of Internet traffic and usage levels are growing twice as fast as the Internet itself.

When you activate one of the links by clicking on it with a mouse or pressing an arrow key, WWW automatically makes the connection, if necessary, to the **host** that houses the document you've requested, and retrieves the document without asking you to manage the details of the underlying file-transfer processes. WWW employs the **client-server model**; you employ a client on your host system, notably **Mosaic**, which contacts WWW servers worldwide. WWW is actually a **hypermedia** system, in that the retrieved documents may be graphics, sounds, or videos as well as text, but the principle means of navigation is by means of hypertext documents.

WWW (also abbreviated as W3) got its start at CERN, a European high-energy physics lab, where Tim Berners-Lee created the original WWW software to help physicists share information. WWW was made available to the Internet community in 1991, and won widespread acclaim. Currently, WWW is experiencing the fastest growth rate of any Internet resource discovery tool: according to one source, WWW traffic increased 300,000 percent in 1994 alone. Much of the Web's recent growth is attributable to the 1993 release of **Mosaic**, a WWW **browser** created by the National Center for Supercomputer Applications (NCSA).

The reasons for WWW's enthusiastic acceptance and rapid growth become clear once you've tried it. The hypertext metaphor is convenient, but what makes the WWW so useful is that every WWW document embodies someone's effort to *explain* what resources are available, and to *organize* them in a way that facilitates their retrieval. A typical WWW document is a page or two of text, which contains several hypertext links along with an explanation of what these do. Very much in line with the community spirit of the Internet, WWW allows users to create their own WWW documents, which can in turn contain links to still other documents—and so the Web grows. WWW perfectly embodies the **community model** of public networking.

WWW is arguably the resource discovery tool of choice for Internet users, because it integrates all the available tools and all the resources they can access. From WWW, you can use **Archie, Telnet, FTP, Gopher** (including **Jughead** and **Veronica**), and **WAIS**. You can even access **Usenet** without loss of the hypertext metaphor; **articles** are listed as documents to which you can jump.

To use WWW, you start a WWW **client,** which displays the default **home page**—the hypertext page that gives you initial access to the Internet's resources. To view any of the highlighted items, you select it and press *Enter*, and the Web software displays the resource you've selected. The following illustrates a WWW home page:

```
ENTERING THE WORLD-WIDE WEB: A GUIDE TO
CYBERSPACE

Table of Contents

* What is the World-Wide Web?
* What is hypertext and hypermedia?
* What is the Internet?
* How was the Web created?
* How popular is the Web?
* What is Mosaic?
* What can Mosaic do?
* What is available on the Web?
* How does the Web work?
```

worm

A rogue program that is designed to replicate itself at high speed, consuming processing resources and bringing the infected computer to a standstill. *See* **Internet worm**.

WWW

See **World Wide Web (WWW).**

X Windows Protocol

A network terminal standard developed at MIT that enables a user to run and display several network applications concurrently. The protocols specify how input and output should be handled in a window (rather than the entire screen). Although the design is **hardware independent**, it is used mainly on **workstations** in colleges and universities.

X Windows has many innovative features but a simpler solution is available: Let the user's workstation and operating system provide the means for displaying multiple applications and handling concurrency. The rapid acceptance of **Eudora** and **Mosaic**, both of which are designed to run in **graphical user interface (GUI)** environments on a variety of machines, demonstrates the appeal of this approach.

X.25

A set of **CCITT** standards that governs the transmission of computer data by means of the telephone system. This standard was developed in the 1970s and is widely used in **public data networks (PDN)**. X.25 is a **connection-oriented** protocol that is designed to provide a **reliable** and private data communication link between two points. For example, a corporation that must relay confidential information between a regional and central office employs a permanent X.25 connection for this purpose. X.25 links can achieve speeds of up to 64 Kbps. See **X.25 network**.

X.25 is concerned with the **physical layer** and **data link layers** of a network—that is, the physical medium over which the data is transmitted coupled with the means by which the data is packaged so that it travels from Point A to Point B reliably.

The X.25 standards include protocols for connecting a computer or terminal, called **Data Terminal Equipment (DTE)** in the CCITT terminology, and a device that links the computer to the network, which is called **Data Circuit-terminating Equipment (DCE)**. These are the same standards that govern the connection between a personal computer's serial port and a **modem**.

Unlike a point-to-point call you place with a PC and a modem, however, X.25 permits calls to be **multiplexed**: data from several computers can be mixed and sent through just one long-haul telephone line. This is done by breaking the data down into **packets** (units of fixed size), each of which contains the address to which it is to be delivered. Thus the connection that is established between two computers using X.25 is a virtual circuit; although the telephone line is shared by several virtual circuits, the users of each circuit do not know this and it seems to them that they have a private, direct line. Terminals that do not directly support X.25 require a device called a Packet Assembler and Disassembler (PAD) to deal with the division of data into packets at the transmitting end and the reassembly of packets at the other end.

X.25 calls can be placed in two ways. With a switched virtual circuit, the caller enters the destination computer's telephone number, and the connection is put through. A permanent virtual circuit works just like a leased line in that it establishes a permanent connection between two computers.

The slow speed of X.25 lines—no more than 64 Kbps—is insufficient to deal with the growing use of **multimedia**. To transfer a Computer Tomography (CT) scan from a medical center to a physician's office, for instance, would require an estimated 40 hours at X.25 speeds.

The X.25 protocols are considered obsolete for another reason: They were designed for use on noisy **analog** telephone lines, and in consequence invest considerable **overhead** in ensuring the **reliable** delivery of data. Now that most long-haul telephone systems employ noise-free **digital** lines, X.25's **robust** error-correction features have less justification. And they have very little justification when Internet packets are **encapsulated** and sent over X.25 networks, since the Internet handles the correction of errors at the **transport layer** (by means of **TCP**). *Compare* **frame relay**.

X.25 network

A **Public Data Network (PDN)** that employs the **X.25** standard to establish a **reliable**, private link between two computers. X.25 networks use their own long-haul lines, satellites, microwave relays, or lines leased from the telephone system.

X.400

A 1984 **CCITT** recommendation for the improvement of **electronic mail**, which was further developed by **OSI** in its **MOTIS** standards (1988). *See* **Message-Oriented Text Interchange Systems (MOTIS)**.

X.500

A **protocol,** as well as the software that implements this protocol, that will permit the construction of a **distributed** global directory of telephone numbers and **electronic mail addresses**: Each organization maintains its own database, but users can access other organization's databases transparently as if the entire phone book were one single entity. The protocol was designed by the **CCITT** and has been slow to gain acceptance.

Xmodem

An early **file transfer protocol** for use with **modems** that allows two computers to exchange data reliably by means of **dialup access.** Xmodem employs a simple (but far from perfect) **error protection** protocol that performs a **checksum** operation on each transmitted byte. Developed in the 1970s by Ward Christiansen, this protocol is considered obsolete and may even degrade the performance of today's fast (14.4 Kbps) modems. A more advanced version is called **Xmodem/CRC.** *Compare* **Kermit, Ymodem, Zmodem.**

Xmodem/CRC

An improved version of **Xmodem,** a **file transfer protocol** that allows two computers to exchange data reliably by means of **dialup access**. Xmodem/CRC employs **Cyclic Redundancy Code (CRC)** error checking on every two bytes transmitted. A variant, Xmodem/1k, performs a CRC check on every unit of 1,024 bytes (1K).

Yellow Pages

See **Network Information Service (NIS).**

Ymodem

A **file transfer protocol** for **modems** that permits two computers to exchange data reliably by means of **dialup access**. Ymodem is a version of **Xmodem/CRC** that allows multiple files to be sent in a single session. *Compare* **Kermit, Xmodem, Zmodem.**

Zmodem

A **file transfer protocol** for **modems** that permits two computers to exchange data reliably by means of **dialup access**. Commonly used on **bulletin board systems (BBS)**, Zmodem incorporates many convenient features, such as the ability to restart a transmission that's interrupted for any reason. *Compare* **Kermit, Xmodem, Ymodem.**

> **Tip:** If you're **downloading** files from a BBS, set your **communications program** so that it uses the Zmodem protocol. This is the most advanced and also the most convenient file transfer protocol for this purpose.

'zine

A low-circulation, high-energy, and non-mainstream magazine with a marked emphasis on the bizarre and the irreverent. The name "zine" is derived from "fanzine" or "magazine," although few contain advertisements and fewer still are produced for profit. Many zines exist in electronic form, generally in **ASCII text** (although some offer **Post-Script** formatting), and can be accessed easily through the Internet.

Sample titles from the edge: *Screams of Abel* (brutal music, including heavy gothic metal and grindcore); *Blink* (an exploration of the intersection of technology and consciousness), *The Neon Gargoyle* (horror, horror films, and monstrosities of every description), *Cousins* (a gathering place of "witches, pagans, nature spirits, fey-folk, and assorted elder kin of the forest," and the redoubtable *Holy Temple of Mass Consumption*, which publishes the works of "cranks, weirdos, freaks, net.personalities, curmudgeons, and anyone else who turns us on at the time."

Topical Index

Access

definition
access control
Access Control List (ACL)
dialup access
dialup IP
gateway
indirect access
unauthorized access

Account

definition
joe account

Address Resolution

definition
Address Resolution Protocol (ARP)
Reverse Address Resolution Protocol (RARP)

Agent

definition
User Agent (UA)

Alternative Newsgroup Hierarchy

definition
alt
bionet
bit
biz
clari
gnu hierarchy
HEPnet
IEEE

full-text database
query

Decryption

definition
key
see also encryption

Dialup Access

definition
dialup site

Dialup IP

definition
PPP (Point-to-Point Protocol)
SLIP (Serial Line Interface Protocol)

Distributed Routing

definition
advertising
convergence
distance-vector routing algorithm
router
routing algorithm
routing domain
Routing Information Protocol (RIP)
routing table

Domain

definition
domain name
domain name system
fully qualified domain name (FQDN)
pseudo top-level domain name
top-level domain

Electronic Mail Terrorism
definition

mail bombing

Electronic Mail
definition

address

alias

attached document

bcc

bounce

cc

electronic mail terrorism

filter

header

mailbox

mailbox name

mailing list

nickname

postmaster

receipt notification

signature

Electronic Mail Programs
Eudora

Pine

Electronic Mail—Technical Terms
mail bridge

mail exploder

mail reflector

mail server

Message-Oriented Text Interchange System (MOTIS)

Multi-Purpose Internet Mail Extensions (MIME)

v.27ter
v.29
v.34

File Compression Program
definition
gzip

File Encoding
file extraction
uudecode
uuencode

File Structure
directory
home directory
subdirectory

File Transfer Protocol
definition
anonymous FTP
File Transfer Protocol (FTP)
Kermit
Trivial File Transfer Protocol (TFTP)
Xmodem
Ymodem
Zmodem

Finding People
CSO name servier
Knowbot Information Service
Netfind
white pages
Whois

network interface card

sneakernet

Legislation

Computer Fraud and Abuse Act of 1984

Digital Telephony Act

Electronic Communications Privacy Act (ECPA)

Electronic Frontiers Foundation (EFF)

Freedom of Information Act (FOIA)

High Performance Computing Act of 1991

High Performance Computing and Communications Program(HPCC)

Markup Language

definition

declarative markup language

HyperText Markup Language (HTML)

parser

Standard Generalized Markup Language (SGML)

tags

Models of Connectivity

broadcast model

community model

Modem

definition

AT command set

baud rate

carrier

demodulation

fall back

modulation

v.22bis

v.32

v.32bis

Modem

v.32terbo
v.42
v.42bis
V.Fast Class (V.FC)
see also fax modem

MUD (Multi-User Dungeons)
definition
bot
god
mobile
MUD client
spamming
wizard

MUD Types
AberMUD
DikuMUD
LPMUD
MOO
TinyMUD

Multicasting
definition
Multicast Backbone (MBONE)
multicast group

Multimedia
definition
codec
full-motion video
multimedia database
multimedia mail

Organizations

Coalition for Network Information (CNI)
Commercial Internet Exchange Association (CIX)
Computer Emergency Response Team (CERT)
Computer Professionals for Social Responsibility (CPSR)
Electronic Frontier Foundation (EFF)
League for Programming Freedom (LPF)
National Science Foundation (NSF)
see also Standards Organizations

OSI Protocol Suite

definition
Abstract Syntax Notation One (ANS.1)

OSI Reference Model

definition
application layer
data link layer
network layer
physical layer
presentation layer
session layer
transport layer

Packet Switching

Asynchronous Transfer Mode (ATM)
cell relay
fragmentation
frame relay
hop
latency
Maximum Transmission Unit (MTU)
packet switching network
Switched Multimegabit Data Service (SMDS)

Page Description Language (PDL)
definition
PostScript (PS)

Parity
even parity
no parity
odd parity
parity checking

Physical Medium
definition
coaxial cable
fiber optic
T1 carrier
T3 carrier
twisted pair

Privacy
definition
Privacy Enhanced Mail
see also Security

Protocol
definition
Address Resolution Protocol (ARP)
connection-oriented protocol
file transfer protocol
OSI Protocol Suite
protocol address
protocol converter
protocol number
protocol stack
protocol suite
Reverse Address Resolution Protocol (RARP)

unreliable protocol

Regional Network

definition
AlterNET
ANS CO+RE
BARRNet
CA*NET
CERFnet
CICNet
CONCERT
CSUnet
EARN
EUnet
JvNCnet
MichNet
MIDnet
MOREnet
MRNet
NEARnet
netILLINOIS
NetNorth
NevadaNet
NORDUnet
NorthWestNet
NYSERnet
OARnet
PREPnet
SURAnet

Resource Discovery Tool
definition
Archie
browser

Resource Discovery Tool

Gopher
Hytelnet
WAIS
World Wide Web (WWW)

Routing
definition
see also distributed routing

Routing Protocols
Interior Gateway Protocol (IGP)
Open Shortest Path First (OSPF)
Routing Information Protocol (RIP)

Security
definition
access control
Access Control List (ACL)
authentication
cracker
The Cuckoo's Egg
encryption
firewall
joe account
password
Security Through Obscurity (STO)
unauthorized accesss
virus

Serial Communication
definition
asynchronous communication
byte stream
synchronous communication

Technical Internet Concepts

distributed routing

Heterogeneous Distributed Computing (HDC)

OSI Reference Model

packet switching network

router

synchronous

transparent adaptive routing

Technical Network Terms

attenuation

Carrier Sense Multiple Access with Collision Detection (CSMA/CD)

contention

distributed computing

handshake

IEEE 802 network

ISDN (Integrated Services Digital Network)

token bus

token ring

Telephone Service

Private Branch Exchange (PBX)

POTS (Plain Old Telephone Service)

Regional Bell Operating Company (RBOC)

T1 carrier

T3 carrier

Television

cable television (CATV)

interactive TV (ITV)

Terminal

line mode terminal

Network Virtual Terminal (NVT)

page mode terminal

UNIX Utilities And Programs
compress
EMACS
finger
grep
gzip
man
ping
vi

Usenet
definition
Call For Votes (CFV)
downstream site
FAQ
Great Renaming
netiquette
.newsrc
Request for Discussion (RFD)
signal-to-noise ratio
subscribe
Usenet site
see also Newsgroup, Usenet articles, Usenet behavior

Usenet Articles
crosspost
digest
expired article
followup posting
junk
test posting
thread

Usenet Behavior

carpet bomb
cascade
dictionary flame
flame bait
flame war
flame warrior
lurk
meme plague
net.character
net.deity
net.police
spamming
spewer
trolling

Usenet Newsreaders

kill file
newsgroup selector
offline reader
subject selector
thread selector
threaded newsreader
unthreaded newsreader

Usenet Newsreaders—software

nn
rn
tin
trn

User Interface

definition
command line interface
front end

X.25

definition

Data Circuit-Terminating Equipment (DCE)

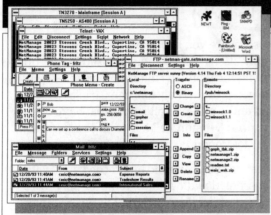

Chameleon Sampler Version 3.11 (Dial-up serial line only)

The Chameleon software you have installed includes several powerful applications most commonly used in dial-up TCP/IP environments including the Internet. This serial-only version of Chameleon provides fully functional copies of FTP, Telnet, Mail, Ping and Custom applications that have been selected from a prior version of NetManage's popular Chameleon TCP/IP for Windows commercial application suite.

With these applications you can send and receive mail with anyone on the Internet, download files from FTP servers or login to remote computers. Also included in this Sampler is a native windows implementation of the TCP/IP Protocol that is 100% DLL and fully WinSock standard compliant. The WinSock industry standard is based on the NetManage TCP/IP specification which was contributed to the standards body.

Installation instructions for the Chameleon Sampler

1. Insert disk in Drive A.

2. To install the program, open the Program Manager in Windows. Enter **a:\setup** in the dialog box, and follow the instructions.

For more information about the Chameleon Sampler please refer to the readme.wri file which you can access through Windows Write in Windows.